THE COMING CREDIT COLLAPSE

AN UPDATE FOR THE 1980s

THE COMING CREDIT COLLAPSE

AN UPDATE FOR THE 1980s

ALEXANDER P. PARIS

ARLINGTON HOUSE PUBLISHERS
WESTPORT, CONNECTICUT

The Coming Credit Collapse: An Update for the 1980s
is an expanded and revised edition of *The Coming
Credit Collapse* published by Arlington House
Publishers, 1974.

Library of Congress Cataloging in Publication Data

Paris, Alexander Perry.
  The coming credit collapse.

  Edition for 1974 published under title: The coming
credit collapse.
  Includes index.
  1. Finance–United States.   2.   Credit–United
States.   3.   Liquidity (Economics).   I.   Title.
HG181.P34   1980   332.7'0973   80–13856
ISBN 0–87000–474–3

Manufactured in the United States of America
9   8   7   6   5   4   3   2   1

TO
Alex, Jason, Greg, David, Tori and
their mother with love

I place economy among the first and most important virtues, and public debt as the greatest of dangers . . . we must make our choice between economy and liberty, or profusion and servitude. If we can prevent the government from wasting the labors of the people under the pretense of caring for them, they will be happy.

—THOMAS JEFFERSON

CONTENTS

PREFACE

This updated version of *The Coming Credit Collapse* is being prepared in the midst of unprecedented confusion among economists and in all financial markets. Gold, in almost panic buying, has gone beyond $800 an ounce, and retreated. In October 1979, interest rates leaped to new modern-day record levels in the largest single week rise in the nation's history. In the same week, the stock market fell with a record one-day volume of over 81 million shares. Mortgage rates were also rising to record levels amid fears of a major housing collapse. The Federal Reserve, which had lost control over the money supply in the prior several months, made a dramatic Saturday night announcement that it was abandoning its long-standing approach to monetary policy implementation. The collective balance sheets of corporations, individuals, and banks have once again deteriorated to postwar lows. At the same time, the nation is poised for another major recession, a new wave of bankruptcies and bank failures, and a new bear market in stocks.

Does it all sound familiar? Ironically, it has all happened before. In fact, it is the third time in just the last decade. In my original work in 1974, I carefully documented the basic underlying long-term process to which all these crises are related. I warned that, if the basic cause was not addressed, the adverse effects would continue to worsen in progressively more painful crunches. It has all unfortunately come to pass but the lesson has not been learned. The dangerous acceleration in credit, which grows larger with each wave, will eventually shake the economy apart unless its basic causes are eliminated. For this reason I have undertaken the task of updating the original work.

Original Purpose

When I began my original work in the early 1970s, the accelerating price inflation and interest rates of the period were generally viewed as an isolated problem related to the Vietnam War or other similar events. My intent was to demonstrate that they were, instead, symptoms of the maturing of a continuing process that had been taking place for several decades. They were also early warning signals of even greater storms to come.

The basic underlying problem is the steadily growing government intervention into the private sector and its excessive credit creation to finance those activities.

I intended to show that a major impact of this process was a massive and continuing financial deterioration that had permeated the economy over the entire postwar period. This deterioration could most easily be measured and tracked through an analysis of the aggregate balance sheets in each of the major economic sectors. This entire credit process, in turn, is the *proximate* cause of our price inflation, rising interest rates, accelerating volatility, declining productivity, and most of the other economic ills troubling the country today.

We also intended to show the existence of a very definable and predictable credit cycle around this secular trend of deterioration. Because the distortions of the previous cycle are never quite corrected completely, each cycle grows progressively worse.

Subsequent Events

In the intervening period since our original work, all our conclusions and our worst fears were confirmed. The basic causes were not treated. The adverse conditions continued to worsen. Credit cycles have become even more violent. Price inflation and interest rates have made two successively higher cyclical peaks. We saw the most severe recession of the postwar period and we have all the ingredients of another of equal or greater magnitude.

In the interim period we have also seen the concepts discussed in our original work creeping into the financial press on a much more regular basis. There is now more talk of the credit cycle, corporate liquidity, banking liquidity, and credit crunches. Government spending and the activities of the Federal Reserve are now finally catching more of the blame for price inflation.

Encouragingly, the causal role of Keynesian economic theory in our problems has been increasingly recognized. Austrian free market economic analysis, upon which I heavily rely for my analysis, has also grown in recognition. Its leading exponent, F. A. Hayek, was awarded the Nobel prize for economics in 1974. It is a venerable school of economics which has always accorded credit a role in its theory of the business cycle.

We have also seen new important sources of instability and risk since our original work. The consumer, formerly a major source of stability in the economy because of his propensity to save, is rapidly abandoning his stabilizing ways. He is finally learning how to react to continued depreciation of his currency. He is saving less, spending more, borrowing even more, and generally beginning a retreat from that currency. This has ominous implications for the future. Through a continual depreciation of the dollar in the international markets, the U.S. has lost its preeminent position among the nations of the world. This has meant growing chaos on the international scene. The growing reluctance of our trading partners to accumulate dollars also means that the U.S. will not be able to export its domestic inflation as easily as before. The greatly enlarged Eurodollar market and the precarious nature of sizable Third World debt are additional new sources of potential trouble. Add all this, plus the potential tinderbox in the Middle East and the high oil prices, to an overall domestic debt structure that has expanded substantially since our original work, and it should be clear that our updated edition is indeed timely.

Revisions in the Second Edition

When producing a new edition of a previous work, one is always tempted to add everything he has learned in the intervening period. This runs the risk, of course, of altering too drastically the original intent of the book. I have also been asked by many readers to update the many statistics in the book.

I decided to leave the first eleven chapters completely untouched. Together, they still represent in my mind the best overall explanation of our current economic troubles. They have really stood the test of time, for there is nothing in the pages I would not also say today. Leaving the chapters untouched, moreover, is an even more dramatic statement on how obvious the basic causes are and how dangerous they can be if left untreated.

I did delete the last two chapters of the original text, which contained some views on the future and investment hints. The conclusions I made regarding the future then, however, are the same ones I still make today—more "business as usual" and growing instability as a result. The investment hints have been greatly expanded.

In their place, I have added three chapters. Chapter 12 offers a complete review of the period since our original work. There is a description of the intervening credit cycles as well as updates of most of the important statistics. Chapter 13 has a fairly detailed description of my view of future conditions. The final chapter provides an overall investment and financial planning framework for surviving the period ahead.

Alexander P. Paris
December 1979

THE COMING CREDIT COLLAPSE

AN UPDATE FOR THE 1980s

Chapter 1

Giving Credit
Where It's Due

On August 15, 1945, an end came to the most violent war in the history of the world and the curtain was raised on the greatest economic expansion in American history. For nearly twenty-five years America remained the military, financial, and moral leader of the world. She was the guardian of the peace while the world regained its economic health and reconstructed its cities. In her magnanimity, she could do no wrong. Now, in a few short years, her image has been tarnished and Americans are increasingly beginning to doubt the wisdom of their government and themselves. Not in several generations have Americans been bombarded with such a myriad of confusing and unprecedented economic, political, and sociological events. It appears as if everything is coming apart at the seams.

Until recently involved in an unpopular war, America has for the first time been cast in the role of international villain, as well as that of the prodigal son among the family of nations. In little more than one year the dollar was devalued twice, and most major currencies, including the dollar, are engaged in a historic currency float. We have finally found the answer to the question, Is the dollar as good as gold, or is gold as good as the dollar? When given the opportunity, foreign bankers and citizens overwhelmingly chose gold. So great was the demand that the dollar could no longer remain convertible into gold and the free-market price of gold tripled in a few short years. The voice of protectionism is growing louder and trade wars are threatening.

At home, investors have been subjected to growing volatility in all financial markets, and have endured some of the most vicious market declines in the nation's history. Interest rates have reached historic high levels as conservative holders of high-quality bonds have suffered huge paper losses with little relief in sight. New words and phrases like *credit crunches, Eurodollars,* and *confidence crises* are entering the investor's vocabulary. Old and cherished financial institutions are being challenged and new ones are appearing in increasing numbers.

9

New postwar lows are being made daily in price-earnings multiples in a stock market that is becoming increasingly dominated by financial institutions. Investors are questioning all of their precepts and are desperately searching for new investment touchstones.

On a broader scale, the nation is facing the most stubborn inflation in its history, approaching, at times, a rate previously reserved only for banana republics. For the first time, inflation expectations are beginning to permeate long-term investment decisions. Peacetime price and wage controls, another historic precedent, are also compounding the confusion. Riots, assassinations, political scandals, as well as questions as to the efficacy of the entire political system, have all added spice to the economic potpourri.

The worst blow to investor confidence has been the growing realization that the government may not have full control over the destiny of the nation. The disappointment is particularly bitter when, having believed in the mid-1960s that the economic millennium had arrived, the investor was greeted by the "stagfiation" of 1969-1970, two credit crunches, and the confusion of more recent years. The record 105-month economic expansion from February 1961 to November 1969, together with the heady rhetoric of the "new economists" of the Kennedy-Johnson years, gave many investors the comfortable feeling that the business cycle was a relic of the past. With the government firmly at the helm, it was promised, a path of steady, stable growth could be maintained indefinitely. By the late 1960s, few colleges still offered courses in business-cycle theory. The euphoric feeling that spread across the country had only one parallel in recent history. That was in the 1920s, when the newly formed Federal Reserve was to be the economic savior. Investors then also believed that serious economic corrections had been abolished. The disappointment that followed led to many of the philosophical changes that laid the foundation for the economic events in the postwar United States.

Now, once again, investors are engaged in the process of attempting to explain what has gone wrong. Many scapegoats have been offered, including the Vietnam War, the gnomes of Zurich, excessive labor strength, politicians, and avaricious businessmen. Political rhetoric and international unrest have added further to the confusion, which has been increasingly reflected in financial markets. The important question, however, is whether the financial and economic problems of recent years are independent but coincidental events, or recurring manifestations of a more basic underlying force. If the latter, is it identifiable and curable?

There does indeed exist a single fundamental cause of all the financial ills. They may all be traced to a long trend of excessive credit growth, which is rapidly approaching its final phase. The problem is very visible, identifiable, and measurable. Over the entire postwar period, the amount of credit outstanding has grown at a rate that, on the average, has consistently been two to three times faster than the growth in the nation's ability to produce goods and services. Moreover, the rate has been accelerating in recent years. We will show that this trend in credit has resulted in a growth in demand that has been highly artificial

10

and, through its primary and secondary effects, has been responsible for most of the economic and financial problems facing the investor today.

Origin of the Credit Trends

At the root of the excessive credit growth has been a steadily evolving philosophy in the federal government and the Federal Reserve. Together, these institutions have created a climate conducive to excessive credit creation, and have supplied the money to allow it to continue unabated throughout the entire postwar period. The seeds of the new philosophy and the current crop of economic problems were sown in the 1930s with the New Deal and the advent of Keynesian economics. The new philosophy gained momentum during World War II, was formalized in the Employment Act of 1946, and reached its zenith with the age of the so-called new economists during the New Frontier and the Great Society.

The philosophical notion that the federal government is "responsible" for the general welfare of the entire population took root in 1946, when the government was legally pledged to maintain full employment at any cost. With this avowed aim of legislating away any serious business corrections, the foundation was laid for the rapid postwar expansion of the government sector. More importantly, the growing belief that any serious social or economic ills would be effectively handled by the authorities, and that business risk was consequently substantially reduced, led business to feel secure in overextended financial positions incurred in search of faster growth.

The unwieldy credit structure that exists today, which far surpasses that of the last period of excess in the 1920s, was accumulated as a result of the new postwar political philosophy and the confidence it engendered. The nature of the present credit structure, however, is quite different from that of the 1920s, and potentially much more dangerous. Unlike the highly speculative but short-lived nature of the excessive credit creation of the 1920s and other past preludes to financial panics, the present credit structure has accumulated over a period of thirty years. It has permeated every corner of the economy and has completely changed the credit ethic of the nation. Credit has been made respectable because the government has been a partner in the process in the name of full employment and economic growth. It has taken the more acceptable form of business risk and consumer credit. Because the credit trends have continued without correction for such an extended period, the ultimate readjustment to a more moderate and sustainable rate of growth may be much more painful and farreaching than that of the 1930s. The confidence in the government, in effect, has led to huge borrowing from the future at the expense of financial stability in the present. With that confidence now beginning to ebb, the future is rapidly approaching.

Growth of Government Spending

Deficit spending in recent years has accelerated drastically and budget surpluses have become rare. The budget is becoming increasingly uncontrollable as government spending has developed its own internal momentum. New programs are expected for every social or economic need, and old programs neither die nor fade away but grow far beyond the original intent. Fiscal discipline has completely disappeared and over half of every dollar is spent by the government. Since growth in the economy has always come as a result of *private* risk-taking, the rapidly growing encroachment of the government sector, and the declining private incentives this implies, contains the seeds of its own destruction.

The Federal Reserve

Much of the damage that has occurred because of the government-spending trends, however, could not have been accomplished without the aid of the Federal Reserve. Our central bank has evolved into an institution far removed from the form intended by the framers of the original act that created it. It has acted as a faithful handmaiden to the federal government, turning government excesses into credit by monetizing the federal debt, and flooding the economy with the monetary raw material necessary to maintain the credit trends. It has conducted itself in a fashion that is far from independent, pursuing many ill-defined and conflicting goals that have only served to intensify the problems caused by excessive government spending.

The National Balance Sheet

In keeping with the government's fixation upon continuing rapid growth and moderation of the business cycle, economists of all persuasions have concentrated upon income flows, while no one has been keeping score on the national balance sheet, where all the damage has been recorded. Following their lead, corporations have dedicated all of their efforts to growing earnings per share, while security analysts and investors avidly search out new growth stocks. Individuals, in the meantime, have run down their personal balance sheets in search of the "good life," while the banking system busily creates money to make it all happen from the raw material supplied by the Federal Reserve. No one seems able to take his eyes off the income statements long enough to examine the balance sheets. Anyone who did, would not have been very surprised by the Penn Centrals or the Equity Fundings, and he would have opposed the recent conglomerate craze. The current deterioration in the national balance sheets, which has resulted from the many years of excessive credit creation and the climate that has made it possible, is clear, unmistakable, and easily measured.

Banking Liquidity

The banking system has been a willing partner in the long postwar financial deterioration that has occurred in the United States and the world. The traditional banking philosophy—that loans should be short term and self-liquidating in nature, and that substantial assets should be maintained in highly liquid form as a buffer against sudden deposit withdrawals or loan

12

demand—has gradually disappeared. It has been replaced by a new philosophy of aggressive liability management and profit maximization. Liabilities are becoming more short term in nature and more volatile, while loans are becoming longer and of lower quality. Because of the unique ability of commercial banks to create money, their actions have permeated the economy and have resulted, as we will demonstrate, in growing volatility and risk in financial markets.

Banking liquidity, by all measures, has deteriorated steadily throughout the entire postwar period, and all former limits of propriety have been far exceeded in the pursuit of profit maximization.

Corporate Liquidity

Paralleling the secular deterioration of banking liquidity has been an equally drastic and continuous rundown of the liquid assets of corporations. The secular decline in corporate liquidity has reached such a mature stage that each business expansion in recent years has precipitated both liquidity "scares" among investors and credit crunches. Corporations react to these scares with massive sales of long-term debt to retire short-term debt. Because this improves the current section of their balance sheets, fears subside until the next scare. The improvement is short-lived, however, and the secular rundown in liquid assets soon resumes.

This is only half of the story, for the short-term debt is not really eliminated, it is transferred to another section of the balance sheet and only the maturity date is changed. Therefore, it is necessary to examine the *entire* balance sheet in order to discover the massive financial deterioration that has befallen the entire corporate sector as a result of the long trend of excessive credit creation. This deterioration is evidenced by high and accelerating corporate-debt ratios and rapidly declining coverage of interest costs. In recent years, financial rating services have begun to reflect the reduced financial condition of many corporations in lower ratings. This combination of deteriorating financial condition and liquidity among both corporations and the banking system, together with excessive government spending and credit creation by the Federal Reserve, is the basic cause of almost all of the financial ills facing the nation today.

Confusing the Causes with the Effects

One of the major barriers to understanding the fundamental causes of our financial ills is the fact that they have been in effect for so long that they have completely permeated the economy. In the process, the major effects of these trends, such as inflation, rising interest rates, growing risk, and increasing volatility, have also been completely established and have fanned out into many secondary effects. They have led, for example, to increasing labor militancy, rising inflationary expectations, rising taxes, international dollar speculation, and declining incentives to invest. As these effects work themselves through the system, they lead to inadequate capital formation, disappointing productivity gains, and declining profit margins. Just as government spending accelerates to the point that it becomes almost uncontrollable, all of these effects join together and interact with each other until they too form a strong self-sustaining momentum. So engrained are these effects, and so strong is their momentum, that they are confused with the basic underlying causes. Many *effects* are blamed as *causes* of our problems. Adding to the confusion is the advent of peacetime price and wage controls, which have become necessary because of the advanced stage of the adverse financial trends. These only help to disguise the underlying problem and do not offer a permanent solution. As long as the basic problem is not recognized and treated, these effects will continue to worsen and accelerate as they have in recent years.

Current Status of the Credit Trends

When the Gross National Product (GNP) surpassed the trillion-dollar mark for the first time in 1971, it was the subject of many awe-inspired articles in newspapers across the country. Serious comments about overheating of the economy were evoked by the strong $100 billion increase in the 1972 GNP. Yet total public and private debt rose over $200 billion in 1972 and reached a total of $2.25 trillion with very little notice. The pyramid of credit, already uncomfortably high, continues to accelerate. No lessons were learned from the nearly disastrous credit crunch of 1969-1970. Many corporations maintain debt structures so top-heavy that they are finding it difficult to finance growth, and certainly will not be able to withstand a prolonged period of either business slowdown or credit stringency. Just as fiscal discipline has been lost and the budget has become uncontrollable, the liquidity and financial trends are also out of control. Inflation and rising interest rates, two of the major effects of the credit trends, have also developed an internal momentum of their own. Expectations of both inflation and credit crunches are accelerating. In the past, consumers always tended to save when threatened with inflation, and this served as a valuable offset to inflation. Recently, they have begun to spend more and contract more credit when their fears of inflation grow. For the first time, they are beginning to add to the inflationary spiral, making it infinitely more difficult to control. With the rapidly growing, uncontrollable nature of inflation, and the steadily deteriorating financial condition of a growing number of corporations, both resulting from the government-spending and credit trends, the hopeless nature of the problem becomes apparent.

To combat inflation requires a government-induced slowdown in business and the application of monetary constraints for a sustained period of time. The financial condition of the corporate sector, however, makes survival in such a period impossible. The financial condition of many companies and the liquidity of the banking system are so poor that any minor slowdown in credit-availability by the Federal Reserve is immediately turned into a credit crunch and a wild scramble for funds. The first quarter of 1973 was an excellent example of this reaction, which is strengthened by supercrunch expectations. With the crunch of 1969-70 still fresh in the minds of many credit-starved corporations, they hoard credit for protection. Because of the growing weight of their debt structures, the Federal Reserve must supply the system with increasingly larger transfusions of credit to keep it all together. The increasing transfusion of credit merely serves to sustain the inflationary credit expansion that the Federal Reserve is attempting to curb, and growing expectations make it even worse. Even in periods when the Federal Reserve restricts bank credit, total credit in the economy continues to grow, demonstrating the uncontrollable nature of the credit trends and the growing ineffectiveness of the monetary authorities. In all its attempts at moderation, the Federal Reserve must be careful not to allow the entire house of credit-cards to fall. The accumulation of debt is so great that once the confidence needed to maintain overextended positions is eroded, a cumulative and self-enforcing liquidation of credit may be put into motion similar to the same upward spiral of credit creation.

How Will It End?

There is no simple, short-term solution to the problems that ail this country, for they are the results of over thirty years of accumulated financial abuse. The basic cause is excessive government spending, and the excessive credit creation that results from both government actions and the climate they foster. Because they have been in effect unchecked for such a long time, the inflation and credit trends now have an internal momentum of their own. No less than a complete change in the philosophy of government, accompanied by major reforms in both congressional and administrative budget techniques, is required. There have seldom been any reversals of strongly entrenched government philosophies without a crisis. There is strong doubt whether any elected government would have the will, ability, morality, and fortitude to engage in the long-term, deliberate action to slow credit growth that would be necessary to cure our financial ills without a serious credit liquidation and financial panic.

The most recent evidence offers little encouragement. Government spending, despite more publicity than ever before, continues to grow at excessive rates. Credit continues not only to grow at historic rates but is accelerating. Volatility in financial markets indicates an economy that is out of control. Banking liquidity is the worst in history and still deteriorating. Like all periods of excessive credit creation in the past, this one will also reverse itself in a very painful fashion. The government will continue with its crisis economics, controls will become more pervasive, but the financial condition of the banks and corporations will continue to worsen until the entire credit structure falls from its own weight. Judging from the intensity of the major effects of these basic credit trends, the end is not far off. In the meantime, the government will supply the credit to make it all possible, and its success in staving off a massive credit liquidation and financial panic will be measured in growing inflationary pressures and diminished personal freedom. The credit crunches of 1966 and 1969-70 were only the first two tremors of the financial earthquake to come. While all attention is now focused upon inflation, it is

15

only the interim problem. The real problems of the 1970s will be financial panic, recessions, and eventually deflation. For thirty years economic growth and the income statement have held the limelight. The day of the balance sheet is coming, when survival will take precedence over growth.

In subsequent pages, we document the existence of the adverse financial trends that have been in existence now for three decades. We trace the basic, underlying credit trends to demonstrate the extent of the damage that has resulted among the balance sheets of corporations and banks. Once the primary and secondary effects of the credit trends are separated from the causes, you should be able to see the true nature of the problem; you will understand how the credit trends have completely permeated the economy, and will be able to more accurately predict the future conditions of our economy—most specifically, those affecting your own investments.

Chapter 2

Traditional Measures of Banking Liquidity

Banking Liquidity Defined

The explosion of the atomic bomb over Hiroshima in August 1945 not only ushered in an era of unprecedented technological change and an end to the most devastating world war in history, but also marked the beginning of important financial trends that continue today. The postwar years have also brought equally rapid and extensive changes in economic and financial theories, as well as important changes in political philosophy and the relationship of the government to the private sector. Even as the new economists of the Kennedy-Johnson administrations were bringing the Keynesian theories to their pinnacle barely twenty years after their birth, the contrary school of the new monetarists was already gaining in popularity.

While controversies have raged between Keynesian economists and monetarist theorists in regard to stabilization policies and the conquest of the business cycle, between advocates of monetary aggregates or interest rates as the proper focus of Federal Reserve policies, and between those who favor either a government-dominated economy or a free-enterprise system, the ravishment of banking liquidity has been largely ignored. From a highly liquid state at the close of World War II, the banking system has undergone a devastating and continuing deterioration of liquidity, the effects of which have been increasingly manifested in rising interest rates, inflation, and growing volatility.

Bank liquidity is a balance-sheet concept, which deals with the adequacy of cash and equivalent resources to meet the withdrawal or loan demands of bank customers. Banking-system liquidity is a basic factor in shaping the lending policies of banks, and therefore a primary determinant of the cost and availability of bank credit to borrowers and of interest-rate levels for the economy as a whole. The portfolio of liquid assets maintained by the individual bank serves as a buffer insulating loans from unexpected variations in deposits or loan demand. It follows that any assets held as such a buffer should possess the quality of being readily exchangeable for cash.

The liquidity of individual assets is essentially a function of time. The greater the length of time between the decision to dispose of an asset and its eventual sale, the closer it may be sold to its maximum price, given prevailing conditions. Quick sales generally require the seller to accept less than the full market value of the asset. This is the essence of liquidity. There is an important but often confused distinction between liquidity and solvency. *Solvency,* in this case, measures the difference between the value of a bank's assets, at maximum expected prices, and its liabilities. *Liquidity* refers to the value of the asset portfolio that may be realized for a given time availability and for a given amount of assets to be sold. A bank may be illiquid and still be solvent.

Cash is perfectly liquid, at least domestically. Government Treasury bills may also be sold rapidly at a very low cost and even on relatively short notice. For all other assets held by a bank, the price received per unit depends also upon the "number" of units sold, prevailing market conditions, and the nature of the individual market for the particular asset. The liquidating price received depends on both the time available prior to the disposal and the number of units sold. At times, there may be no market at all for certain assets. The amount of the most liquid assets relative to less liquid assets, therefore, has a great deal to do with the loan policy of the individual bank and the interest rate it must charge. If individual banks are illiquid, then the entire banking system is illiquid; the interest rates that must be charged by individual banks become the general level of interest rates in the economy and, of course, important determinants of many major economic trends. It is the aim of this book to trace these trends in banking liquidity to their ultimate effects upon the economy, to explain the unusually frantic financial markets of recent years, and to construct the investment environment that may be expected for the balance of the 1970s.

Indications of Bank Liquidity

The levels and changes in the aggregate money supply are at the very root of the problems discussed in this book. It is ironic, however, that while considerable attention has been devoted to the changes in money supply, the relationship between money and stock prices, interest rates, inflation, and economic growth, the effects of all of the short-term policies upon total banking liquidity is almost entirely ignored, except in periodic credit squeezes. An important element of the total long-term condition of the entire financial system and interest-rate trends is largely excluded from concern.

Since the lending policies of every bank cannot be observed directly and individually, and since our concern here is with the condition of the entire system, it is necessary to substitute broader and more indirect indicators of liquidity.

Although there is no single perfect measure of liquidity, there are many historical relationships for which data are available and which give a consistent and objective standard of comparison over time. The period studied here includes all the postwar years for which there is uninterrupted data. The period begins with a condition of extremely high liquidity, which represented a peak for the long trend of liquidity-building that began in the 1930s. This trend itself was a reaction to the massive credit expansion that led to the 1929 crash and the credit-liquidating depression that followed. In fact, all the financial panics of the past were in some way related to the overexpansion of credit. The indicators presented in this book demonstrate that the nation has reached a condition of credit expansion that far exceeds the levels of the late 1920s. Rather than selecting a single indicator of banking liquidity, a number of different but confirming measurements are used in the following chapters.

The Investment Component of Total Bank Credit

The first two indicators of banking liquidity are the two most traditional measures of liquidity. They are both closely related with one, the ratio of bank holdings of government securities relative to total bank credit, a much more stringent or exacting measurement of liquidity than the other. The term *total bank credit* refers simply to the total of banking assets within the system, and is a summary of the manner in which banks have put their deposits to work. The bulk of all bank assets are in either loans or investments, as demonstrated in Table 2.1.

TABLE 2.1

Assets for all Commercial Banks as of January 1973
(In Billions of Dollars)

Loans and investments	$588.9
Reserves, cash, and bank balances	94.7
Other assets	28.9
Total assets	$712.6

As deposits are received by a bank, a decision must be made as to how they are to be invested. The decision is simply one between maximum return and safety. Loans represent the generally higher return while also offering the greater risk and lower liquidity. The investment account, which is comprised of the very liquid U.S. Treasury securities and other securities, primarily municipal bonds, offers lower yields but represents the liquid buffer against sudden changes in loan demand or deposit levels.

Ratio of Bank Investments to Total Bank Credit

Relating the entire bank-investment portfolio to total bank credit has been a customary measure of banking liquidity for many years. A glance at Table 2.2 and Figure 2.1 will clearly demonstrate how bankers have decided the question between maximum safety and maximum return. Using this measurement, there is no question that the entire postwar period has seen a continuous secular decline in banking liquidity, interrupted only periodically by feeble cyclical upturns. There are, in fact, only six years in the entire period that saw a slight improvement in liquidity, and those, coincidently, occurred during recessionary periods, if one counts the mini-recession of 1966. Thus, it would appear that even these attempts to rebuild liquidity were probably involuntary. It is, of course, difficult to declare exactly what is the optimum level of liquidity within the system. It is equally difficult, however, to

TABLE 2.2

Traditional Measures
of Banking Liquidity[1]

Year	Ratio of Bank Investments to Total Bank Credit	Ratio of U.S. Governments to Total Bank Credit
1948	0.63	0.55
1949	0.65	0.56
1950	0.59	0.49
1951	0.57	0.46
1952	0.55	0.45
1953	0.54	0.44
1954	0.55	0.44
1955	0.49	0.38
1956	0.46	0.35
1957	0.45	0.34
1958	0.47	0.36
1959	0.41	0.31
1960	0.41	0.30
1961	0.42	0.31
1962	0.41	0.28
1963	0.39	0.25
1964	0.37	0.22
1965	0.34	0.19
1966	0.32	0.17
1967	0.34	0.17
1968	0.34	0.16
1969	0.31	0.13
1970	0.33	0.13
1971	0.34	0.13
1972	0.32	0.11

Source:
Business Statistics 1971, U.S. Dept. of Commerce.
Survey of Current Business, U.S. Dept. of Commerce.

[1] All Commercial Banks.

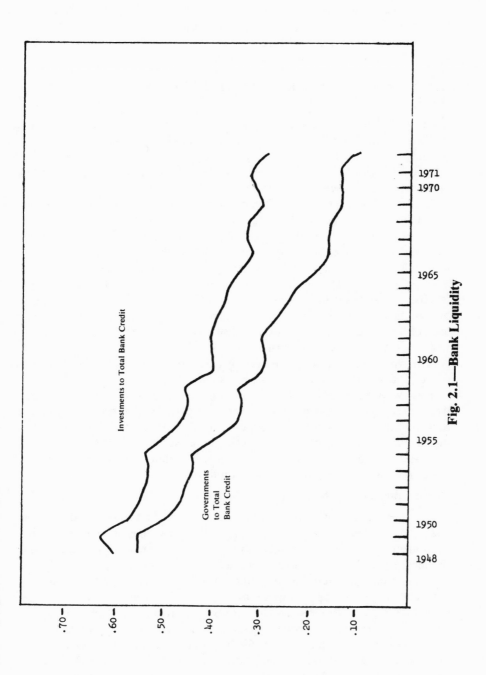

Fig. 2.1—Bank Liquidity

Investments to Total Bank Credit

Governments
to Total
Bank Credit

1948
1950
1955
1960
1965
1970
1971

.70
.60
.50
.40
.30
.20
.10

21

ignore the facts that banking liquidity has declined by 50 percent from 1948 to 1972, that the trend has been inexorable and continues to the present day, and that each minor peak has been followed by a recession. This is particularly harrowing when one reflects upon the increasingly violent credit crunches of recent years, which may be indicating that the economy is rapidly approaching the limits to which this trend may extend.

Ratio of Government Securities to Total Bank Credit

An examination of the second measure of liquidity among banks is even more instructive and unsettling because it is a much better indicator of true liquidity. Aside from vault cash, which is quite minor in amount, *absolute* bank liquidity can only be measured by bank holdings of U.S. government securities, since they are the only assets that can be sold quickly and in quantity into declining markets at or near their maximum value levels.

Another reference to Table 2.2 and Figure 2.1 will illustrate even more convincingly the magnitude of the unrelenting nature of the deterioration that has occurred in banking liquidity. There have been only three years of recovery in liquidity during the entire postwar period, again during recessions. Unlike the first indicator, however, there has been no year of improvement since 1961. Any attempts at rebuilding liquidity in this important category have been quite impotent. Not only has the trend been more relentless than that of the first indicator, but the damage has been considerably more severe. The ratio declined from a level of 0.55 in 1948 to 0.11 at the end of 1972. This means that of all the invested assets of the banking system, only 11 percent have been placed in U.S. government securities, which are the only true source of liquidity during periods of credit stringency, as we will show below.

Thus, while the total investment portfolios have been steadily declining relative to loans, the internal mix of the investment portfolios has been deteriorating as well. Tax-exempt securities, with their much lower marketability but much higher aftertax yields, have been resolutely substituted for U.S. government securities, making the broader measurement of liquidity decidedly less meaningful as an indicator of true banking liquidity.

Credit Crunch of 1969-70

It is interesting to note that during the recession of 1969-70 and the sluggish recovery that followed, the broader indicator managed an extended improvement, though modest relative to the liquidity scare of those years, while the more critical measurement continued to make new record lows. By this measure, banking-system liquidity has never been worse. The small liquidity that remains can disappear rapidly as major cyclical loan demand continues, should the Federal Reserve decide to drastically reduce bank reserves to halt inflationary pressures, or should rapid disintermediation suddenly occur.

During the credit squeeze of 1969-70, prices of tax-exempt bonds fell far faster and to a greater extent than prices of government bonds. In Table 2.3 it can be seen that from January 1969 to the peak in interest rates in June 1970, municipal bond yields rose 43 percent, as compared to 22 percent for government bonds. It is particularly instructive to note that in the twelve months of 1969 alone, the municipal yields rose 39 percent, while during the same period, holdings in bank portfolios of U.S. government securities fell nearly $10 billion. Holdings of other investments, however, held substantially unchanged. Banks obviously sold only modest amounts of municipal bonds relative to their total holdings, preferring to sell the more liquid government securities. As Table 2.3 shows, holdings of U.S. government securities, even by the end of 1971, had still not recovered to the level of year-end 1968. It was not a chance decision that led banks to liquidate governments rather than municipal bonds to offset their sharp loss of deposits in that year. Liquidity of tax-exempt bonds in 1969 almost disappeared completely for any large-quantity orders. Not only was there little demand for their holdings, except at sharp discounts from current prices, but liquidating them would have also turned the huge paper losses in bank portfolios into real ones. If bank portfolios had been priced at the market rather than at cost during that year, the questions of solvency and liquidity might have been discussed during that

TABLE 2.3

		Bond Yields	
Year	Month	State & Municipal[1]	U.S. Treasury[2]
1969	Jan.	4.95	5.74
	Feb.	5.10	5.86
	Mar.	5.34	6.05
	Apr.	5.29	5.84
	May	5.47	5.85
	June	5.83	6.06
	July	5.84	6.07
	Aug.	6.07	6.02
	Sept.	6.35	6.32
	Oct.	6.21	6.27
	Nov.	6.37	6.51
	Dec.	6.91	6.81
1970	Jan.	6.80	6.86
	Feb.	6.57	6.44
	Mar.	6.14	6.39
	Apr.	6.55	6.53
	May	7.02	6.94
	June	7.06	6.99

Source:
Business Statistics, 1971 U.S. Dept. of Commerce.
Federal Reserve Bulletin.

[1] Standard & Poor's five High Grade Domestic Municipal Bonds.
[2] Fully taxable marketable bonds due or callable ten years and over.

period. It is well to keep in mind that during periods of sharply rising interest rates, even our frightening statistics on banking illiquidity are drastically understated, since the investment portfolios are priced at cost. It is fortunate that the banking system did not have to resort to wholesale disposal of municipal bonds during 1969. As it was, many firms specializing in municipal bonds were forced to close their doors, while many more were in serious trouble.

With this pronounced difference in liquidity between municipal bonds and U.S. government securities, and with the considerably changed mix in investment portfolios that has occurred, it has become exceedingly misleading to use the broad ratio of total investments to total bank credit as an indicator of bank liquidity. When one turns to the more rigorous liquidity indicator, the current condition becomes much more disturbing, with the indicator still moving into new low ground for the postwar period and approaching the very illiquid condition of the late 1920s.

TABLE 2.4

Year	U.S. Government Holdings	Other Investments
	(In Billions of Dollars)	
1968	61.0	71.4
1969	51.5	71.2
1970	58.0	85.9
1971	60.3	103.9
1972	62.0	115.6

Turning to Table 2.4, one can see that in the two years following the disastrous year of 1969, banks added a total of $32.7 billion to the "other investment" portion of their investment portfolios, while adding only $8.8 billion of U.S. government securities, which, as mentioned, is still below the level for the year preceding the crunch, though total bank credit has grown considerably. If the events of 1969 were disturbing, then the condition currently is potentially chilling. At year-end 1972, holdings of U.S. government securities had still only managed to reach $62 billion. Between 1970 and 1972 the holdings had grown a scant $2 billion, while total loans outstanding *grew by $86.1 billion.* If the investment portion of bank assets is to continue to serve its traditional role as a reservoir of loanable funds to satisfy rising loan demand, then there are clearly problems ahead for any future economic expansions. Either the expansions will be shortened for lack of sufficient loanable funds or interest rates will soar to further postwar highs. With the extremely low levels of U.S. government securities, it will be necessary for banks to liquidate tax-exempt bonds in much larger quantities than in 1969 in the next period of credit tightness. Yields on municipal bonds may easily exceed all previous record levels, and the volatility of the market should be much greater than at any time in the past. The resulting writedown of bank

24

portfolios will demonstrate even more clearly the extent to which illiquidity threatens bank solvency. Should banks call in loans instead, and given the increase in the level of loans outstanding since the last crunch, a self-enforcing credit liquidation could easily be touched off, which could be extremely difficult to control. The only alternative would be a rapid increase in the supply of reserves by the Federal Reserve, with the resulting expansion of money and credit, inflation, and an ultimate worsening of the liquidity situation. These possibilities will be discussed in further detail in subsequent chapters. First, we must disclose additional evidence of the deteriorating liquidity trends.

Loan Ratio

All of our attention, up to this point, has been focused upon the investment segment of total bank credit. As mentioned above, total bank credit is the total of investments plus loans. We have shown how the ratio of total investments to total bank credit has declined throughout the postwar years. This is, of course, due to the fact that banks have gradually decided to place more of their deposits to work in the form of loans at the expense of lower-yielding but more liquid investments. The *loan-ratio*, the percentage of total bank credit represented by loans, is naturally the mirror image of the investment ratio, and it has been rising over the same period, as evidenced in Table 2.5.

By now concentrating our attention on the loan side of bank credit, we will begin to see the true nature of the problem. Looking at the loan ratio, and in the next section at the loan-deposit ratio, you will gain further insight into banking liquidity and the probable sources of the growing volatility in money and capital markets that has occurred in recent years. For the problem is not only that banks are buying too few government securities, but also that loan expansion has been far too rapid.

Given certain deposit characteristics, the greater the portion of total assets represented by loans, the greater the probability that a bank may be forced to dispose of some portion of its loan portfolio at unfavorable terms or disappoint good customers. If an individual bank is to be induced to carry more loans relative to total assets, it must ultimately be compensated for the increased risk, due to the higher probability that sudden deposit withdrawals will have to be offset by loan sale rather than sale of securities. The bank with the higher loan positions must ask for higher interest rates. Since most banks are interested in showing higher earnings per share every year, those with high loan ratios must work all the harder to replace loans as they are repaid. In times of slack loan demand, the pressure will be great to take lower quality credits, which will also raise the overall risk level of the bank's asset structure, which must also be compensated for by charging higher interest rates. If the entire system is carrying relatively more loans, there should then be an upward pressure on the general level of interest rates, as indeed we have seen over the entire postwar period with increasing intensity. The increasing loan content of bank credit, as demonstrated in Table 2.5, has predictably been mirrored by rising interest rates. We will have much more to say about the level, the growth, and the nature of bank

25

TABLE 2.5

Loan and Loan-Deposit Ratios

Year	Total Loans (Billions of Dollars)	Loan Ratio	Demand Deposits (Billions of Dollars)	Time Plus Demand Deposits (Billions of Dollars)	Loans Demand Deposits	Loans Time Plus Demand Deposits
1948	41.5	0.37	86.2	121.0	0.48	0.34
1949	42.0	0.35	85.7	121.0	0.49	0.35
1950	51.1	0.41	89.1	125.8	0.57	0.41
1951	56.5	0.43	93.7	130.9	0.60	0.43
1952	62.8	0.45	98.5	138.2	0.64	0.45
1953	66.2	0.46	100.6	143.4	0.66	0.46
1954	69.1	0.45	102.8	149.7	0.67	0.46
1955	80.6	0.51	106.8	156.0	0.75	0.52
1956	88.1	0.55	108.1	158.9	0.82	0.55
1957	91.5	0.55	108.5	163.6	0.84	0.56
1958	95.6	0.53	110.0	172.8	0.87	0.55
1959	110.5	0.59	114.4	181.2	0.97	0.61
1960	116.7	0.59	112.6	181.7	1.04	0.64
1961	123.6	0.58	114.8	193.3	1.08	0.64
1962	137.3	0.59	116.9	208.0	1.18	0.66
1963	153.6	0.61	119.7	225.2	1.28	0.68
1964	172.9	0.64	123.7	243.2	1.40	0.71
1965	198.2	0.66	128.6	266.2	1.54	0.74
1966	213.9	0.68	133.6	287.6	1.60	0.74
1967	231.3	0.66	138.4	311.8	1.67	0.74
1968	258.2	0.66	148.5	341.0	1.74	0.76
1969	279.4	0.70	157.0	355.8	1.78	0.79
1970	292.0	0.66	162.3	370.7	1.80	0.79
1971	320.6	0.68	180.1	434.1	1.80	0.74
1972	378.2	0.68	191.6	485.0	1.96	0.78

Source:
Business Statistics, 1971 U.S. Dept. of Commerce.
Survey of Current Business, U.S. Dept. of Commerce.

loans. Examination of the *Loan-deposit ratio* will show still another facet of the postwar monetary trends.

Loan-Deposit Ratio

Since deposit levels are, in large part, outside the direct influence of the bank, the higher the ratio of loans to deposits of the bank, the greater the risk that a sudden loss of deposits might force the bank to dispose of loans on unfavorable terms. This is the specific risk that the bank with a high loan-deposit ratio must compensate for by an increase in its interest rates. When we are talking about an individual bank with an abnormally high loan-deposit ratio, there is no lasting problem. The higher interest rate that such a bank must charge, reflecting the greater risk due to the high loan-deposit ratio, will eventually cause the bank to lose loan business to competitors who do not have the same high loan-deposit ratio. The ratio of the first bank would then gradually decline, the need for the higher interest rates would diminish, and the bank would then regain its market share with the overall interest rates of the system being relatively undisturbed. What is the effect, however, if the entire banking system suffers from the same rising loan-deposit ratio? The answer must be an inexorable upward pressure upon the general interest-rate level.

A second examination of Table 2.5 undeniably confirms that the long-term trend of loan-deposit ratios is distinctly upward. The aggregate loan-deposit ratio for the system has, without a single interruption, moved from 0.48 to 1.84 in the postwar period. In other words, total bank loans moved from a position of being 48 percent of total demand deposits in 1948 to 184 percent at the end of 1971. Just as the loan-deposit ratio imparts useful knowledge as to the disposition of the resources of individual banks, it is equally enlightening in a study of the system as a whole. It tells us that the most illiquid asset of total bank credit has been growing steadily relative to the most liquid of the liabilities of the banking system, its demand deposits. If bank loans are rising at a much faster pace than deposits, as this indicator demonstrates, the public's position is becoming less liquid, for these loans all belong to someone. For the banks, there is increasingly less room for future loan expansion. It is obvious that, over the entire postwar period, credit outstanding has expanded relentlessly relative to money. Is it any wonder that interest rates have also been steadily rising throughout the same period?

This ratio tells nothing of the liquidity of the other assets of the banking system, which was covered in our first indicators. It does, however, clearly confirm the implications for declining liquidity indicated by the first two measurements. Nor does this indicator take into account the nature of the deposit liabilities of banks, which will be dealt with separately. There are two additional considerations involved. One is a continuing shift from demand deposits into time deposits over the entire postwar period, which will be considered shortly. Second, the banks, acknowledging these dismal statistics, advance the counter-argument that they now practice improved "liabilities management," which will also be discussed in detail below.

A part of the magnitude of the decline in the loan-deposit ratio can be explained by the fact that time deposits have been growing faster than demand deposits, and to the extent that funds have been switched away from demand deposits, the ratio would be worsened. This has also been considered in Table 2.5 in column showing the ratio of loans to time plus demand deposits. It may be seen that, although the trend is mitigated to some extent, it is nevertheless still quite pronounced; as we will see, the shift to time deposits is only one more confirming indicator of the changing liquidity and also a contributor to the trend.

Summary

We have seen that by traditional measures of banking liquidity, there has been an unrelenting and extensive secular decline since the end of World War II, which remains intact today. The trend has in fact been accelerating in recent years, and the effects are becoming apparent. Due to the pervasive nature of the traditional indicators used in this chapter, the evidence presented here should be sufficient to alarm even the most casual observer. One may argue that the measurements began from a period of excessive liquidity in the system, and that we are only now reaching a more normal state of liquidity. One answer to such an objection may be that the nation has always undergone broad trends from excessive liquidity to deficient liquidity, with each extreme always unleashing corrective forces. The last period of extreme illiquidity was the late 1920s. The replacement of liquidity was a primary causal factor of the problems of the 1930s. The illiquidity, as measured today by the same indicators, is considerably worse. The second answer to the objection is that at some point the trend has gone too far, and there should be some predictable effects in evidence to support this conclusion. These effects, which are becoming increasingly evident, will be presented in the balance of this book.

If one accepts the alarms being sounded here, he would be tempted to conclude that the banks are completely at fault, and that all we require is a few changes in banking regulations. Though there has been a fairly drastic change in banking philosophy during this period, which we will discuss in Chapter 3, this is not the complete story or even the primary cause. More importantly, banks are merely reacting to the philosophy and actions of the federal government and the Federal Reserve, which are setting the pace for the decline in liquidity among corporations, individuals, and the banking system.

Chapter 3

Contemporary Banking Theory and Practice

A Bold New Approach or A Study in Desperation?

Current banking theory would seem to hold that much of the asset-liability relationship discussed in Chapter 2 is part of an outmoded banking philosophy. Under the old order, the proper composition of assets required to achieve the optimum balance among income, liquidity, and safety was the primary concern of banks. Before we survey the arguments of the "new bankers," a few comments may be made. Given the drastic deterioration in the indicators presented thus far, it would be difficult for a responsible banker to admit to himself that the old standards are still valid. Moreover, there is considerable evidence that this new philosophy was born of necessity and is not the result of a bold new innovative approach to banking. That is, the system is playing a strong game of "defensive ball" rather than developing aggressive new offensive strategy.

Liabilities Management

The new approach is called "liabilities management," or the ability to compete aggressively for new funds by attracting new deposits and to maximize profits. The argument is made that deposits are no longer all determined exogenously, or outside the control of the banking system. Banks no longer have to take the level of deposits as given to them and thus protect themselves against sudden changes. Endogenous deposit determination has become possible for banks. That is, individual banks and the entire system can now much more aggressively determine their own level of deposits from an unlimited supply of potential deposits. Since they can now determine their own deposits more readily, there is much less to fear from sudden reversals of deposit flows. It is said that the development of the market for Federal Funds and the secondary market for large Certificates of Deposit (CDs) now allows banks, within limits, to determine the size and the nature of their deposits. The argument follows that this development has the tendency to reduce the size of the buffer needed in the form of very liquid assets. Hence, bank investments, and particularly the U.S. government securities portion of it, should rightfully be reduced in the interest of profit maximization. The cost of portfolio adjustments previously made necessary by sudden swings in exogenously determined deposits is also reduced, and thus the upward pressure on interest rates, mentioned in Chapter 2, is not real. This argument would also seem to justify the much higher loan-deposit ratios of today, since the volume of loans is no longer determined solely by the level of exogenous deposits but by the total size of the portfolio. Asset liquidity is no longer critical under this new philosophy.

Counter-Arguments

There are a number of counter-arguments to this new approach to banking liquidity—or, perhaps more accurately stated, this excuse for bank illiquidity. First, it is difficult to be convinced that the problem of adjusting a bank's portfolio to unpredictable and capricious changes in deposits can be drastically improved by attracting larger average deposits, the owners of which are considerably more interest-rate sensitive (referring here to large negotiable CDs, whose minimum size is $100,000). In these days of increasing sophistication among corporate treasurers in the management of excess corporate funds, it may be easier to make the case that the volatility of bank deposits is becoming increasingly worse. Corporate treasurers are not only more aware of other forms of securities, such as preferred stocks, as a tax-free haven for surplus funds, but they are also becoming more aware of the advantages of being alert as to which country their surplus funds are invested in. Incidentally, in Chapter 5 an equally alarming mass of evidence as to corporate illiquidity is presented. The primary argument against the case that corporate liquidity is too low is also that more sophisticated corporate treasurers manage their surplus funds more efficiently and therefore do not require the same quantity of liquid assets as formerly. It would seem that the same argument cannot be applied in both places in a positive vein. We will show in Chapter 6 that the corporations to which these CDs are sold are also becoming illiquid.

Since a major part of such large individual deposits is not covered by deposit insurance by the Federal Deposit Insurance Corporation (FDIC), the wise depositor should favor banks with a higher degree of liquidity. In the new approach, it would seem that the bank that is successful in attracting these large deposits would steadily become more illiquid, given the predilection of bankers to immediately put all deposits to work in high-yielding assets. The new philosophy's increased drive for profit maximization regardless of liquidity costs would also imply such a tendency. As an individual bank becomes less liquid, the possibilities for the loss of some large depositors increase. In the quest for profit maximization, the tendency would be to bid even higher rates in the market to replace the deposits to avoid loan liquidation. This would be particularly true if the same bank had allowed its holdings of U.S. government securities to decline, which, of course, is a part of the plan of the new approach. Further, since the bank is now dealing with the more sophisticated investor, it must compete not only with other banks but also with alternative fixed-income and money-market instruments. As banks compete more strenuously with each other as well as with alternative investments, becoming increasingly illiquid in the process, the upward pressure upon the general interest-rate level continues. Even if the advocate of the new banking philosophy should convince someone that the present structure of the banking system is not in a precarious condition, despite the dismal readings of the traditional indicators, he would be hard-pressed to deny that one clear effect of the new policy is a rising general level of interest rates.

In addition to the long-term upward pressure upon interest rates, the growing usage of the large negotiable CDs introduces increasing volatility and potential distortions into money and capital markets since they are fairly short-dated. An examination of the action of these large CDs during the last money squeeze demonstrates the potential dislocations they introduce.

In 1969, as has already been mentioned, interest rates had their sharpest rise. During the year, municipal bonds became practically illiquid and banks were forced to rely upon their dwindling supply of U.S. government securities to avoid serious loan liquidations. As Figure 3.1 demonstrates, the major contributor to the intensity of the crunch was the very large CDs, which experienced an extremely sharp runoff from the beginning of 1969 to the trough in January 1970. Such CDs declined from their new record level slightly over $23 billion to around $10 billion, placing unreasonably high liquidity pressures upon the banking system. It is interesting that the decline in CDs was almost exactly offset by the decline in the system's holdings of U.S. government securities.

A major reason for the severity of the runoff in CDs during 1969 was the existence of Regulation Q interest-rate ceilings on CDs, which led to disintermediation as yields on competing instruments exceeded the return available on large CDs. These ceilings were enacted over twenty-five years before in the belief that destructive rate competition among banks was one of the basic causes of bank failures in the 1930s. It was not until the late 1950s that rates finally began to bump against these Regulation Q ceilings. In the credit crunches of both 1966 and 1969, when the ceilings became restrictive, banks were able to partially offset the runoffs that occurred by obtaining Eurodollars, which were not subject to the ceilings. In 1966, Eurodollars held by U.S. banks increased from slightly over $1 billion to over $4 billion. In 1969, holdings of Eurodollars were expanded even faster to a level of $15 billion, and from November 1969 to August 1971 they again decreased by over $14 billion. The existence of such interest-rate ceilings undoubtedly led to a much faster expansion of the Eurodollar market than would have occurred in their absence and also probably contributed greatly to today's volatile international flow of dollars. The rapid changes in Eurodollars (see Figure 3.2) is only one of many examples we will

Outstanding Volume

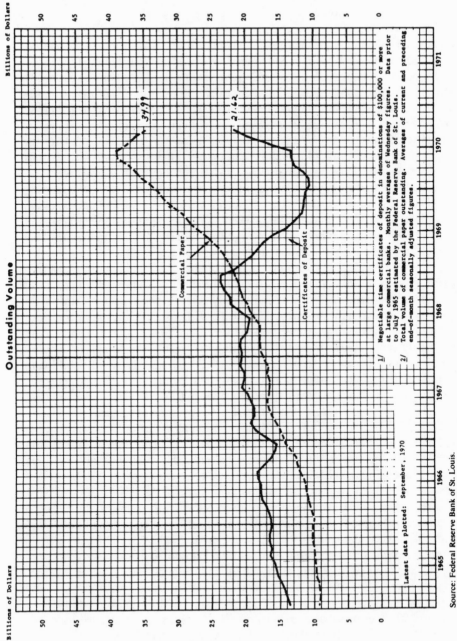

Source: Federal Reserve Bank of St. Louis.

Fig. 3.1—Certificates of Deposit and Commercial Paper

Billions of Dollars

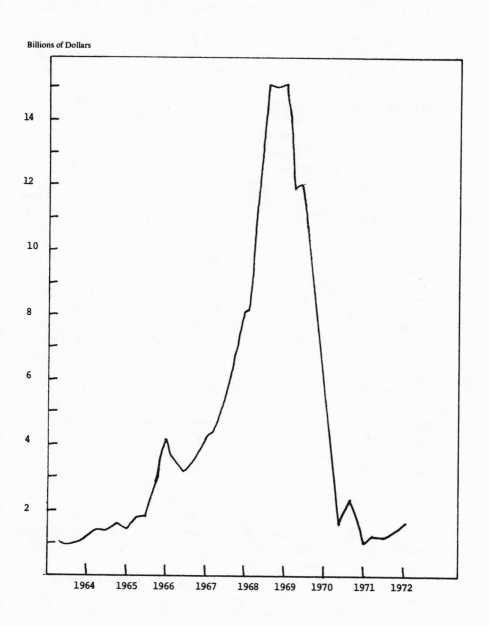

Fig. 3.2—Eurodollar Borrowing by the U.S.

show of increasing volatility in financial markets.

The ceilings were removed on large denomination CDs of 30-89 days maturity in 1970, and such CDs outstanding recovered rapidly from the low of $10.3 billion in early February 1970 back to $23.5 billion by the end of October 1970. This timely action probably averted a run on the commercial-paper market as well as a much more serious credit collapse than what occurred. The action probably also removed, for a while, much of the possibility for a repeat of such violent disintermediation as occurred in 1969. As abhorrent as most government controls have been, one wonders if the ceilings, though they caused many unnecessary dislocations in the past, might better have been replaced after the emergency had passed. Perhaps the threat of a recurrence of such a disintermediation might serve to force banks to have greater care regarding their liquidity ratios until action can be taken to get at the root of the excessive credit expansion of the Federal Reserve, which we will describe further on. Perhaps what was gained in lower near-term volatility will be more than offset by increased upward pressure on interest-rate requirements for bank loans, since banks must pay up for deposit money in periods of higher interest rates for alternative investments. The level of large CDs outstanding at this writing has already surpassed $60 billion, more than doubling the record levels of 1970. When one observes the aggressive actions of large commercial banks today in bidding for large CDs, one wonders whether the original fears of destructive rate competition felt by the enactors of the first ceilings were not well taken. It is also conceivable that from the sheer size of the present levels of CDs there may be as much potential volatility in the system as there was under the Regulation Q ceilings.

The combination of the steadily declining liquidity ratios and the rapidly growing CD levels may mean that a new magnitude of volatility has been introduced into the system. We do not have perfect information on just who the holders of the CDs are. Presumably most of them are the sophisticated corporate treasurers referred to above, who may soon use the funds for the capital goods boom that is in progress or to build depleted inventory levels, or conceivably the funds may be shifted to other countries. The holders may be institutional investors who are only awaiting clearer investment opportunities before shifting the funds elsewhere. Finally, they may also be foreign investors who may repatriate the funds on short notice. The growing size of this pool of aggressive money should be a greater source of concern to banks than is evidenced by their continued disregard of liquidity.

There are other ramifications to the increasing use of negotiable CDs, aside from the problem of the size of the pool. They concern the question of liquidity and upward pressure upon interest rates. When banks issue the large negotiable CDs and then loan the funds received, they run the risk that the CD-rate will rise prior to the maturity date of the loan since it is fairly short-term money. When they renew the CD at a higher rate, their margin of profit on the loan is reduced. Given the present aggressiveness of banks in the pursuit of CD money, the large size of the pool, and the growing dependence of banks on this source of funds, there is little doubt that the volatility in this market will grow. There is also a very pronounced trend, which will be discussed later in more detail, for the average maturity of bank loans to lengthen. Thus, there is a very good chance that this condition of borrowing short and lending long by banks will continue to spread. This should cause bank profit-margins to narrow unless it is offset by much higher interest rates to compensate for the added risk. Everything considered, this new endogenous deposit determination will not be the blessing to the individual bank that it is represented to be by the proponents of the new banking philosophy, and it certainly will not be a blessing to the economy.

A second and perhaps more basic counter to the new approach in banking is the argument that what may be true for one bank is not necessarily true for the system as a whole and certainly not for the economy. An individual bank may become more profitable, or even more liquid, by its actions, but it must do so at the expense of another bank. All banks are competing for a given pool of potential savings. If one illiquid bank succeeds in attracting deposits from another by raising deposit rates, it makes the unsuccessful bank more illiquid, and it in turn must reduce loans or investments or raise rates to attract deposits from a third bank. Thus, when one considers the system as a whole, the negative implications of the growing illiquidity, as measured by traditional indicators, have meaning again. The sophisticated banking approach of today only encourages overextended positions in the interest of profit maximization, growing illiquidity, increasing volatility, and upward pressure upon interest rates. To retreat toward better liquidity is not considered sound strategy for a bank in today's violently competitive market for deposits and profit maximization.

A Recent History of New Banking Techniques

A brief review of the events of the credit crunch of 1969-70 should give you a better insight into the new innovative banking management. Prior to the crunch, large commercial banks were generally losing deposits to smaller banks. Since their liquidity ratios had already reached a serious state, they began to bid aggressively for CDs, which grew rapidly in amounts outstanding until reaching the peak of over $23 billion at the beginning of 1969. Then, as mentioned above, the crunch began, with CDs running off to $10 billion in scarcely one year. The loss had to be replaced, and was partially offset by sales of U.S. government securities as far as practicable. Then began a series of aggressive new techniques.

Some of the problem was alleviated by the increased use of federal funds, which are funds that banks without adequate reserves borrow on a short-term basis from banks with excess reserves. Generally, the large banks—the sellers of the large CDs—are the borrowers. Federal Funds sales rose 50 percent in 1969 and have continued to grow since (see Table 3.1). Due to the general lack of liquidity in the system, there were no excess reserves available to stem the decline in reserves in 1969.

TABLE 3.1

(In Billions of Dollars)

Month	Year	Federal Funds Rate (Percentage)	Federal Funds Sold	Commercial Paper, Bank-Related	Liabilities of U.S. Banks To Foreign Branches Eurodollars
Dec.	1968	6.02	6,747	—	6,039
Jan.	1969	6.30	—	—	—
Feb.	1969	6.64	—	—	—
Mar.	1969	6.79	—	—	9,621
Apr.	1969	7.41	—	—	—
May	1969	8.67	—	—	—
June	1969	8.90	7,226	1.2	13,269
July	1969	8.61	—	1.9	—
Aug.	1969	9.19	—	2.3	—
Sept.	1969	9.15	—	2.6	14,349
Oct.	1969	9.00	—	3.7	—
Nov.	1969	8.85	—	4.2	—
Dec.	1969	8.97	9,928	4.2	12,805
Jan.	1970	8.98	—	5.5	—
Feb.	1970	8.98	—	5.0	—
Mar.	1970	7.76	—	6.4	11,885
Apr.	1970	8.10	—	6.7	—
May	1970	7.94	—	7.6	—
June	1970	7.60	11,193	7.6	12,172
July	1970	7.21	—	7.8	—
Aug.	1970	6.61	—	7.3	—
Sept.	1970	6.29	—	4.6	9,663
Oct.	1970	6.20	—	3.7	—
Nov.	1970	5.60	—	3.1	—
Dec.	1970	4.90	16,241	2.3	7,676
June 30,	1971	4.91	15,663	1.7	1,492
Dec. 31,	1971	4.14	19,954	2.0	909

Source: *Federal Reserve Bulletin.*

The Eurodollar Boom

The void was next filled by increased use of a relatively new tool, Eurodollar borrowing. The term *Eurodollar* refers to American dollars borrowed or loaned by foreign financial institutions as well as foreign branches of American banks. Most Eurodollar borrowings are for terms of less than one year. Prior to the liquidity squeezes of 1966 and 1969-70, little use was made of Eurodollars by American banks. Table 3.1 depicts the rapid increase since that time. In the beginning, this borrowing was not subject to interest-rate ceilings or the reserve requirements of the FDIC. Banks could afford to pay the higher rates necessary to obtain such funds. Before the end of 1969, however, the Federal Reserve placed a 2 percent reserve requirement against Eurodollar borrowing, as well as against assets sold by member banks to their foreign branches. The levels of Eurodollars have since declined considerably.

Commercial Paper

The next tool discovered by banks was commercial paper, which is a short-term promissory note, usually less than six months in maturity, used by non-financial organizations. Short-term notes with maturities of less than two years, if issued by banks, are subject to the same restrictions as deposits. Banks, however, found a loophole. The restrictions did not explicitly cover bank-holding companies or their nonbank subsidiaries. Thus, when Eurodollar borrowing became more expensive with the new restriction, banks turned rapidly to commercial paper and the amount outstanding burgeoned from less than $2 billion in the summer of 1969 to close to $8 billion by mid-1970 (see Table 3.1). With the sale of commercial paper by the holding company, the operating bank subsidiary was able to sell its existing loans to the holding company for the proceeds of the commercial-paper sale and was then free to make new loans to accommodate its customers or to meet deficient reserve conditions. This loophole was fairly quickly closed also, and the growth of such commercial-paper offerings slowed and finally declined from the peak levels. Total commercial-paper outstanding, including both bank-related and nonbank, continued to increase rapidly even after the sharp rise during the credit crunch. As you can see in Table 3.2, the overall level of commercial paper outstanding grew fourfold from 1965 through the end of

TABLE 3.2

Commercial Paper Outstanding
(In Billions of Dollars)

End of Period	Total Commercial Paper Outstanding	Bank Related Commercial Paper
1965	9.1	0.0
1966	13.3	0.0
1967	16.5	0.0
1968	20.5	0.0
1969	31.7	4.3
1970	31.8	2.3
1971	31.1	2.0
1972	34.7	2.6
1973 (Jan.)	35.7	2.7
1973 (Feb.)	35.2	3.1

37

1972. The level of commercial paper outstanding is a good confirming indicator to track commercial-bank liquidity. When banks have trouble fulfilling loan demands due to such liquidity problems, the unfilled demand often switches to commercial paper.

A number of minor new techniques attempted in 1969 and 1970 never became as widespread as those mentioned above but remain as a testimony to the ingenuity, or desperation, of commercial banks. One such technique in 1969 was the practice by a number of banks of purchasing short-term funds from corporate clients, paying the going Federal Funds rates. The Federal Reserve very quickly eliminated this procedure, reasoning that the practice was akin to paying interest rates on demand deposits, which is not allowed.

Also in 1969, some banks began selling loans, under repurchase agreements, to corporate customers. Since the liability for loans sold in this manner was not considered a deposit, there were no reserve requirements. The Federal Reserve was once again quick to amend Regulations D and Q to classify such obligations as deposits and thus subject to reserve requirements.

Although the list of new techniques of liability management was not exhausted, it was long enough to demonstrate the tone of the new philosophy of banking under stress. Though praised by many authors as sound, innovative banking, it seems to be more an expression of the old proverb that necessity is the mother of invention. We saw that, in a period of stress, there was more scrambling than planning. One of the cornerstones of the new liability management, the large CDs, caused much of the problem in 1969 with the sharp runoff. It is true that, with the relaxation of the interest-rate ceilings, the deposits were quickly replaced, but the system suffered extreme volatility in the process. The substitution of one type of purchased money, such as Eurodollars or Federal Funds, for CDs and then back again accomplishes very little in reconstituting the internal liquidity that banks have lost. The fact that the level of the volatile CDs has reached well beyond $60 billion leaves the system once again quite vulnerable.

Conclusions

The new liability management discussed in this chapter seems to be more a desperate reaction to the overwhelming illiquidity problem than the application of bold new managerial techniques. The increased use of nondeposit sources of funds only mitigates the effects of illiquidity in the short run. In the process, however, it introduces further volatility into the system. The aggressive search for funds at any cost, described above, leads to higher costs of money for the banks, which must be passed along to borrowers in the form of higher interest costs, contributing to the long-term upward trend in interest rates throughout the postwar period. Clearly, the new liabilities management is a direct reaction to the lower investment portfolios, high loan ratios, and high loan-deposit ratios.

Perhaps worst of all, the time bought by the new techniques helps to extend the long-term trend of liquidity deterioration by putting off any debt liquidation during business recessions, which in the past acted as natural corrections to trends toward lower liquidity. The techniques detract attention from the low levels of liquidity and promote confidence among bankers that buffers are not needed. We will discuss the effects of illiquidity in the banking system in greater detail later. In the next chapter, we examine other indicators that confirm the findings in Chapter 2. We then examine liquidity in other sectors of the economy.

Chapter 4

Additional Indicators of Banking Liquidity

The measurements of banking liquidity discussed in Chapter 2 are the indicators that have traditionally been used to assess liquidity among banks or in the banking system. As pointed out in Chapter 3, many bankers would argue that such indicators no longer reflect accurately the condition of the industry, since there have been significant changes in the philosophy and practice of banking. The financial data discussed in this chapter offer further evidence of the illiquid state of the banking system as measured by the traditional indicators. The trends presented in evidence confirm the growing illiquidity, though they are not strictly measurements of liquidity. Other trends serve to intensify the effects of illiquidity and aid in furthering it. Still other trends are evidence that the liquidity is even worse than indicated by our indicators, though the amount is not measurable.

Time Deposit-Demand Deposit Relationship

Throughout the entire postwar period the relationship between time and demand deposits has changed drastically. While demand deposits scarcely doubled, time deposits increased nearly sevenfold over the same period. The ratio of demand deposits to time deposits moved from 249.1 percent in 1947 to 68.2 percent at the end of 1971, with only minor and infrequent interruptions in the trend. The trend is depicted in Table 4.1 and Figure 4.1

While there may be several explanations for this phenomenon, the causes are not as important as the effects. One important reason for the trend, if not the primary reason, is that savers tend to move idle money out of demand deposits and into time deposits as real interest rates rise since it becomes more expensive to hold cash.

Our findings in Chapter 2 demonstrated that banks have generally used any

41

TABLE 4.1

Time and Demand Deposit Relationships

Year	Demand Deposits (Billions of Dollars)	Time Deposits (Billions of Dollars)	Demand Deposits as a Percentage of Time Deposits
1947	85.2	34.2	249.1
1948	86.2	35.8	240.8
1949	85.7	36.3	236.1
1950	89.1	36.7	242.8
1951	93.7	37.2	251.9
1952	98.5	39.7	248.1
1953	100.6	42.8	235.0
1954	102.8	46.9	219.2
1955	106.8	49.2	217.1
1956	108.1	50.8	212.8
1957	108.5	55.1	196.9
1958	110.0	62.8	179.2
1959	114.4	66.8	171.3
1960	112.6	69.1	163.0
1961	114.8	78.5	146.2
1962	116.9	91.1	128.3
1963	119.7	105.5	113.5
1964	123.7	119.5	103.5
1965	128.6	137.6	93.5
1966	133.6	154.0	86.8
1967	138.4	173.4	79.8
1968	148.5	192.5	77.1
1969	157.0	198.8	79.0
1970	162.3	208.2	78.0
1971	180.1	254.0	71.0
1972	191.6	293.4	65.3

Source:
Business Statistics, 1971, U.S. Dept. of Commerce.
Federal Reserve Bulletin.

extra reserves to increase their loan portfolios rather than their investment portfolios. Since reserve requirements have always been lower on time deposits than on demand deposits, this long postwar trend has had the effect of supplying additional reserves to the banking system. These reserves, in turn, have enabled banks to further accelerate their lending activities, making this shift in deposits a contributing factor to the decline in liquidity by further expanding total bank credit relative to the deposit base.

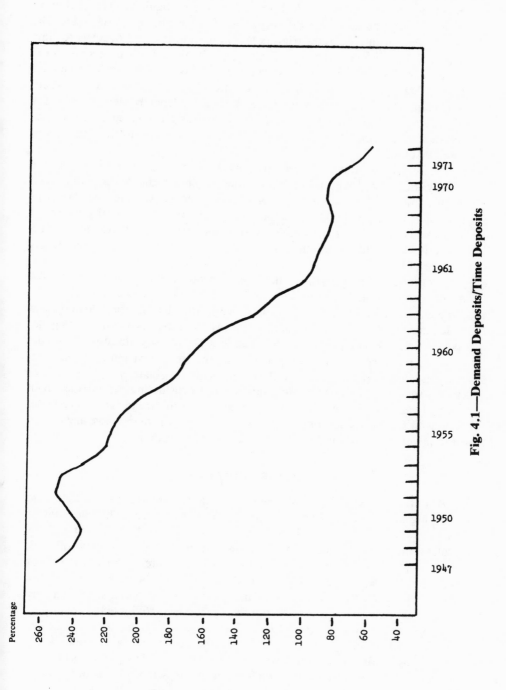

Percentage

260 — 240 — 220 — 200 — 180 — 160 — 140 — 120 — 100 — 80 — 60 — 40 —

1971
1970
1961
1960
1955
1950
1947

Fig. 4.1—Demand Deposits/Time Deposits

We see, then, the first of many circular or self-enforcing trends helping to maintain and accelerate the decline in the nation's liquidity. The decline in liquidity, as pointed out, has the very clear effect of raising interest rates. The rising trend in interest rates triggers the shift from demand deposits to time deposits. The excess reserves so created give bankers further impetus to expand their loan portfolios at the expense of the investment portfolios and deposits, thereby accelerating the trend toward lower liquidity, which is where we began. The creation of excess reserves resulting from the deposit shift may also be said to be stimulative and, all things being equal, inflationary. The inflation, according to monetarist theory, serves to add a further premium to interest rates.

As we will continue to point out, most of the indicators discussed are closely interrelated, and all serve not only to confirm the deteriorating trend in banking liquidity but also to enforce it. Further on, we point out that similar trends of corporate liquidity, spurred by actions of the federal government and the Federal Reserve, combine with banking liquidity trends to create a self-propelling and accelerating force, which is at the root of the current financial ills of the nation.

The trend in time deposits, when traced through, can be seen to contribute to the declining investments-bank credit relationship, the declining U.S. government securities-bank credit relationship, the deteriorating loan-deposit relationship, and the rise in general volatility from the portion of the time deposits that are comprised of the mobile CDs already discussed. Finally, through the effects of all these phenomena, the trend contributes to the postwar rise in interest rates. It is always difficult to isolate the effects of one trend, such as this time-deposit shift, without considering the interaction of several variables. We will return to a discussion of this trend again in conjunction with trends in loan content of bank credit, interest-rate trends, and deposit turnover. The latter is discussed in the following section.

Deposit Turnover

A useful indicator in gauging banking liquidity—or, more specifically, the changing loan content of bank credit—is deposit turnover. This indicator of money velocity has historically correlated well with the loan-deposit ratio as well as with interest rates. The turnover rate is derived as a ratio of bank debits to demand deposits and is a traditional measure of the circulation of money. Bank debits are simply a compilation of total checks written, cleared, and finally debited to the account of the writer of the check, and as such they provide an important measurement of total economic activity in the country.

As the record indicates (see Table 4.2 and Figure 4.2), the turnover rate has not declined in any year, thus paralleling the decline in bank liquidity, the loan-deposit ratio specifically, and rising interest rates. The particularly sharp acceleration since 1960 is very reminiscent of the action of this indicator in the late 1920s. Although the ascent is quite pronounced in New York, the trend is the same even when more SMSA's are considered.

TABLE 4.2

Deposit Turnover at New York

Year	Percentage	Year	Percentage
1947	23.8	1960	60.0
1948	26.9	1961	70.0
1949	27.9	1962	77.8
1950	31.1	1963	84.8
1951	31.9	1964	93.8
1952	34.4	1965	98.8
1953	36.7	1966	109.0
1954	42.3	1967	120.3
1955	42.7	1968	135.5
1956	45.8	1969	143.6
1957	49.5	1970	154.4
1958	53.6	1971	196.1
1959	56.4	1972	229.2

Source:
Supplement to Banking and Monetary Statistics: Bank Debits, Section 5, Board of Governors of the Federal Reserve System.

Relationship of Deposit Turnover to Other Measures of Liquidity

Deposit turnover has historically correlated well with the loan content of bank credit for a very basic reason. The banking system, as we know, may create money by investment in government bonds or by granting loans. Investments have always served as a buffer, particularly in the case of the most liquid investments, or as a residual awaiting an increase in loan demand to be loaned at higher interest rates. They represent relatively idle money as far as the economy as a whole is concerned. Borrowers, on the other hand, do not borrow money to leave it idle but to use in more dynamic pursuits. A higher loan content of bank credit, then, implies higher turnover of money. The higher the percentage of money derived from bank loans to the private sector, the faster the money will circulate. Just as the rising loan-deposit ratio is a major factor in increasing deposit turnover, so is that turnover a testimony to, and confirmation of, the growing indebtedness of the economy and the delining liquidity of the banking system specifically.

When examining relationships among the indicators discussed up to this point, we see that there is not only correlation and confirmation but, as mentioned earlier, a self-enforcing trend among them. We begin our study from a period of admittedly high liquidity with a low level of loans and a correspondingly low velocity of deposits. Demand for money was obviously low relative to the supply, and interest rates were low. Then, as demonstrated, a

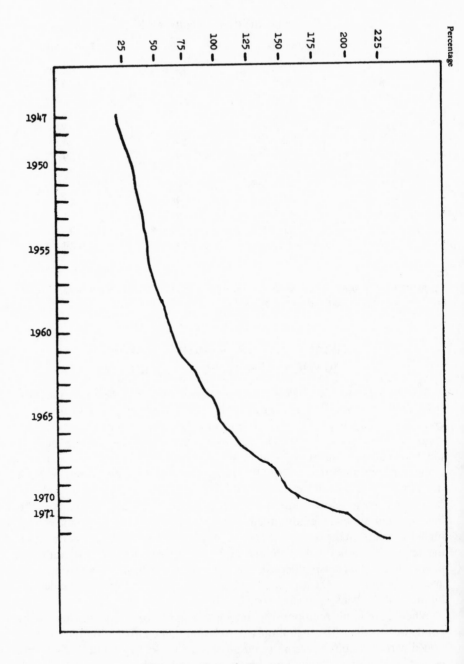

Fig. 4.2—Deposit Turnover

46

number of important trends began, which have continued intact to the present time. The banking system has consistently liquidated bonds to meet rising credit demands. Increases in velocity of deposits have paralleled the increased loan content of bank credit as idle investment money has been turned into more active loans to the private sector. The increases in velocity have been accelerated by the more rapid growth in time deposits relative to demand deposits. The increased velocity and the relative decline in demand deposits have both combined to increase the loan-deposit ratio and decrease bank liquidity as a result. The decline in banking liquidity, in turn, has stimulated the rise in postwar interest rates. But rising interest rates, as we saw, lead to the shift from demand deposits to time deposits. This shift, in its turn, increases excess reserves, which eventually leads to a stimulation of loan demand and creation of money, all of which contributes to the rising loan-deposit ratio and velocity, which completes the circle of self-generating liquidity deterioration.

While we discuss the inflationary aspects of the liquidity decline at greater length further on, they should be mentioned briefly here. Rapid increases in the velocity of circulation are quite characteristic of periods of rapid expansion of money and credit in the private sector. With the rapid price inflation eventually accompanying such a trend, holders attempt to pass money off as quickly as possible for assets. Rising velocity is clearly an indicator of the condition of declining liquidity described here.

There is nothing portentous in the close correlation of these indicators, or even in the self-sustaining, circular relationship. These indicators have always moved in close harmony, reaching peaks in the 1920s, prior to the economic collapse, and reaching their troughs in the 1930s, when demand for money was low, velocity of bank deposits reached its lowest point ever, and activity in general was quiet, The concern lies in the length of the period of uninterrupted trends of each of the indicators and the unprecedented levels of the readings. We reserve the analysis of the reasons for this for a subsequent point in this book.

Excess Reserves

Historically, the level of excess reserves has varied with the changing moods of bankers from pessimism to optimism. In the 1930s, at times, bankers held excess reserves almost equal to their required reserves, reflecting an extreme lack of confidence. When the Federal Reserve attempted to "mop up" the excess reserves by doubling reserve requirements in 1936, banks proceeded to reduce loan commitments in 1937 and 1938 to bring the excess reserves back up to the same levels. This action was probably a significant causal factor in the recession of 1937-38.

It can be seen from Table 4.3 that excess-reserve relationships had improved considerably by the beginning of the postwar period, with excess reserves only about 6 percent of required reserves. Since the loan content of total bank credit was relatively low at that time, due to the massive increases in government securities in the banking system during the war, the level of excess reserves was probably adequate. With the long and continuous rise in the loan content and

47

TABLE 4.3

Excess Reserves

(In Millions of Dollars)

Year	Excess Reserves	Required Reserves	Total Reserves
1929	48	2,347	2,395
1930	73	2,342	2,415
1931	60	2,010	2,069
1932	526	1,909	2,435
1933	766	1,822	2,588
1934	1,748	2,290	4,037
1935	2,983	2,733	5,716
1936	2,046	4,619	6,665
1937	1,071	5,808	6,879
1938	3,226	5,520	8,745
1939	5,011	6,462	11,473
1940	6,646	7,403	14,049
1947	986	16,275	17,261
1948	797	19,193	19,990
1949	803	15,488	16,291
1950	1,027	16,364	17,391
1951	826	19,484	20,310
1952	723	20,457	21,180
1953	693	19,227	19,920
1954	703	18,576	19,279
1955	594	18,646	19,240
1956	652	18,883	19,535
1957	577	18,843	19,420
1958	516	18,383	18,899
1959	482	18,450	18,932
1960	756	18,527	19,283
1961	568	19,550	20,118
1962	572	19,468	20,040
1963	536	20,210	20,746
1964	411	21,198	21,609
1965	452	22,267	22,719
1966	392	23,438	23,830
1967	345	24,915	25,260
1968	455	26,766	27,221
1969	257	27,774	28,031
1970	272	28,993	29,265
1971	165	31,164	31,329

Source:
Supplement to Banking & Monetary Statistics, Section 10, Member Bank Reserve and Related Items, Board of Governors of the Federal Reserve System.
Business Statistics, 1971, U.S. Dept. of Commerce.

decline in banking liquidity discussed above, one would expect the level of excess reserves relative to required reserves to rise, reflecting the increasing risks in the system. It can be seen in Table 4.3 that the opposite is true. Not only has the ratio of excess reserves to total required reserves moved steadily downward, but the absolute amount of excess reserves has declined over the entire period. A low level of excess reserves must surely represent at least a potential risk that, should bankers' sentiment change to a more realistic appraisal of the level of risk in the system, loan commitments could be reduced sharply to bring excess reserves to a more reasonable level. The reduction in the absolute level of excess reserves would have been bad enough in itself if all other banking statistics had remained relatively stable or moved in the same direction. This was clearly not the case (see Table 4.4). Since other statistics moved to much higher levels over the same period, a much larger retrenchment in loans would be necessary to bring excess reserves up to a more conservative level. Notice particularly the extremely large expansion in total loans. When the increase in loans outstanding is related to the trend in excess reserves, one can see the extent to which the banking system is overextended today relative to the early postwar years. Imagine the loan liquidation that would have to take place if the Federal Reserve attempted to slow down the rate of credit expansion by raising reserve requirements.

TABLE 4.4

Banking Statistic Changes, 1948-71
(All Commercial Banks)

Total loans	+668%
Demand deposits	+101%
Total deposits	+171%
Excess reserves	− 79%
Total reserves	+ 56%
Required reserves	+ 62%

Source:
Business Statistics 1971, Department of Commerce.
Federal Reserve Bulletin.

The decline in excess reserves is even more significant when we consider the changes during the period that should have had the tendency to raise excess reserves. The shift from demand deposits to time deposits has already been discussed. With the lower reserve requirements for time deposits, excess reserves are automatically raised as the shift continues. There has generally been a shift of total deposits away from reserve city banks, especially New York, to country banks, where once again the reserve requirements are lower (see Table 4.5). The classifications of banks were restructured in 1972, and reserve requirements applicable to demand deposits of member banks are now levied according to the

TABLE 4.5

Change in Total Deposits by Class of Bank
(In Millions of Dollars)

	Dec. 1974	Dec. 1971	% Change
All commercial banks	144,103	524,890	264
Reserve city member: New York	25,216	70,247	178
Reserve city member: Chicago	6,402	16,340	155
Other reserve city	46,467	151,249	225
Country member	44,443	178,734	302

Source: *Federal Reserve Bulletin.*

amount of such deposits, regardless of a bank's location rather than the older classification of reserve city bank versus country bank. This too has the effect of raising the level of excess reserves. Moreover, the overall level of reserve requirements for both time deposits and demand deposits for banks of all categories has been steadily reduced, and in some instances drastically, over the entire postwar period. The history of the regulation of reserve requirements reflects a philosophy that has generally been evolving away from the earlier role of insuring proper sources of liquidity to the role of a tool of monetary policy. State regulations are usually even less restrictive than those for member banks. Reserve requirements on large commercial banks have been reduced almost 50 percent in the postwar years. Finally, after 1960, banks were permitted to count vault cash as part of their reserves, which added to reserves immediately and measurably. Thus, in spite of a number of significant measures, all of which have the effect of increasing excess reserves, the absolute level of excess reserves has declined drastically even as total reserves, required reserves, and loans have all increased.

So it can be seen that excess reserves, like the other indicators examined so far, also confirm the secular decline in liquidity and the increase in risk in the entire banking system. As with the other indicators, it is difficult to decide just when the level is dangerous and when it must begin to improve. Often the phrase "Liquidity is only a state of mind" is used to dispel the concern for poor liquidity figures. While this idea may be true, it ignores the facts that the level of risk in the system is increasing, that each economic expansion will run out of money sooner, that the upward pressure on interest rates will continue, and that the potential for extreme dislocations from any change in sentiment is everpresent. Until recently, the general state of mind favored the rundown in liquidity. As we will discuss fully, this state of mind was fostered by the government and by the Federal Reserve, which together played the key roles in the rundown of liquidity. The state of mind is changing, however, as both populace and financial institutions are being given constant reminders that perhaps the trend has gone far enough. Some examples are the recurring credit crunches and atten-

Percentage

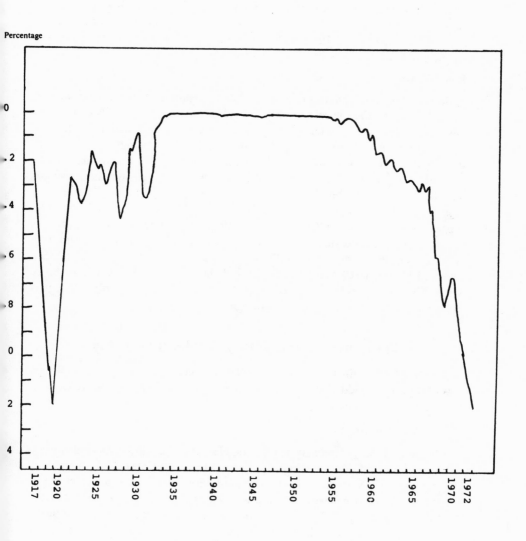

Fig. 4.3—Ratio of Bank Borrowings to Reserves

51

dant volatility, America's loss of world prestige, several devaluations, stubborn inflationary pressures, and rising interest rates. As sentiment changes, the liquidity structure becomes more meaningful. Just as the level of excess reserves in the 1930s represented an extreme of banking pessimism, the current level probably indicates much more optimism than is warranted, considering the increasing risk in the system. Perhaps it is not just optimism but also a lack of concern with the low levels of liquidity, due to a pervasive feeling that the government, in its expanding militant role in business-cycle management, will simply rescue any bank that gets into financial trouble.

Bank Borrowings

Still another confirming indicator of banking liquidity is presented in Figure 4.3. It illustrates the relationship of bank borrowings, primarily comprising bank borrowings of Federal Funds and securities sold under repurchase agreements, to total bank reserves. The ratio of borrowings to reserves is plotted inversely. For example, if the reading is 0.40, then borrowings are 40 percent of reserves, while if over 1.00, borrowings are greater than reserves and the system is illiquid.

It can be seen that in past periods, when the ratio rose substantially, problems ensued. In 1920, when the ratio rose drastically to 1.20, it was followed by a period of recession, market decline, and strains on liquidity. After recovering in the later 1920s, it again declined to nearly 0.50 in 1928, followed by the 1929 market collapse and the recession of the 1930s. Since 1960, after a long period of good behavior, the ratio has steadily risen; it is presently hovering near the 1.20 mark again.

Additional Indications of Banking Liquidity

The indicators already presented definitely confirm a trend of declining bank liquidity. In addition, several less documentable factors indicate an even lower degree of illiquidity.

Hidden Bond-Portfolio Losses

We have already demonstrated the deteriorating condition of bank-investment portfolios relative to total bank credit. The picture presented, though disturbing in itself, was probably understated, since banks are not required to recognize a loss on an investment unless it is sold. Investments are stated on the books at original cost. Table 4.6 reviews the uptrend in interest rates for municipal and U.S. government bonds, which has been in effect throughout the entire postwar period, with a decided acceleration in the most recent years. Paralleling the rise in interest rates, of course, is the corresponding decline in bond prices, which has the effect of understating bank portfolios, especially with the rapid rise of interest rates in recent years.

Although banks may have adjusted somewhat to the rising interest rates by going "shorter" in their municipal-bond investments lately, it is safe to assume that there are still a great number of "paper losses" in every portfolio,

52

TABLE 4.6

Domestic Municipal & U.S. Government Bond Yields

Year	Bond Buyers' 20 Bonds	Standard & Poors' 15 Bonds	U.S. Treasury Taxable Bonds
1947	1.93	2.01	2.25
1948	2.35	2.40	2.44
1949	2.15	2.21	2.31
1950	1.90	1.98	2.32
1951	1.97	2.00	2.57
1952	2.20	2.19	2.68
1953	2.73	2.72	2.94
1954	2.38	2.37	2.55
1955	2.49	2.53	2.84
1956	2.80	2.93	3.08
1957	3.28	3.60	3.47
1958	3.18	3.56	3.43
1959	3.58	3.95	4.07
1960	3.51	3.73	4.01
1961	3.46	3.46	3.90
1962	3.14	3.18	3.95
1963	3.18	3.23	4.00
1964	3.20	3.22	4.15
1965	3.28	3.27	4.21
1966	3.83	3.82	4.66
1967	3.96	3.98	4.85
1968	4.47	4.51	5.25
1969	5.79	5.81	6.10
1970	6.34	6.50	6.59
1971	5.46	5.70	5.74
1972	5.11	5.03	5.63

Source:
Business Statistics, 1971, U.S. Dept. of Commerce.
Survey of Current Business, U.S. Dept. of Commerce.

particularly during periods of sharp credit constraint, as in 1966, 1969, and 1970.

Further, if rates continue to rise in response to the steadily declining bank liquidity, there will be continuing undercover deterioration in bank investments and, hence, in liquidity. Declining bank liquidity thus reinforces itself through the upward pressure it places upon interest rates by reducing, in turn, the real level of bank investments, further reducing liquidity and raising interest rates. Thus, should loan demand accelerate, or should the monetary authorities decide to restrict reserves, banks will either take real losses by liquidating investments to meet loan demand, or be more willing to liquidate loans rather than show actual losses. The latter alternative, if followed, would have the effect of restraining economic expansion as well as exacerbating any credit crunches.

Pledging of Liquid Assets

Another factor that tends to understate further the actual level of banking liquidity is the amounts of liquid assets pledged by banks against deposits of public funds by state and local governments. This fairly widespread practice takes a large amount of the collective investment portfolios out of the liquid fund available to meet sudden deposit withdrawals or increased loan demand.

Public funds, at present, qualify for only the same $20,000 in deposit insurance available to the private sector. Banks generally pledge municipal bonds to guarantee the uninsured balance of public deposits. Although the Federal Reserve does not regularly report on such pledged securities, a recent article reported the current amount at $57 billion, or roughly 55 percent of the "Other Securities" portion of total bank-investment accounts.

Although these securities are not available to meet loan or deposit withdrawal demands, they are not deducted or in any other manner accounted for in the liquidity ratios we have presented up to this point. Therefore, our ratios drastically overstate the amounts of investments available to meet liquidity needs.

Lengthening Bank Credit

Still another factor not considered in the traditional indicators of banking liquidity is the gradually increasing length of average bank loans, particularly in larger banks. Adequate data are not available to trace the entire postwar trend, but the Federal Reserve has begun to report regularly on the "term" loans outstanding at large commercial banks. At the end of 1969, near the peak in the credit squeeze of 1969-70, such term loans (defined as all loans that had an original maturity of more than one year) reached a level of 40.2 percent of all commercial and industrial loans outstanding. This percentage represented a level considerably higher than the one prevailing during the early postwar years. When the increasingly shorter-term nature of the new sources of bank deposits described earlier and the increasing volatility are juxtaposed with the increasing length of loans, the combination represents a significant deterioration of bank liquidity. Banks violate the advice they commonly give to customers to avoid borrowing short to invest long. As we will see in Chapter 5, a decline in corporate liquidity has paralleled the decline in banking liquidity. The increase in term loans is evidence of reduced banking liquidity and also implies that corporations are looking to banks for financing of a more permanent nature.

Summary

We have tried to demonstrate that by traditional measures as well as others, banking liquidity has steadily declined, with banks currently being more illiquid than at any time in recent history. While there has been some cyclicality in the decline, with each postwar recession serving to temporarily interrupt the trend by restoring some liquidity, there is little doubt that a well-defined and unmistakable downward trend is in effect and continues to the present day. There has been a pronounced acceleration in the trend since the early 1960s. There appears to be little resiliency left in the banking system to absorb further deterioration in liquidity, let alone such shocks as the sudden declines in deposits in 1969 or the highly restrictive Federal Reserve monetary policy. The manifestations of this lack of resiliency or cushion in the system are the increased volatility in capital and money markets, and the steady upward interest-rate pressure throughout the entire postwar period, as well as the vicious cyclical swings in recent years, inflationary pressures, and a generally rising level of risk, as indicated by interest-rate spreads.

The banking industry excuses much of the liquidity deterioration with its new aggressive deposit determination, which, it is claimed, makes unnecessary the conservative liquidity ratios of the past. Even if the ratios of the early postwar years were overly conservative, they have now reached levels that are clearly in the opposite extreme, as evidenced by the desperate scrambling for funds at any cost that has characterized the industry in recent years. Certainly, the willingness of the banking industry to accept lower standards of liquidity has been the major factor in the liquidity rundown in the postwar years. But this is not the entire story. As we will point out, illiquidity exists in all sectors of the economy, and banking illiquidity is but one facet of the problem.

The central bank has generally aided the postwar deterioration in liquidity in many ways, as we will discuss at greater length later. Indeed, it has played a major role through its rapid increase in money and credit. It has also lowered reserve requirements, progressively lowered the quality of acceptable collateral required for Federal Reserve advances, and readily supplied reserves during credit squeezes only to cause further credit expansion later. The federal government, in turn, has had the major role in forcing the Federal Reserve to expand credit excessively through its fiscal policy, and it has, in general, set the tone for the long liquidity decline.

Finally, the corporate sector has experienced the same pronounced liquidity decline found in the banking system. In Chapter 5 we present the evidence of this decline before going on to describe the role of the government and the Federal Reserve.

Chapter 5

The Importance of Liquidity In Corporations

We have already examined the nation's balance sheet in terms of one of its most important sectors, the banking system, and found a record of consistent deterioration in liquidity throughout the entire postwar period and until the present day. In this chapter, we show that the same forces are at work in the aggregate corporate balance sheet of the nation. The data used include, for the most part, all nonbank corporations.

Liquidity for the corporation is much the same as liquidity for the individual bank. It is simply the ability to meet cash demands as they become due, with a minimum of interference in the daily operations of the firm. Like a bank, a corporation may be solvent but still illiquid. Also as with banking liquidity, there is no single perfect measure of corporate liquidity; thus, it becomes necessary to examine a number of indicators to determine the overall liquidity trends. Since events of recent years have focused considerable attention on this subject, a review of the most recent concerns may be helpful.

The 1970 Liquidity Crisis

We have already dissected the so-called credit crunch of 1969-70 from the viewpoint of the banking system. Much more prominently covered in newspapers at the time, however, was the liquidity crisis among corporations, highlighted by the sensational failure of the Penn Central. The failure of the Penn Central, which had a sizable amount of commercial paper outstanding, could have started a run on the commercial-paper market and precipitated a sizable financial crisis, but the intervention of the Federal Reserve provided the reserves to supply short-term financing.

The Federal Reserve had maintained a highly restrictive monetary policy in 1969 and in early 1970, which precipitated not only the events mentioned above but also the runoff in CDs described in Chapter 3. It also precipitated a renewed interest in corporate balance sheets among security analysts. Their analyses found that despite declining internal cash flow, high bond yields, and a depressed stock market, corporations, probably spurred on by the inflationary pressures of the overheated economy earlier, continued large investment expenditures. By financing much of this long-term investment by short-term credit, they managed to reduce their liquidity to record low levels and were hence quite vulnerable to the sharp credit restraint applied by the Federal Reserve. Many corporations were in the same condition as the Penn Central, or in even worse straits, and the sudden reversal by the Federal Reserve gave them the time to put their houses in order. Once again, corporations learned the importance of adequate liquidity, at least for a while.

In the period that followed, the most massive demand for long-term financings in the history of the United States took place, in the form of bonds, common stocks, and preferred stocks. Short-term borrowing dropped off precipitously, and much of this debt was retired by the proceeds of the long-term financings. Corporations added generously to their cash balances and reduced their accounts payable. To add to the liquidity recovery, corporate cash flow began to rise for the first time in a number of years, and the liquidity crisis became a nightmare of the past. Was it only an unfortunate combination of events and a onetime phenomenon? Or was it, like the milder crunch of 1966, a manifestation of deeper, underlying problems that will be recurring regularly in increasingly terrifying fashion?

In the pages that follow, you will be shown that the dramatic decline in banking liquidity during the postwar years has been paralleled by an equally startling deterioration in corporate liquidity. While it is not possible to accurately determine beforehand exactly when such a long and pronounced trend of declining liquidity has reached its limits, we would look upon the credit crunch of 1966, and the more serious liquidity crisis of 1970, as evidence that the limits may be near. The corporate scramble to restore liquidity described above is simply a small delay or cyclical interruption of the trend. Banking liquidity, as mentioned above, is worse than ever, and corporate liquidity, while modestly improved by the long-term financings, is already showing signs of an end to the good intentions of corporations and has ceased to improve despite rising cash flow. Before presenting the evidence, it may be useful to discuss some of the consequences of deficient corporate liquidity.

The Illiquid Corporation

In our discussion of banking liquidity, it was seen that the illiquid bank was inflexible and thus vulnerable to sudden shifts in demand deposits and unable to capitalize on surges in loan demand. The illiquid corporation has the same lack of resiliency to sudden shocks and the same inability to profit from rising demand or changing demand, or to plan for future expansion in an orderly manner. The problem of illiquidity is probably more intense for the nonbank corporation than for the bank. Not only is the government much more likely (read expected) to intercede to aid a failing bank, because of the obviously more psychologically dangerous impact of such failures on the economy, but the sudden shocks that may face a nonbank corporation are more varied and numerous. A few examples of such shocks follow.

Labor Strife

The corporation with deficient liquidity is not able to cope with a strike as well as a more liquid firm. First, the deficient firm would be unable to hold out as long, due to its finances, and would generally have to submit to a much higher wage settlement than others in the industry. Because of this, the firm would eventually lose competitiveness in its industry. Second, the firm would have a difficult time regaining the market share lost during the strike because it would not have sufficient funds to cover the increased advertising and promotion costs as well as other start-up costs needed to get back fully on stream. Finally, in the extreme case, the firm may not survive the strike. This is only one of many possible shocks that may face any firm, but such a situation is doubly disturbing to the firm that is illiquid or highly leveraged. Such firms lack the resiliency to snap back from adversity as fast and as effectively as more healthy firms. As we will discuss later, growing labor militancy and strength is one of the effects of declining liquidity and can be expected to continue.

Competition

Many other shocks facing the average corporation are much more normal than strikes and are part of the competitive nature of the industry within which it operates. They can be expected to occur often, sometimes with little notice. Some of the well-known examples of such shocks are the shift to the compact car, the shift to filter cigarettes, the advent of the discount store in retailing, the shift to suburban stores and to shopping centers, the advent of trading stamps or discount pricing in supermarkets. The list is endless, but each shock represents a costly challenge that must be met by the corporation if it is to survive in its competitive environment. The solutions may entail higher research-and-development spending, retooling, shifting of store locations, or other expensive changes. Each such shock might represent a fresh challenge to the average firm, but to the illiquid and overextended firm it could represent a disaster from which recovery is difficult or impossible.

External Shocks

Many other pressures, imposed upon the individual corporation from outside the industry, are difficult to foresee or to plan for but require a strong financial condition to withstand. One need only observe the vagaries of government spending, particularly in the adjustment from wartime to peacetime expenditures, to see the exposure of firms highly dependent upon government contracts. Foreign competition also represents an increasing source of external disturbance to healthy as well as illiquid firms. Government-imposed restrictions are also becoming increasingly common. They include the imposition of safety regulations upon the automobile and others, restrictions on television advertising of toys and cigarettes, the more stringent requirements of "efficacy" in the drug and medical industry, the increasingly more demanding and more expensive antipollution regulations of recent years, and many others. Compliance with the new rules, delays in production, call-backs, and increased spending on alternate products all impose financial burdens upon the corporation that may or may not be readily passed on to the consumer. There is very little evidence that such demands upon the private sector will diminish in the near future. Once again, the illiquid firm fares badly in this climate, and, as we will show, firms are generally becoming less liquid.

The Internal Effects of Illiquidity

There are at least two other reasons why the illiquid individual corporation will continue to encounter problems and lose competitiveness even in the absence of the many shocks that are bound to touch any firm at any time. Illiquidity implies an excessive debt structure, high interest costs, and deficient cash assets. A firm whose management is incessantly occupied with servicing its present debt structure, struggling daily or weekly for cash to sustain its operations and to fight the financial fires caused by the shocks mentioned above, must certainly be at a disadvantage to the management that is able to allocate all its time to the more constructive pursuits of planning, expanding, increasing market share, and so on. Second, the illiquid firm within an otherwise healthy and growing industry is unable to plan and finance future expansion, and must eventually lose market share to financially healthy and aggressive competitors.

The Illiquid Corporation in the Business Cycle

Some corporations are, of course, more sensitive to the vicissitudes of the business cycle than others. Illiquid firms that are also highly responsive to the vagaries of the business cycle are sure to be battling for their very corporate life with every downturn in business, no matter how mild. It is probably safe to assume that a large proportion of the growing number of illiquid firms are such companies, since a large number of cyclical companies are engaged in manufacturing activities, particularly heavy industry, and are found to be operating early in the manufacturing process. Such firms are in the extractive industries, capital equipment, machine tools, and other enterprises of this type. These very companies are generally capital-intensive, highly leveraged financially and productively, and plagued by the most militant unions.

We saw a chilling example of the problems outlined here during the business recession and liquidity squeeze of 1969-70. While the recession was one of the mildest on record, we saw many firms on the verge of serious trouble and a great number, including the sensational Penn Central failure discussed above, that became bankrupt. As mentioned, it was only the timely easing of credit by the Federal Reserve in the summer of 1970 that ended the credit squeeze before a sustained domino effect of failures and credit liquidation could be triggered. As the liquidity trends described here continue, we may expect more frequent and more severe recessions in the years immediately ahead.

The Aggregate Effects of Deficient Corporate Liquidity

What is true for the individual corporation must also be true for the economy as a whole, which is only a composite of all corporations. Although it is instructive to discuss the aggregate effects of corporate illiquidity at this juncture, much of the discussion is reserved for a later chapter, in which the combined effects of corporate and banking liquidity are examined.

As deficient liquidity extends to corporations in general, a number of destabilizing forces are introduced into the economy, as well as many forces that stifle growth, incentives, and capital formation, and tend to reduce competitiveness in world markets. The effects upon business cycles are apparent from the preceding discussion. The length and the magnitude of the recessionary phase of the cycle are bound to be extended as the number of illiquid firms in the economy rises. A growing number of firms will fail in each recession and, through the effect of these failures upon healthier firms, will add to the severity of the business slowdown. Increases in unemployment should become larger in each slowdown, and as increasing fears of job loss serve to reduce consumer spending further, the saving rate will rise. Many other firms, approaching failure, will retrench their positions by layoffs, cost cutting, inventory cutbacks, cancellation of expansion plans, and other methods of insuring survival. These actions will have the same effects upon the economy as the failures. For the illiquid firms that survive the recession, lack of cash and strong desire to rebuild liquidity after the scare of the recession will add measurably to the sluggishness of the ensuing recovery, thereby stretching the length of the recession. This was certainly the situation in the recovery following the recession of 1969-70, which was a source of constant frustration to business forecasters. Many blamed the sluggish recovery upon the fact that the recession was quite mild, but this was not the case. It was simply a case of fear caused by the seriousness of the crunch. Though many economic statistics, such as the unemployment rate, did not show the intense decline of other postwar recessions, the liquidity scare and potential economic collapse were greater than any recession of the postwar years. The reason was simply the advanced stage of liquidity deterioration that had been reached.

Effect upon Interest Rates

One of the major effects of the declining corporate liquidity is a pronounced upward pressure upon interest rates, which adds to the pressure on interest rates from diminishing bank liquidity. As corporations become more illiquid, they become more reliant upon external financing. Their reliance upon the banking system and capital markets for expansion funds and funds for daily operations places a continuing upward pressure upon interest rates, even when they do not find themselves in a period of recession. During business contractions and liquidity squeezes, the combined struggle of all the illiquid firms for funds necessary for their very existence placed great burdens upon capital markets and money markets, causing extremely sharp cyclical swings in interest rates. The volatility brought to these markets adds a large degree of risk to individuals and financial institutions that regularly deal with and invest in fixed-income securities. The rabid activities of dangerously illiquid corporations during periods of credit constraint, and the funding of short-term debt afterward, also explains why interest rates no longer fall as far as they did in past periods during recessions and the recovery that followed. Even as these firms borrow in capital markets to alleviate their liquidity woes, their growing debt structure and consequent diminished creditworthiness raise their continuing interest costs further, and their heavy debt-service load compounds their woes by taking more flexibility away. In recent years, the credit markets have been dislocated further by debt-financing activities of the federal government at precisely the same time that the private sector is at the height of its financing needs. This competition by the federal government in the credit markets for funds, at the very time when corporate demand is highest, introduces additional volatility to the markets and, of course, upward pressures on interest rates. The increasing illiquidity of corporations, and their inability easily to cope with temporary reverses, adds to risk in the companies, as both investments and borrowers, and to risk in the entire economy when the individual firms are aggregated. This risk must ultimately manifest itself in terms of higher interest rates.

The phenomenon of rising risk due to increasing debt burdens and declining cushions of corporations is injurious to the economy in another long-lasting way. The effect upon long-term growth of the economy must be considered. The more obvious effects upon growth have already been mentioned in the discussion of the individual illiquid firm that simply does not have the wherewithal to effectively plan and implement a long-term expansion plan when it is engaged in a struggle for its day-to-day existence. It is difficult for management to plan for the distant future when the near-term life of the corporation is in doubt, or time is spent on short-term financing. Risk-taking in general diminishes also because of the climate of higher levels of risk and the higher levels of interest rates, which require a higher-yielding project before money is committed. As we shall see, capital formation by the United States has been quite low relative to the rest of the industrialized world. One manifestation of the effects of this trend is the steadily rising balance-of-payments deficits suffered by the United States.

Finally, aggregate corporate illiquidity has important effects upon the rate of inflation, which in turn adds a further premium to the level of interest rates. Though no one simple explanation of the causes of inflation will find universal agreement, deficient liquidity among corporations and the banking system is certainly to be regarded as a major cause, as we will show. The cause-and-effect relationship between monetary inflation and price inflation has been well established and documented by monetary theorists. When we discuss the role of the federal government and the Federal Reserve, the cast will be complete. The federal government and the Federal Reserve are directly responsible for the rundown in liquidity, and now that it has reached such low levels, they have no choice but to continue in their role.

Fully committed by the Employment Act of 1946, the government, through its influence upon the Federal Reserve, must and does step in to relieve the pressures of credit squeezes as they occur, just as it did in the summer of 1970. The result is always the massive increases in the money supply and credit leading eventually to price inflation. We will return to this discussion of the effects of deficient liquidity after a consideration of the evidence of corporate liquidity trends in the postwar period.

Indicators of Corporate Liquidity

Corporate liquidity is basically the relationship between corporate holdings of liquid assets, such as currency and other short-term marketable securities, and current liabilities. Therefore, a logical beginning for any study of corporate liquidity should be an analysis of such liquid assets and short-term liabilities. Unfortunately, too many studies end there with some "reasonable" explanation of deteriorating liquidity, such as the more efficient use of cash, just as bankers explain away illiquidity with a new banking philosophy. At the time when the overall conditions of liquidity become disturbing, corporations generally turn to the capital markets to fund the excessive short-term debt that has been incurred and to replace depleted cash accounts, and the liquidity scare ends with comments that liquidity has been replaced. This approach does not take into consideration the cumulative effect of each short-term encounter with illiquidity. In Chapter 6 we examine the traditional measures of corporate liquidity and make an attempt to trace the illiquidity to other areas in the balance sheet.

Chapter 6

Indicators of Corporate Liquidity

The postwar history of corporate liquidity is much the same as that of banking liquidity. During economic upswings there is a steady rundown in liquidity, which continues to business peaks; during the ensuing recession and its aftermath, a portion of the liquidity is replaced. The longer-term trend, however, continues downward. More important, the illiquidity is not cured but accumulates instead. It seems to be cured, however, and the concern over liquidity evaporates for a time.

Analysis of the corporate liquidity problem is essentially a balance-sheet analysis, a practice that had almost been forgotten completely by most security analysts until the liquidity squeeze of 1970 reminded them. The analysis of the entire corporate sector should be attacked in exactly the same way as a balance-sheet analysis of any individual firm. The same ratios that should be meaningful to the security analyst can be applied with aggregate figures.

Comparative Balance Sheets

Perhaps the best way to begin a study of corporate liquidity trends for the postwar period is through a comparison of balance sheets for all nonfinancial U.S. corporations at year-end 1971 with those at the end of 1947. The results are summarized in Table 6.1.

One factor stands out quite clearly in the figures. The role of cash and equivalents in the current section of the corporate balance sheet declined considerably over the entire period. Most of the change in this category was absorbed by the increase in trade receivables, which, at 46.7 percent, became the largest category of all current assets. We will have much more to say about this growth in receivables.

TABLE 6.1

	1947	1971
Cash and equivalents as percentage of current assets	30.9	12.6
Trade receivables as percentage of current assets	32.8	46.7
Other assets as percentage of current assets	1.4	7.1
Inventories as percentage of current assets	34.8	33.5
Current ratio	2.08	1.64
Cash and equivalents as percentage of current assets	64.34	20.7

Compound Growth Rates 1947-71	
Receivables	8.7%
Cash and equivalents	3.2%

The decline in the cash accounts has garnered the most attention by analysts of corporate liquidity. This figure is pointed out when investors and economists are alarmed during credit squeezes. A sigh of relief is given when the level recovers somewhat, and the recovery is a signal to forget about corporate liquidity until the next crisis. As we will see, it is not the cyclical trends but the secular trend that should be considered. Obviously, as shown by the comparative data in Table 6.1, the periods of recovery have been much less intensive than the periods of decline. Before examining this trend in detail we will look at a very familiar balance-sheet ratio.

The Current Ratio

Our study of banking liquidity began with a review of the long-term trend in the relationship of bank investments to total bank credit. A close corporate equivalent would be the current ratio. Like the banking indicator, it is a ratio comparing an assortment of current assets, of varying degrees of liquidity, with current liabilities. It is a good, rough single-figure assessment of the ability of a corporation to pay its liabilities as they become due—that is, of corporate liquidity.

The comparative data in Table 6.1 indicate a distinct decline for all U.S. corporations during the postwar period. The yearly record for all manufacturing firms is presented in Table 6.2, which confirms the decline. After reaching a postwar high of 3.08 in 1949, the trend has been steadily downward with some periodic improvements, usually during periods of recession. It is evident that the attempts to improve liquidity were weak ones that did little to stem the long-term trend, which still seems to be intact at this writing. It is interesting to note the extremely weak recovery during the most recent recession in 1969-70 and the recovery that followed.

The trend in this single-figure indicator probably does not seem particularly ominous. Like our banking indicator counterpart, this ratio may also be

TABLE 6.2

Current Ratio
(All Manufacturing Firms)
as of Dec. 31.

1947	2.67	1960	2.51
1948	2.70	1961	2.48
1949	3.08	1962	2.47
1950	2.54	1963	2.46
1951	2.25	1964	2.39
1952	2.29	1965	2.27
1953	2.33	1966	2.16
1954	2.47	1967	2.20
1955	2.41	1968	2.14
1956	2.36	1969	2.01
1957	2.43	1970	1.98
1958	2.63	1971	2.03
1959	2.51		

Source:
Quarterly Financial Report for Manufacturing
Corporations, Federal Trade Commission.

deceptive. If current assets of lower liquidity have come to dominate total current assets, this measure of liquidity is overstated, in addition to displaying a declining trend. Therefore, current assets must be examined as thoroughly here as banking liquidity was in Chapter 4. Nor should we be satisfied with only one indicator. Therefore, we have used a number of indicators to uncover the extent of the deterioration that has taken place in the corporate sector.

Receivables/Current Assets

Among the current assets included in the comparative data in Table 6.2, we saw that the most pronounced changes occurred in trade receivables and the cash-and-equivalents category. Over the entire postwar period the most rapid growth occurred in receivables, one of the least liquid components of current assets, at the expense of cash and equivalents, which are the most liquid components. Thus, even as current assets in total have failed to keep pace with rising current liabilities over the period, the mix of current assets has also been changing for the worse in terms of liquidity. Over the entire period, trade receivables grew over 700 percent while total current assets grew less than 400 percent. Receivables grew at an average compound rate of nearly three times that of cash and equivalents.

Receivables versus Sales Growth

The growth of receivables is even more startling when compared to the growth in total manufacturing and trade sales over the same period. These annual sales expanded by only 224 percent from 1948 through 1971, a rate less than one-third that of receivables. These figures are the first, to this point, to disclose another facet of the liquidity trends, which we have not yet discussed. So far we have limited our discussion to only one aspect of the liquidity trend, the increasing risk as a result of the deterioration of liquidity and the consequent effects of higher interest rates and volatility. Now we begin to see another dimension to the problem.

The relative growth rates of receivables and sales inform us that increased sales, to a large extent, have been made only through the extension of trade credit and at the expense of liquidity. This introduces a note of artificiality to the great postwar economic expansion. Table 6.3 includes the entire postwar record of receivables, current assets, and sales and their relationships on an annual basis for all U.S. corporations. Like all our indicators, the figures reveal unmistakable and continuous trends over the entire period. Also like our other indicators—and our entire thesis, for that matter—it is not possible to accurately pinpoint the levels at which the trends become critical. Certainly the security analyst, examining the individual firm whose extension of credit is rising faster than its sales over a prolonged period of time, should be put on his guard. If the trend has been in effect for over twenty-five years, he should definitely be alarmed.

The final column of Table 6.3 gives the ratio of receivables at year-end to the total sales for the year. In 1947, for every dollar of sales it was necessary to carry $0.09 of trade receivables. By the end of 1970, this ratio had more than doubled to a new high of $0.21 for each dollar of sales, before recovering somewhat in 1971 as short-term indebtedness was reduced after the scare of 1970 by record offerings of long-term bonds and stocks. This record represents a significant impairment of liquid assets, thereby reducing liquidity. It also represents a steadily rising demand for short-term funds by corporations, and steady upward pressure upon short-term interest rates and, later, upon long-term rates as the credit needs are eventually funded. It also means that interest costs for debt required to support sales has doubled over the period. When one considers that interest rates also doubled over the same period, the interest costs have quadrupled. This is hardly an insignificant rise in costs for the average firm. In the mature stages of every business expansion, receivables as well as inventories rise, creating higher credit demands. The concern, however, is that the liquidity is not being restored during each recessionary stage as the trends in the tables indicate.

Age of Receivables

When trade receivables are compared to an average month's sales over the same period, as is done in Table 6.4, still another facet of the problem can be

TABLE 6.3
Trade Receivables

Year (as of Dec. 31)	Receivable* (Billions of Dollars)	Current Assets* (Billions of Dollars)	Receivables/ Current Assets	Manufacturing and Trade Sales* (Billions of Dollars)	Receivables/ Sales
1947	38.2	116.6	0.33	—	
1948	38.7	123.2	0.31	423.1	9.1
1949	40.3	128.6	0.31	405.5	9.9
1950	50.0	150.5	0.33	463.2	10.7
1951	55.2	170.7	0.32	520.3	10.6
1952	61.8	181.1	0.34	538.1	11.5
1953	65.3	184.5	0.35	575.8	11.3
1954	66.2	187.8	0.35	557.3	11.9
1955	77.3	208.1	0.37	620.3	12.5
1956	84.1	218.6	0.39	648.8	13.0
1957	99.8	244.7	0.41	670.5	14.9
1958	106.9	255.3	0.42	650.8	16.4
1959	119.0	278.7	0.43	715.9	16.6
1960	126.5	287.4	0.44	728.9	17.4
1961	134.5	303.0	0.44	733.6	18.3
1962	145.5	322.8	0.45	785.0	18.5
1963	159.7	349.9	0.46	827.6	19.3
1964	169.9	372.2	0.47	884.2	19.2
1965	190.2	410.2	0.46	963.3	19.7
1966	205.1	443.4	0.46	1,046.1	19.6
1967	214.5	470.4	0.46	1,076.5	19.9
1968	237.1	513.8	0.46	1,162.7	20.4
1969	261.0	555.9	0.47	1,231.9	21.2
1970	268.1	572.1	0.47	1,264.4	21.2
1971	277.6	601.5	0.46	1,371.1	20.3

* (Billions of Pounds)

Source: *Working Capital of U.S. Corporations*, U.S. Securities & Exchange Commission.

69

TABLE 6.4

Receivables-Sales Ratio

Year (as of Dec. 31)	Receivables (Billions of Dollars)	Average Monthly Sales (Billions of Dollars)	Receivables-Sales
1948	38.7	35.3	1.09
1949	40.3	33.8	1.19
1950	50.0	38.6	1.30
1951	55.2	43.4	1.27
1952	61.8	44.8	1.38
1953	65.3	48.0	1.36
1954	66.2	46.4	1.43
1955	77.3	51.7	1.50
1956	84.1	54.1	1.55
1957	99.8	55.9	1.79
1958	106.9	54.2	1.97
1959	119.0	59.7	1.99
1960	126.5	60.7	2.08
1961	134.5	61.1	2.20
1962	145.5	65.4	2.22
1963	159.7	69.0	2.31
1964	169.9	73.7	2.31
1965	190.2	80.3	2.37
1966	205.1	87.2	2.35
1967	214.5	89.7	2.39
1968	237.1	96.9	2.45
1969	261.0	102.7	2.54
1970	268.1	105.4	2.55
1971	277.6	114.3	2.43

Source:
Working Capital of U.S. Corporations, U.S. Securities and Exchange Commission.
Business Statistics, 1971, U.S. Dept. of Commerce.
Survey of Current Business, U.S. Dept. of Commerce.

seen. By comparing one month's sales with the total receivables outstanding in each period, rough approximations of the average age of the receivables can be determined. A ratio of 1.0 would indicate that it requires thirty days to collect the receivable, while a ratio of 3.0 would indicate that ninety days are required to collect. Table 6.4 indicates an almost continuous trend toward longer repayment throughout the postwar period, from a figure slightly over thirty days in 1948 to one of slightly over seventy-five days in 1970 (thirty days times 2.55) before shortening somewhat in 1971.

Not only are the more illiquid receivables becoming a larger portion of total current assets, nearly half, but they are also rapidly and steadily becoming more illiquid, as indicated by their average age. Corporations are carrying larger receivables in relation to sales every year, *and they are being forced to carry them longer*. This trend forces corporations into larger debt burdens as well as higher interest costs. Because the declining corporate liquidity itself is a force behind rising interest rates, there is a self-enforcing nature to this problem. Interest costs are rising due to greater amounts of debt per dollar of sales, as well as the higher rates of interest that must be paid. As the trend continues, corporations can be expected to grow more illiquid earlier in each business expansion, thereby helping to cut short each business recovery sooner as firms are forced to find the necessary short-term funds to finance their ongoing business. To the extent that liquidity is not replaced during periods of economic decline or sluggish recovery, as is increasingly the case, the problems become more acute and they occur more frequently.

Aside from the increasing cyclical problems with liquidity, there are also the questions of how long the secular trend can continue, and what will be the rate of growth of the economy should the trend reverse itself, as it eventually must. Corporations have been "buying" sales at the expense of their financial condition. The credit extended is growing at three times the rate of sales, collections of the debt are more than twice as slow, and the costs of the credit have doubled.

The Quick Ratio

The final test and basic source of corporate liquidity is the level of cash and its equivalents related to the short-term claims against it. This measure, the quick ratio, corresponds to the relationship of government securities to total bank credit discussed in the section on banking liquidity. Table 6.5 depicts the yearly record for this relationship over the postwar period for all manufacturing firms. It demonstrates, like the comparative balance-sheet analysis earlier for all U.S. corporations, the most drastic long-term deterioration of all the indicators.

From a postwar high in 1949 of $1.07 of cash and equivalents for every $1.00 of current liabilities, the ratio declined almost continuously to a low of $0.20 in 1970. On a quarterly basis, the ratio reached an even lower level of $0.19 in the third quarter of 1970 before a recovery finally occurred. This decline reflects and confirms what was seen above as an increasingly wider diffusion of credit throughout the economy as business continues to extend credit to consumers and other firms at a rate that far exceeds the rate of increase in total sales. This indicator, like the others discussed to this point, confirms the same consistent deterioration of liquidity.

At least two common responses are usually made to persons who express a concern about the long-term deterioration in this indicator, which is the most commonly quoted indicator of corporate liquidity. The first is that the liquidity at the beginning of the period under study was much too high anyway

TABLE 6.5

Cash & Equivalents as Percentage of Current Liabilities
(All Manufacturing Firms)
as of Dec. 31

1947	0.83	1960	0.52
1948	0.78	1961	0.49
1949	1.07	1962	0.48
1950	0.84	1963	0.46
1951	0.68	1964	0.43
1952	0.64	1965	0.37
1953	0.67	1966	0.30
1954	0.71	1967	0.29
1955	0.69	1968	0.28
1956	0.55	1969	0.23
1957	0.55	1970	0.20
1958	0.62	1971	0.25
1959	0.57	1972	0.24

Source:
Quarterly Financial Report for Manufacturing Corporations.
Federal Trade Commission.

and the present readings reflect a more normal level. The second is the argument that corporate managements are now more sophisticated in their employment of excess funds and internal cash needs, and that much lower levels of liquidity will now suffice.

We have already admitted that it is difficult to determine just when the trend has progressed too far. The fact remains, however, that liquidity for both corporations and banks does seem to move in long secular cycles, with the troughs in liquidity usually proceeding some correcting credit-liquidation phase that gradually starts a long trend toward improving liquidity. The last trough in liquidity occurred in the late 1920s, and it was followed by a long period of credit liquidation and rebuilding of liquidity. The next peak, made in the 1940s, roughly marks the beginning of this study. We have since been in the period of declining liquidity and the levels reached are now lower than those reached during the last trough in the 1920s. Now the trend may be able to go even further because of such things as sophisticated corporate management of funds and the new liabilities management of banks, but the levels are such that an alert is certainly not out of order. The point that efficient corporate management of cash excuses the low quick ratio might be acceptable if it were not for the fact that many other indicators lead one to the same conclusion regarding the dangerous levels of liquidity. This is, of course, the primary reason for using many indicators, since we are thus protected against the possibility of some structural change rendering any one indicator meaningless. The other approach to determining whether the decline has reached a terminal stage is to hypothesize what the identifying effects of an intolerable level of liquidity would be and then to determine whether those effects are present. We have already pointed out many of these effects casually, and we will present them more formally later on in this book. Some of the effects would be rising interest rates; volatility in capital, money, and stock markets; inflationary pressures and rising levels of risk. Those who give sanguine responses to the lower levels of the quick ratio, in the aggregate, fail to apply accepted minimum levels for ratios of individual corporations. One of the leading textbooks on security analysis recommends a minimum level of 1.00 for the quick ratio for most industrial firms. Yet an aggregate figure of 0.20, which implies many firms well under this level, does not alarm them. It is also curious that this ratio comes into the limelight during periods of recession and sharp credit constraint or squeezes, and that fears of deficient corporate liquidity are voiced daily by investors and periodicals. Once the crisis is passed, however, the fears subside and the indicator is relegated to obscurity. Show the long-term record of the indicator to the same people who expressed such concern during the squeeze, and they will reply that liquidity has been restored and is no longer a cause for alarm. This is, of course, the problem with watching only one indicator. A small recovery removes any concern for the level of the ratio even though the secular trend of deterioration continues. Nor is the illiquidity really improved in the long-term sense, since it is merely removed to accumulate in another section of the balance sheet, as we point out in Chapter 7.

Chapter 7

The Permanent Nature of Short-Term Liquidity Problems

Most studies of corporate liquidity end with the several indicators discussed in the preceding chapter. In fact, as pointed out, most studies do not go beyond a simple reading of the quick ratio. A liquidity squeeze is always followed by a wave of long-term financing, bank-loan reduction, cost-cutting, and cash replacement. The periodic fears of corporate illiquidity are once more laid to rest for a time, to rematerialize when the traditional measures of liquidity take another cyclical decline. Once the problem leaves the current section of the balance sheet it seems to disappear. This viewpoint does not take into consideration the cumulative effects of liquidity problems. This is not strange, since almost the entire focus of most security analysts and many corporations is on growth of earnings and specifically on earnings per share. This too is only a part of the even broader fascination with growth in the level of GNP. To analyze the corporate liquidity trends completely, one must consider the trends in the *entire* balance sheet.

It is obvious that the average liquidity of all corporations is declining, but there has still been enough resiliency to periodically recover some of the lost liquidity without pushing the economy into a financial collapse, although many feel the brink was reached in 1970. The critical point will be reached when the number of firms not able to survive a credit crunch is sufficient to seriously affect the healthier companies. This will not be so much a matter of liquidity, in the strict sense of the quick ratio, but one of the accumulation of prior short-term debt that has been funded. Periodically, corporations begin to compete aggressively for short-term funds in a manner so intense that short-term interest rates rise rapidly as supplies of short-term funds are outstripped by the demand for such funds. This is the climate that is usually present in the latter stages of an economic expansion, and credit constraint by the Federal Reserve is usually also in effect to slow the economy. Finally, the competition and liquidity fears become so intense that the corporations must turn to the long-term capital markets to fund the excessive short-term debt that has been incurred and to replace depleted cash balances. This usually begins as the business expansion matures and lasts well into the ensuing decline and subsequent recovery. The rundown in liquidity is a primary cause of the slowdown in business as well as an aggravating factor in the subsequent recovery.

TABLE 7.1

New Corporate Security Issues
(In Billions of Dollars)

Year	Bonds & Notes	Common Stock	Preferred Stock	Total
1947	5,036	779	762	6,577
1948	5,973	614	492	7,078
1949	4,890	736	425	6,052
1950	4,920	811	631	6,361
1951	5,691	1,212	838	7,741
1952	7,601	1,369	564	9,534
1953	7,083	1,326	489	8,898
1954	7,488	1,213	816	9,516
1955	7,420	2,185	635	10,240
1956	8,002	2,301	636	10,939
1957	9,957	2,516	411	12,884
1958	9,653	1,334	571	11,558
1959	7,190	2,027	531	9,748
1960	8,081	1,664	409	10,154
1961	9,420	3,294	450	13,165
1962	8,969	1,314	422	10,705
1963	10,856	1,011	343	12,211
1964	10,865	2,679	412	13,957
1965	13,720	1,547	725	15,992
1966	15,561	1,939	574	18,074
1967	21,954	1,959	885	24,798
1968	17,383	3,946	637	21,966
1969	18,348	7,714	682	26,744
1970	30,315	7,240	1,390	38,945
1971	31,883	10,459	3,683	46,025
1972	28,896	9,694	3,367	41,957

Source:
Business Statistics, 1971, U.S. Dept. of Commerce.
Survey of Current Business, U.S. Dept. of Commerce.

Funding the Liquidity Problem

Table 7.1 shows the results òf declining liquidity upon the capital markets. In 1967, the year after the credit crunch of 1966, postwar record highs were made for the sale of both new corporate bonds and notes and new preferred stock. The following year, a new postwar record in the issue of new common stock was also set. With this action, the fears of corporate illiquidity were once again retired, along with much of the short-term debt.

With liquidity continuing to decline, the upheavals in the capital markets were even more dramatic in the years surrounding the credit crunch years of 1969 and 1970. As we saw in earlier Tables, despite the credit scare of 1966 and the ensuing capital financing, the indicators of corporate liquidity continued to fall up to and through the credit scare of 1969-70 and even through the recession and into the sluggish recovery that followed. Finally, in 1971, some modest improvement was seen in corporate liquidity, although banking liquidity continued to deteriorate. The improvement in liquidity, however, came only after three years of record common-stock financings and preferred-stock sales in 1971, totaling over 400 percent more than any record year prior to 1970. Add to this activity two years of long-term corporate debt offerings in excess of $30 billion each year. In the process, interest rates reached highs not seen since Civil War days. The high rate of offerings of all types continued into 1972.

Each cycle of liquidity deterioration, credit scare, funding, and slightly improved liquidity seems to be followed by a period of relative contentment during which fears of illiquidity are put to rest. Corporate or banking liquidity were seldom topics of conversation among institutional investors during 1972. More important, none of these periods of funding cures the real problem, even temporarily, as the return of confidence seems to imply. They merely transfer the problem to the long-term section of the national corporate balance sheet, while only slowing the deterioration of the current assets section. The deterioration of the entire balance sheet continues unabated even throughout the short reprieves for current liquidity. It is only when the deterioration in liquidity, as measured by the traditional measures of the current section of the balance sheet, reaches such dire straits that business pauses to replace cash balances by financing long-term that there appears to be an improvement in liquidity. The problems, though, are only being accumulated, not dissolved.

Because the government is committed to intervene to moderate the nature of every postwar recession, there is never enough debt actually retired to seriously slow down the trend of rapid credit expansion that is at the root of the liquidity problem. Once the short-term debt is transferred to the long-term category, where concern seems to be absent, everyone relaxes until the next critical period of illiquidity. As long as short-term indebtedness can be transferred to long-term status, there seems to be no limit to the deterioration in the liquidity indicators. It will be instructive to examine the cumulative effects of this transference of debt upon corporate balance sheets. One way to examine the effects is the *debt-to-equity ratio*.

Debt-To-Equity Ratio

A common method for measuring risk in a corporation and its securities is the amount of debt present in the capital structure of the corporation relative to the amount of equity or ownership money in the firm. The larger the amount of debt in the capital structure, the greater the risk in the corporation. The large amount of debt in the balance sheet affords a degree of "financial leverage" to the corporation, which is a two-edged sword. In an economic upswing, the leverage results in a higher return to the equity holders of the firm, but in a downswing much sharper declines in earnings are likely. The result is a higher degree of volatility in the operating results of the firm as well as the price of its stock, and, therefore, risk to the holder is increased.

The Federal Trade Commission has, for some years, maintained a series for all manufacturing firms measuring the relationship of their total stockholders' equity to their total short-term bank loans plus long-term debt. The inversion of these figures (total debt as a percentage of total stockholders' equity) is presented in Table 7.2

TABLE 7.2

Debt-Equity Ratio
(All Manufacturing Firms)
as of Dec. 31

1955	21.1	1963	25.3
1956	23.9	1964	25.8
1957	24.2	1965	28.2
1958	23.9	1966	32.1
1959	23.7	1967	35.0
1960	24.6	1968	37.7
1961	25.0	1969	41.1
1962	25.3	1970	44.4
		1971	44.4

Source:
Quarterly Financial Report for Manufacturing Corporations, Federal Trade Commission.

It is evident that the same inexorable trend of balance-sheet deterioration in the current section is present in this section of the balance sheet as well. It is obvious that the liquidity that was of such concern in 1970 cannot be disposed of simply through the floating of long-term debt. It can only be disposed of by actually liquidating some debt, not by changing its expiration date, which can only delay the ultimate effects of excessive debt creation. From 1955 through the end of 1971, debt rose as a percentage of stockholders' equity from slightly over 20 percent to a figure approaching one-half. Though this particular series has only been maintained since 1955, it is safe to assume from other evidence that change has been much more pronounced if measured from 1947. Once again, we do not know the absolute limits to which this deterioration can carry before it substantially affects the entire economy. We can say, however, that the effects in the system would be increasing risk and volatility, just as they would be for the individual corporation. As the average for all corporations continues to rise, the effects upon the system must be stronger each year and the number of individual firms that have reached dangerous levels must be rising. A recent study provided data for *all* active corporations, giving the percentage of long-term debt as a percentage of total capital—that is, the debt ratio. The results are given in Table 7.3. These data would seem to

TABLE 7.3

All Active Corporations, Long-Term Debt as a Percentage of Total Capital

Year	Percentage
1968	42.9
1965	39.2
1960	37.7
1955	32.1
1947	27.8

easily confirm the indicator maintained by the Federal Trade Commission for all manufacturing firms. If all short-term bank loans were added to the total of long-term debt, the relationship of total debt to total capital would prove quite alarming. Although the latest year for the data in Table 7.3 is 1968, the current percentage must certainly be much higher, what with the massive financing in the last several years, which is described in Table 7.1. One would also expect that with the debt-equity ratios climbing, the quality of credit must also be declining. The same study that is summarized in Table 7.3 points out that in the first seven months of 1972, bond ratings of seven utilities, one telephone company, and two industrials were reduced, and that further downgradings were expected. Although there is no accurate account of such downgradings, the pace quickened considerably in the latter months of 1972 and into 1973. Standard & Poors has said that its "typical single-A ratings" require a borrower's earnings to cover debt service by 2.25 to 2.5 times after taxes.

Debt Service

Although it is difficult to state with assurance just what is the optimum debt load for any individual corporation, let alone the entire system, it may be stated with certainty that there is some limit commensurate with acceptable levels of risk. It may also be stated with certainty that interest costs must also

TABLE 7.4

Debt Service as a Percentage of Profits

Year	Corporate Profits After Tax (Billions of Dollars)	Net Interest Payments (Billions of Dollars)	Total (Billions of Dollars)	Ratio of Interest to Profits & Interest
1947	20.2	1.9	22.1	0.086
1948	22.7	1.8	24.5	0.073
1949	18.5	1.9	20.4	0.093
1950	24.9	2.0	26.9	0.074
1951	21.6	2.3	23.9	0.096
1952	19.6	2.6	22.2	0.117
1953	20.4	2.8	23.2	0.121
1954	20.6	3.6	24.2	0.149
1955	27.0	4.1	31.1	0.132
1956	27.2	4.6	31.8	0.145
1957	26.0	5.6	31.6	0.177
1958	22.3	6.8	29.1	0.234
1959	28.5	7.1	35.6	0.199
1960	26.7	8.4	35.1	0.239
1961	27.2	10.0	37.2	0.269
1962	31.2	11.6	42.8	0.271
1963	33.1	13.8	46.9	0.294
1964	38.4	15.8	54.2	0.292
1965	46.5	18.2	64.7	0.281
1966	49.5	21.4	70.9	0.302
1967	47.3	24.7	72.0	0.343
1968	47.8	26.9	74.7	0.360
1969	44.8	29.9	74.4	0.402
1970	40.2	34.8	75.0	0.464
1971	45.9	38.5	84.4	0.456

Source:
Business Statistics, 1971, U.S. Dept. of Commerce.
Survey of Current Business, U.S. Dept. of Commerce.

be rising relative to earnings, given the much higher growth rates of debt relative to growth in sales. Table 7.4 conclusively confirms this intuitive suspicion. From 1947 through 1971, net interest payments of all corporations rose over *ten times faster* than total corporate aftertax profits. Interest costs for all corporations rose from less than 9 percent of total aftertax profits plus interest costs to over 40 percent at the end of 1971.

The deterioration of this indicator is obviously caused by two factors: the increasing amounts of debt indicated in Table 7.2 and the steadily rising level of interest rates in the postwar period. There is a self-enforcing nature to this indicator in that the decline in corporate liquidity is responsible, at least in part, for the rising interest rates. The rising debt levels exert an increasing upward pressure upon interest rates by both the demand for funds and the increasing risk level in the securities themselves, which must therefore carry a lower rating and higher interest rates. The rising debt-service load leaves a smaller amount of profits to finance business needs internally. Coupled with the declining banking liquidity mentioned previously, we once again are reminded of the growing influence of declining liquidity upon interest rates. The fact that corporate profits move down as well as up, as demonstrated in Table 7.4, and that interest payments move higher *every* year, should gradually make increasing numbers of companies more vulnerable to adverse business swings. Since corporate aftertax profits now amount to less than 5 percent of GNP, the lowest rate since before World War II, the moment of truth for many companies may not be far off. The increasing vulnerability of a growing number of firms to periods of credit scarcity introduces a source of continually increasing volatility to the system as well as upward pressure upon interest rates.

It also introduces a growing deflationary pressure into the system, which, as we will see, is offset only by a steadily rising level of money supply and credit supplied by the Federal Reserve, which only serves to extend the declining trend of overexpansion of credit and growing illiquidity and puts off the ultimate solution to the problems.

Coverage of Fixed Charges

With debt growing as a percentage of stockholders' equity, and interest costs growing as a percentage of profits, the question of the quality of debt, as mentioned, should be brought to mind. It was mentioned that decreases in the ratings of a considerable number of major companies, particularly among utilities, offer some qualitative evidence of a decline in quality. "Coverage of fixed charges" is a major consideration in ratings placed upon corporate securities and is a good quantitative measurement of quality and risk. Table 7.5 represents a rough approximation of the trend in coverage of fixed charges on a national balance-sheet basis.

In preparing Table 7.5 we attempted to approximate the annual interest expense on total long-term corporate debt. Moody's average interest rate for all grades of corporate bonds was used for each year and applied to total long-term corporate debt to arrive at interest expense. The actual stated interest rate was used up until 1957 and applied to all of the long-term debt outstanding. This had the effect of overstating the interest expense and understating the coverage figure, since interest rates were slowly rising, and we used the higher rate for all the debt outstanding while prior debt was only subject to the lower rates. From 1957

TABLE 7.5

Coverage of Fixed Charges
(In Billions of Dollars)

Year	Corporate Profits Before Tax	Total Long-term Corp. Debt	Interest Rates Percentage Actual Assumed*	Interest Expense	Coverage
1947	31.5	46.1	2.86	1.3	24.2
1948	35.2	52.5	3.08	1.6	22.0
1949	28.9	56.5	2.96	1.7	17.0
1950	42.6	60.1	2.86	1.7	25.0
1951	43.9	66.6	3.08	2.1	20.9
1952	38.9	73.3	3.19	2.3	16.9
1953	40.6	78.3	3.43	2.7	15.0
1954	38.3	82.9	3.16	2.6	14.7
1955	48.6	90.0	3.25	2.9	16.8
1956	48.8	100.1	3.57	3.6	13.6
1957	47.2	112.1	4.21 4*	4.5	10.5
1958	41.4	121.2	4.16 4*	4.9	8.4
1959	52.1	129.3	4.65 4*	5.2	10.0
1960	49.7	139.1	4.73 4*	5.6	8.9
1961	50.3	149.3	4.66 4*	6.0	8.4
1962	55.4	161.2	4.62 4*	6.5	8.5
1963	59.4	174.8	4.50 4*	7.0	8.5
1964	66.8	192.5	4.57 4*	7.7	8.7
1965	77.8	209.4	4.64 4*	8.4	9.3
1966	84.2	231.3	5.34 5*	9.5	8.9
1967	79.8	255.6	5.82 5*	10.7	7.5
1968	87.6	280.9	6.51 5*	12.0	7.3
1969	84.9	307.4	7.36 7*	13.9	6.1
1970	74.3	341.3	8.51 7*	18.2	4.1
1971	83.3	380.3	7.94 7*	19.0	4.4

Source:
Business Statistics, 1971, U.S. Dept. of Commerce.
Survey of Current Business, U.S. Dept. of Commerce.

through 1965, a flat interest rate of 4.0 percent was applied to all debt outstanding, although rates were higher each year. Since the amount of debt outstanding for this period doubled, a 4.0 percent rate was quite appropriate on the whole. From 1966 through 1968, a period of rapidly rising interest rates, 4.0 percent was assumed on all debt prior to 1966 and a flat 5.0 percent rate was used on the incremental debt for each of the three years. Starting in 1969, a 7.0 percent rate was assumed on all incremental debt outstanding.

The important figure is the resulting coverage number, which is obtained by dividing total corporate profits before tax by the interest expense. The results are an astounding decline from a high 25.0 in 1950 to a reading of 4.4 at the end of 1971. Since the method of calculation understated earlier coverage ratios and overstated more recent ratios, the actual results are probably even more alarming.

Since earnings coverage is a key factor in bond-quality ratings, it is evident that the quality of corporate debt is declining. It is no wonder that interest rates are rising to reflect this declining quality. Should the trend continue, corporations will have an increasingly difficult time raising capital to fund the excessive short-term debt that is periodically amassed by corporations during each business expansion. The interest rates that will have to be paid will make it progressively more difficult to justify many expansion projects, which should be reflected in future rates of capital formation. As long as the trends in liquidity continue, interest rates should continue to rise and corporations should gradually find themselves with growing inflexibility in financing their operations.

According to a well-recognized authority on security analysis, a minimum coverage figure for industrial companies on average pretax earning power is seven times. Clearly, this indicator has fallen well below that figure for the average corporation. With the average below the acceptable coverage figure, there must be a great number of corporations that have reached extremely dangerous levels. The increasing number of rating reductions tells us that the limits for the economy may be very near. As the number of firms reaching dangerous coverage figures increases, they will have a growing effect upon the economy as a whole and upon other more healthy firms in particular.

In Table 7.6, additional confirmation of the long deterioration in the quality of debt is presented. In that table, total pretax corporate profits are compared to total interest charges as computed in the national income accounts. The net interest figures presented there measure the excess of interest payments of the domestic business system over its interest receipts. This figure differs from the one used in Table 7.5 in that it includes interest on short-term debt as well as long-term. It is also broader in scope in that it includes all business, while Table 7.5 deals exclusively with corporations. It may be seen that the results very closely parallel our rough approximation of coverage on long-term debt only. If anything, the trend is even more alarming than that presented in Table 7.4, for it discloses that both corporations *and* nonincorporated businesses are overextended.

TABLE 7.6

Coverage of Interest Charges
(In Billions of Dollars)

Year	Corporate Profits Before Tax	Net Interest	Coverage
1947	31.5	1.9	16.6
1948	35.2	1.8	19.6
1949	28.9	1.9	15.2
1950	42.6	2.0	21.3
1951	43.9	2.3	19.1
1952	38.9	2.6	15.0
1953	40.6	2.8	14.5
1954	38.3	3.6	10.6
1955	48.6	4.1	11.9
1956	48.8	4.6	10.6
1957	47.2	5.6	8.4
1958	41.4	6.8	6.1
1959	52.1	7.1	7.3
1960	49.7	8.4	5.9
1961	50.3	10.0	5.3
1962	55.4	11.6	4.8
1963	59.4	13.8	4.3
1964	66.8	15.8	4.2
1965	77.8	18.2	4.3
1966	84.2	21.4	3.9
1967	79.8	24.4	3.3
1968	87.6	26.9	3.2
1969	84.9	30.5	2.8
1970	74.3	34.8	2.1
1971	83.3	38.5	2.2

Source:
Business Statistics, 1971, U.S. Dept. of Commerce.
Survey of Current Business, U.S. Dept. of Commerce.

Corporate External-Financing Needs

Unfortunately, it is not only increased inventory and accounts-receivable financing that periodically increase corporate short-term debt to unsustainable levels, resulting in the increasingly frequent credit squeezes. Superimposed upon the above credit needs in each economic expansion, and with varying lags, is a boom in plant and equipment expenditures. Much of the cash needs for this expansion is initially paid from existing short-term assets and borrowing, depending upon conditions. In 1968 and 1969, for example, overreliance upon short-term financing threw the corporate debt structures far out of balance, contributing to the credit squeeze in the next year. Manufacturing firms often attempt to delay their long-term financing in the early stages of a capital-goods boom, for in these periods there is usually a climate of monetary restraint due to the historical interventions of the Federal Reserve to cool the speculative climate. Later, the climate for long-term financing is often better.

In effect, corporations go through a period of heavy reliance upon short-term borrowings to finance long-term investments. In recent years, particularly after the squeeze of 1966, they have shown remarkable imagination in finding new sources of funds. Table 3.2, for example, shows the record of commercial-paper offerings. From 1965 through 1971, the amount outstanding more than tripled. A part of this surge was the novel offering of commercial paper by bank-holding companies. As discussed earlier, the banking system faced the necessity to become equally inventive in keeping the proverbial ball in the air. The fact that the level of commercial paper was still quite high in 1972 is an indication of continuing illiquidity.

Ultimately the debt must be funded. When the capital markets become more hospitable, usually during the ensuing business slowdown and the following recovery, they reflect a lagged surge in long-term financing, as was experienced in 1970 and 1971, as shown in an earlier table.

Corporate Profitability

The situation would be much improved if the results of the massive leveraging process described above were successful in terms of leading to much higher levels of corporate profits. Once again, corporations must take a failing mark. Figure 7.1 depicts the postwar record, for all manufacturing firms, of pretax profit margins and aftertax return on stockholders' equity. Since at least one of the aims of leveraging, if not the only one, is to increase the return on stockholders' equity, one would hope that the corporations would at least be able to hold returns equal instead of suffering the 50 percent decline from 1947 to 1971. Pretax profit margins also showed a pronounced downward bias over the entire postwar period. Although there are undoubtedly many reasons for this record, the decline in liquidity, the resulting high debt-service loads, and the periodic preoccupations with financing their way out of excessive short-term debt, as well as other effects of illiquidity, all worked against corporations.

The postwar record of comparative growth-rates of corporate profits and corporate debt is summarized in Table 7.7. Throughout the entire postwar period from 1947 through 1971, while corporate profits about kept pace with the growth in real GNP, corporate debt grew at more than twice the rate. In the later six-year period, while corporate profits showed little or no growth, the rate of growth of corporate debt expansion accelerated. Clearly, the disappointing profit growth worsens the liquidity situation and puts further upward pressure upon interest rates, for corporations are forced to use external financing in a period when the trend of interest rates is definitely upward.

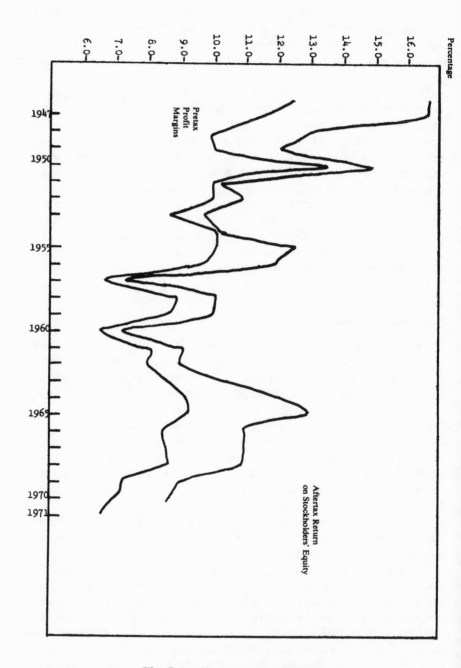

Fig. 7.1—Corporate Profitability

86

TABLE 7.7

Trends in Corporate Debt
(In Billions of Dollars)

Year	Corporate Profits Before Tax	Corporate Profits After Tax	Total Corporate Debt	Total Long-Term Corporate Debt
1947	31.5	20.2	108.9	46.1
1950	42.6	24.9	142.1	60.1
1955	48.6	27.0	212.1	90.1
1960	49.7	26.7	302.8	139.1
1965	77.8	46.5	454.3	209.4
1966	84.2	49.5	506.6	231.3
1967	79.8	47.3	553.7	255.6
1968	87.6	47.8	628.0	280.9
1969	84.9	44.8	714.8	307.4
1970	74.3	40.2	773.6	341.3
1971	83.3	45.9	827.3	380.3

Growth Trends			1947-71	1965-71
Corporate profits B.T.			4.1%	1.2%
Corporate profits A.T.			3.5%	0.0%
Total corporate debt			8.8%	10.5%
Total long-term corporate debt			9.2%	10.4%

Source:
Business Statistics, 1971, U.S. Dept. of Commerce.
Survey of Current Business, U.S. Dept. of Commerce.

Financing Postwar Investment

The postwar record of investment by corporations, as related to the wherewithal to finance it, is presented in Table 7.8. The table lists the record of annual corporate capital spending and inventory accumulation. This total is then related to the postwar record of corporate cash flow (retained earnings plus depreciation). Any shortfall between the two must be financed externally and, of course, exerts upward pressures upon interest rates. This pressure is in addition to that made necessary by the growth of trade credit among current assets at the expense of cash assets.

Although there have been many deficit years since World War II, it is easy to see that the years from 1965 to the present have been the worst sustained period of the era under study. This explains why, while new corporate offerings of bonds and equities have been at record levels by far, there has been scant improvement in liquidity among corporations. It is not coincidental that interest rates have also been at record levels for the century. There is a very close correlation between this indicator and interest rates throughout the entire period of study as well as in previous periods. Corporate cash needs, along with those of the government, which we will discuss later, are the two major determinants of interest rates. In recent years, unfortunately, the peak cash needs of both sectors coincided.

TABLE 7.8

Corporate External Financing Requirements
(In Billions of Dollars)

Year	New Plant & Equip. Expenditures	Change in Business Inventories	Total Investment	Cash Flow	Surplus or Deficit
1947	19.33	—0.5	18.93	19.2	0.27
1948	21.30	4.7	26.00	22.0	—4.00
1949	18.98	—3.1	15.88	18.7	2.82
1950	20.21	6.8	27.01	24.3	2.71
1951	25.46	10.3	35.76	22.5	—13.26
1952	26.43	3.1	29.53	21.7	—7.83
1953	28.20	0.4	29.60	23.8	—5.80
1954	27.19	—1.5	25.69	25.3	—0.39
1955	29.53	6.0	35.53	32.8	—2.73
1956	35.73	4.7	40.43	33.6	—6.83
1957	37.94	1.3	39.24	33.8	—5.44
1958	31.89	—1.5	30.39	31.7	1.31
1959	33.55	4.8	38.35	38.4	0.05
1960	36.75	3.6	40.35	37.1	—3.25
1961	35.91	2.0	37.91	38.5	0.59
1962	38.39	6.0	44.39	44.8	0.41
1963	40.77	5.9	46.67	46.8	0.13
1964	46.97	5.8	52.77	53.5	0.73
1965	54.42	9.6	64.02	60.1	—3.92
1966	63.51	14.8	78.31	66.8	—11.51
1967	65.47	8.2	73.67	66.1	—7.57
1968	67.76	7.1	74.86	68.9	—5.96
1969	75.56	7.4	82.96	70.8	—12.16
1970	79.71	2.8	82.51	69.8	—12.71
1971	81.21	2.2	83.41	80.9	—2.51

Source:
Business Statistics, 1971, U.S. Dept. of Commerce.
Survey of Current Business, U.S. Dept. of Commerce.

There is good reason to believe that the deficits we have seen since 1965 will continue with only a brief interruption. First, the corporate offerings have been continuing at historically high levels, indicating that the need is still present. Second, with inventories at this writing still historically low, inventory accumulation should be stimulated as the economy continues to improve, as predicted by most economists. Third, many writers on the subject attest to the fact that a large portion of our present capital is obsolete or old and must be replaced. Add to this the usual stimulus to capital spending of a rising economy and inflation, as well as the burgeoning demand for pollution-control spending, and we should see a continued high level of capital spending. The Council on Environmental Quality has estimated that between now and 1980 industry will need $25 billion in new capital funds for pollution-control spending. There are also some key industries that will be large spenders in the 1970s, such as the oil and gas industry, where there is not only a shortage of supply of product but also of refining capacity. Utilities and communications will also be large spenders. One estimate has placed the spending for these three industries at over $350 billion during the 1970s, as compared to less than $90 billion for the last five years of the 1960s. Fourth, it is obvious that during periods of inflation, all capital-intensive industries overstate their profits since they depreciate their plants on a cost basis, not on a replacement basis. Finally, corporate profits should continue their disappointing long-term trends, interrupted by only brief cyclical improvements.

Sales Growth versus Credit Growth

Earlier, we examined the growth in trade receivables as related to sales growth and learned that although sales were growing throughout the postwar years, receivables were growing much faster. That indicator, like most of the others we have examined so far, is meaningful whether applied to the individual firm or to an aggregation of all firms. We concluded that there is a certain amount of artificiality to rapid sales growth that is paced by a considerably larger rate of growth in receivables. The same reasoning applies to the data presented in Table 7.9

A security analyst would be alarmed if, in analyzing a company, he found a growth in sales but a far faster growth in credit extended *to* that firm. Any profits accruing to the firm because of the rising sales might be thought to be illusory. This seems to be the situation for the entire corporate sector. We saw earlier that sales growth by the corporate sector was totally eclipsed by a growth in trade credit, signifying that corporations were financing much of the growth in their sales for their customers. Next, we saw that total corporate profits have been growing at less than one-half the rate of total corporate credit. The sluggish growth in corporate profits relative to growth in debt could be excused if the quality of profits were higher than that indicated by the actual figures because of higher depreciation or research and development spending. If this were the case, then sales performance would have at least been able to keep pace with the growth in credit. Table 7.9 confirms that this is not the situation. There we see a complete record of the postwar growth in sales and debt. From 1948 through 1971, manufacturing and trade sales grew 224 percent. Over the same period, total corporate debt, both long and short term, grew over 600 percent, and long-term corporate debt alone grew by 624 percent. The comparative annual compound growth-rates from 1948 to 1971 are summarized in Table 7.10. These data unmistakably lead to the conclusion that the trends cannot continue. If a corporation continues to borrow at a faster rate than its sales grow, its return on capital must decline, and if, by the process of excessive debt creation, the total level of interest rates is increased, the day of reckoning must draw even closer.

TABLE 7.9

Sales Growth versus Credit Growth
(In Billions of Dollars)

Year	Manufacturing & Trade Sales	Total Corporate Credit	Total Corporate L.T. Debt
1948	423.1	117.8	52.5
1949	405.5	118.0	56.5
1950	463.2	142.1	60.1
1951	520.3	162.5	66.6
1952	538.1	171.0	73.3
1953	575.8	179.5	78.3
1954	557.3	182.8	82.9
1955	620.3	212.1	90.0
1956	648.8	231.7	100.1
1957	670.5	246.7	112.1
1958	650.8	259.5	121.2
1959	715.9	283.3	129.3
1960	728.9	302.8	139.1
1961	733.6	324.3	149.3
1962	785.0	348.2	161.2
1963	827.6	376.4	174.8
1964	884.2	409.6	192.5
1965	963.3	454.3	209.4
1966	1,046.1	506.6	231.3
1967	1,076.5	553.7	255.6
1968	1,162.7	628.0	280.9
1969	1,231.9	714.8	307.4
1970	1,264.4	773.6	341.3
1971	1,371.1	827.3	380.3

Source:
Business Statistics, 1971, U.S. Dept. of Commerce.
Survey of Current Business, U.S. Dept. of Commerce.

TABLE 7.10

Manufacturing and trade sales	5.3%
Total corporate debt	8.9%
Total long-term corporate debt	9.0%

Summing Up

We began this section on corporate liquidity trends by outlining some of the effects of deficient liquidity upon the individual corporation. These effects include inflexibility, vulnerability to sudden adverse shifts in business, inability to perform long-term planning, loss of market share, and generally inefficient management due to preoccupation with debt management.

We followed with the conclusion that what is true for the individual firm must also be true for a composite of all firms, though the effects may take slightly different forms. The process of losing liquidity, for the composite, tends to stifle overall growth of the economy, increases risk of failure of a number of firms and thus risk for the entire economy, reduces incentives, and restricts competitiveness in world markets. Most important, the growing illiquidity places great upward pressure upon interest rates and prices.

Examining the evidence, we found that there has been a long and rarely interrupted deterioration in liquidity, in the aggregate, throughout the entire postwar period, which paralleled similar trends in the banking system. This deterioration was evident in a number of indicators, such as the current ratio, the trade receivables relationship to current assets as well as the age in receivables, and the quick ratio, which underwent a pronounced decline. This trend has been largely ignored by most investors and economists, except for the severe cyclical declines in liquidity when attention is temporarily focused upon the problem. During the recessions that usually follow these periods, much of the short-term debt is funded. With the decline in liquidity temporarily halted, the problem is forgotten.

We then traced the gradual shifting of the excessive short-term debt into other sections of the balance sheet and found that far from disappearing, the excessive debt accumulation is simply transferred to long-term debt. This process is manifested by the increasing percentage of debt relative to equity, a rapidly growing interest-expense load relative to profits, and drastically declining coverage figures. The problem is compounded by sluggish profit growth and declining profit margins.

The end-result of the entire process is a series of unmistakable confirming financial trends among corporations, which have been in force throughout the entire postwar period and are beginning to reach unsustainable proportions. Traditional liquidity, as measured in the current section of the balance sheet, has been steadily reduced, except for periodic cyclical recoveries. In addition to this, the sins of the past have also accumulated in the long-term section of the balance sheet, bringing risk not of liquidity but of insolvency. Finally, the growth of the economy, as measured by sales in the corporate sector and the GNP, has been bought, in large part, by excessive debt creation. The same trends of debt creation cannot be continued without rendering corporations totally inflexible because of heavy debt and interest loads.

Thorough analysis of the full effects of the declining corporate liquidity cannot be accomplished without also considering the same trend in banking liquidity. Before discussing the final effects, however, it is necessary to consider the role of the government in the entire process and, finally, the role of the Federal Reserve.

Chapter 8

The Role of the Government

So far we have discussed the existence of the long continuous secular trend of deteriorating liquidity among corporations and commercial banks within the United States, exploring the evidence and discussing in a broad fashion the effects of the trend. We have said very little about the causes of the trend. The primary culprits are the federal government and the Federal Reserve, working in concert to supply both the philosophical underpinnings of the trend and the wherewithal to keep it intact to the point where it probably cannot end without disastrous consequences.

Early Precedents

There have already been too many books written on the economic events of the 1930s and the crash that preceded it. The period was a rich source for economists and stock-market analysts alike as they poked around in the rubble of the collapse. The collapse, and the disaster that followed, was in part a product of the monetary excesses of the 1920s. In the extreme conditions that followed, the seeds of our present predicament were sown. It was then that there took shape a body of economic thought holding that the U.S. economy could not move on its own, that an equilibrium at very low levels of activity could exist. It was then that our mixed economy began, with the government taking an active role in the management of the economy and in the management of the lives of the people of this country. No longer was that government best that governed least. No longer could the economy be relied upon to correct its own excesses. The framework of the economic theory that guided the postwar years was developed during this period. The precedents set in this period, and during World War II, were welded into the Keynesian theory of the 1950s and 1960s.

Employment Act of 1946

The behavior of the government and the budding Keynesian theory was formalized in the Employment Act of 1946. With the passage of this act, the federal government officially declared war on unemployment and assumed responsibility for the maintenance of full employment regardless of cost. It hoped to legislate away the business cycle and, so it was claimed, would never again allow the country to sink to the depths reached in the 1930s. This act, plus the deeds that followed, began the trend away from the excessive liquidity that had been amassed during the war years. This was accomplished in a number of ways: First, government spending and the resulting deficits financed by the Federal Reserve, as we will see in Chapter 9, served to stimulate the economy. Second, the management of the business cycle through fiscal and monetary policy eliminated many of the natural corrective forces of the cycle, which had served, in the past, to moderate the rate of increase in the growth of credit. Finally, the success of limiting the extent of any economic corrections, together with the rhetoric by government and economists regarding the demise of the business cycle, served to create a climate in which individuals changed their credit ethic and corporations and banks changed their business approach. The growing belief that serious business recessions had been eliminated also led to the belief that much of the business risk had been eliminated, or, in the case of banks particularly, shifted to the government. This led banks to feel safe in reducing drastically the size of the buffers once thought necessary to protect against risk of deposit withdrawals. It served as justification for the new banking philosophy described in previous chapters. The same attitudes led corporations to feel comfortable with lower levels of liquidity and with debt-heavy capital structures. These attitudes reached a peak in the early 1960s with the ascension of the so-called new economists.

The New Economists

In 1961, after two long terms out of the White House, the liberal Keynesian economists once again found themselves in a position of power. They soon, in word and deed, made up for the long absence. War was declared on every aspect of American life where money had not previously been thrown. Not only would the economy be "fine-tuned" as never before, but once the economy was "moving again" the growth would be continuous. Not even the mild recessions of the early postwar years would be allowed. There followed the most massive spending spree in years and a record 105-month economic expansion that removed any remaining doubts that the business cycle had not been finally eliminated.

Even the Vietnam War could not slow the progress of the Great Society. While war expenditures began to mount, nondefense expenditures continued at their high levels, deficits mounted, and money from the Fed flowed to finance it all. This final acceleration in spending, deficits, and credit expansion pushed the trend in liquidity deterioration so far that it may already be too late to extricate the country without either a serious credit contraction or a long period of stagflation, which we will discuss later in more detail. Before we discuss exactly how the government, with the aid of the Federal Reserve, has accomplished this financial deterioration, we must first examine the extent of the encroachment of the government sector upon the private economy.

The Postwar Record

Government Spending

When the postwar record of government spending is examined closely, it is easy to see where the inspiration and the impetus for the long postwar run-down in liquidity in the private sector originated. Table 8.1 discloses an upward trend in government spending that is even more pronounced and continuous than the private-sector trends discussed in previous chapters. In terms of absolute growth, the average compound rates of growth that prevailed over the entire period from 1947 through 1972 are as shown in Table 8.2

With both federal spending and total government spending growing at a rate 50 percent higher than the private sector, it is obvious that the same rates that prevailed over this twenty-five-year period cannot continue without a complete change in the structure of the economy. When this country's GNP finally surpassed the trillion-dollar mark it was the cause of many articles treating the mind-boggling amount with a sense of both tribute and amazement. Consider then what total government spending will be in the years ahead if the same growth were to continue: In fifteen years such spending will be beyond the $1.5 trillion level, and at the end of a twenty-five-year period it will be approaching a level of $6 trillion.

Nor is there any sign of a slowdown as yet, despite the strong appeals of the Nixon administration for drastic slowdowns in government spending. The year 1972 finished with a growth in federal spending of over 10 percent, or well above the long-term trend rate. As might be expected from the highly inflationary period since 1965, the rates of growth from 1965 through 1972 were sharply accelerating, as shown in Table 8.3. It can be seen from these figures that total federal spending grew at a rate one and one-half percentage points higher than the secular growth rate, while the growth in state and local spending was two full percentage points higher than the long-term trend. With the pitched battle between Congress and the President in the closing months of 1972 and into 1973 on the budget, impounding of funds by the President, and drastic cutbacks in government programs, one might conclude that the growth rate can now be expected to decline. Not so, according to the preliminary budget for federal spending through fiscal 1975. The projected growth-rates for federal spending in 1973, 1974, and 1975 are, respectively, 8 percent, 7 percent, and 10.5 percent. Although the estimates are somewhat below the long-term trend, it must be remembered that these are only "opening bids," for it is very seldom that budgeted spending has not be exceeded by large amounts when the final record is tabulated. Moreover, the estimates given here do not consider the projected state and local spending, which has been accelerating at an even faster rate than the federal spending levels.

TABLE 8.1

Government Spending Trends
(In Billions of Dollars)

Year	Federal Government Expenditures	State & Local Expenditures	Total Government Outlays	GNP	Government Spending Percentage of GNP
1929	2.5	7.8	10.3	103.1	10
1947	29.8	13.8	41.9	231.3	18
1948	34.9	17.4	50.3	257.6	19
1949	41.3	20.0	59.2	256.5	23
1950	40.8	22.3	60.8	284.8	21
1951	57.8	23.7	79.0	328.4	24
1952	71.0	25.3	93.7	345.5	27
1953	77.0	27.0	101.2	364.6	28
1954	69.7	29.9	96.7	364.8	27
1955	68.1	32.7	97.7	398.0	25
1956	71.9	35.6	104.2	419.2	25
1957	79.6	39.5	114.9	441.1	26
1958	88.9	44.0	127.3	447.3	28
1959	91.0	46.8	131.0	483.7	27
1960	93.0	49.7	136.2	503.7	27
1961	102.1	54.1	149.0	520.1	29
1962	110.3	57.6	159.9	560.3	29
1963	113.9	62.2	167.0	590.5	28
1964	118.1	67.8	175.5	632.4	28
1965	123.5	74.5	186.9	684.9	27
1966	142.8	83.9	228.7	749.9	30
1967	163.6	95.1	242.9	793.9	31
1968	181.5	107.5	270.3	864.2	31
1969	189.5	119.0	292.3	930.3	31
1970	204.5	132.2	312.3	976.4	32
1971	220.8	147.0	339.5	1050.4	33
1972	246.8	162.7	371.6	1151.8	33

TABLE 8.2

Total federal spending	9%
Total state & local spending	10%
Total government spending	9%
Private sector growth	6%

TABLE 8.3

Growth in Government Spending, 1965-72

Level of Government	Growth-Rate (Percentage)
Federal	10.5%
State and local	12.0%
Total	10.0%

Government Spending Relative to GNP

The growth in the absolute levels of government spending is, of course, quite astounding, but it becomes much more meaningful when compared to the growth in the entire economy. While the entire economy increased slightly under four times since 1947, the various categories of government spending grew by between nine and twelve times. Table 8.1 depicts the postwar record of total government spending as a percentage of total GNP. From 18 percent in 1947, the relationship rose to the level of 33 percent in 1972. If one went back as far as 1929, the percentage relationship would be less than 10 percent. Even these statistics do not tell the entire story, for masked by the overall government spending figures is an even more quickly changing relationship between federal-government purchases of goods and services and the GNP.

The ratios computed in the last column in Table 8.1 include state and local spending as well as all federal-government spending, comprising both purchases of goods and services and nonpurchase expenditures, such as social-security benefits, interest, other transfer payments, and other expenditures that do not constitute direct demands on the nation's productive capacity. Only the purchases of goods and services are included in the GNP figures. Prior to the 1930s, when "little government" was still the prevailing philosophy, federal expenditures were far exceeded by state and local spending. It was not until the economic holocaust of the 1930s that the role of the federal government changed. If one compares the level of federal-government purchases in 1929, for example, with those at the end of 1972, he would see a much more dramatic change. The level of federal-government purchases over this period grew by *eighty-one times,* while the entire economy grew by only eleven times. In terms of the percentage representation in the GNP, this category of spending grew from 1.2 percent to 9.2 percent from 1929 through 1972, or roughly nine times the representation, as compared to a growth of roughly three times for total government spending as a percentage of total GNP. As we will see, the growth in federal spending has the greatest meaning for the decline in liquidity in the postwar years. It is not only the changes in the levels of federal-government spending, but also the important change in philosophy as to the role of the government, that is crucial in our study of liquidity trends. It is not only the increase in federal-government purchases of goods and services that has been dramatic. The federal government has steadily added scores of programs that serve to redistribute income within the economy but do not have an impact upon the GNP. They do not give the government anything in return. These nonpurchase expenditures include welfare payments, subsidies, social security, and unemployment benefits. In terms of the effect of the government upon the liquidity trends discussed here, it is this total amount of government spending that is important. All government spending must be financed by taxation or borrowing, and this is where the problem lies. In 1929, total federal-government spending comprised 2.4 percent of total GNP. By the end of 1972 this relationship had grown to over 18 percent, also a growth factor of nine times. As it began from a higher level, this rapidly changing relationship is masked, as mentioned, by the slower growth of state and local spending since 1929. In recent years, however, state and local spending has been growing even faster, compounding the problem.

Public versus Private Spending

The figures just presented can be rearranged to perhaps more dramatically display the trends in government spending and their effects upon personal choice and freedom. Table 8.4 relates the record of total government spending to spending by the private sector. The ratio of government or public spending to spending by private citizens grew from 22 percent in 1947 to 48 percent by 1972. In other words, an increasing amount of the wealth produced in this country is spent by the government and not by private citizens. By 1972 nearly half of every dollar spent in the economy was spent by the government in one way or another. The change is even more dramatic if we look all the way back to 1929, when the percentage was only 11 percent. Once again, if one separates federal expenditures, a much more alarming change is seen. In 1929, federal expenditures represented only 2.7 percent of private expenditures, while in 1972 it comprised 32 percent, or an increase of ten times.

It is not difficult to understand why such a changing governmental role in the affairs of the economy has wreaked such tremendous changes in the philosophy of banks, business, and individuals. It has triggered, among other things, the deterioration in liquidity.

Government purchases of goods and services compete directly for the nation's production and productive resources in terms of goods and services as well as the labor force. The growing nonpurchase expenditures alter the income distribution in the nation through transfer payments without consider-

TABLE 8.4

Public versus Private Spending

Year	Total Public Spending (Billions of Dollars)	Private Spending (Billions of Dollars)	Ratio of Public to Private Spending
1929	10.3	92.8	11
1947	41.9	189.4	22
1948	50.3	207.3	24
1949	59.2	197.3	30
1950	60.8	224.0	27
1951	79.0	249.4	32
1952	93.7	251.8	37
1953	101.2	263.4	38
1954	96.7	268.1	36
1955	97.7	300.3	33
1956	104.2	315.0	33
1957	114.9	326.2	35
1958	127.3	320.0	40
1959	131.0	352.7	37
1960	136.2	367.5	37
1961	149.0	371.1	40
1962	159.9	400.4	40
1963	167.0	423.5	40
1964	175.5	456.9	39
1965	186.9	498.0	38
1966	228.7	521.2	44
1967	242.9	551.0	44
1968	270.3	593.9	46
1969	292.3	638.0	46
1970	312.3	664.1	47
1971	339.5	710.5	48
1972	371.6	780.2	48

ation being given to the effects upon future growth of the economy. One result of these first two effects of government spending is a reduction in incentives. Since most of the gain in the economy in terms of production, innovation, and invention have come as a result of risk-taking by the private sector, there is little doubt that the diminishing role of the private sector in total spending has already been felt. Further on we will look in greater detail at changes in capital formation and productivity in the United States. The growing evidence of the diminishing competitiveness of the United States in foreign markets already testifies to the effects of these trends in declining incentives. A third major effect of the rising level of government spending is the change in the public's understanding of the role of government, which has a two-barreled effect. The first effect is the growing expectation that the government will take on new programs as problems arise, as well as the expectation that it will continue to expand existing programs, such as social security and other socially oriented programs. We all saw this carried to extremes during the New Frontier and the Great Society of the 1960s under Kennedy and Johnson. The second, and more relevant, effect of our thesis is the feeling that business risk has been substantially reduced. This has helped, as mentioned, to form the new banking philosophy and corporate cash management, which have played a major role in the liquidity deterioration. Finally, the most important effect of all lies in the financing of the spending, which must be done by either taxation or borrowing. Much, of course, has been done through taxation, as the average tax rate has doubled in the last twenty-five years. This alone is reason to believe that reduced incentives to commit capital and take risks have resulted from the increased government activity. To the extent that taxation has not generated sufficient revenues to finance the spending, the level of government debt must rise, as indeed it has. It is the interaction of the federal government and the Federal Reserve in the financing of the debt that underlies the liquidity trends, as we explain in Chapter 9. Before examining this procedure in depth, it will be helpful to see the magnitudes of the amounts involved.

Government Deficits and Debt

The final reckoning of the government's spending activities appears in Table 8.5. It is evident that government revenues, in spite of rising average rates of taxation, have not kept pace with government spending. This is not surprising in light of the difference in attractiveness to Congress between proposing new spending programs and proposing higher taxes. A quick glance at Table 8.5 will also disclose the increasing frequency with which deficits are occurring. On a National Accounts basis, there have been fourteen deficit years in the twenty-five-year period encompassed in the table. Nine of the deficits, however, occurred in the twelve years since 1960. The Unified Budget, which replaced the administrative budget as the government's basic planning document and includes government trust funds and sponsored agencies, has shown only *one* budget surplus since 1960.

In the early postwar years, the budget deficits usually occurred in conjunction with business recessions and later were balanced according to good Keynesian theory. During the record 105-month business expansion of the 1960s, however the unified budget was in deficit every year but one throughout the entire period. Both the frequency and the size of the deficits are rising. It also seems that each recession requires larger government spending to turn business upward again.

The deficits, of course, must be financed by government borrowing, as is evidenced by the growing levels of debt outstanding by both the federal government and its agencies. State and local debt is growing even faster than debt on the federal level.

TABLE 8.5

Government Finance
(In Billions of Dollars)

Year	National Income Budget Calendar Year	Unified Budget Fiscal Year	Federal Debt	Federal Agency Debt	State & Local Debt	Total Public Debt
1947	13.4	0.0	221.7	0.7	15.0	237.4
1948	8.4	0.0	215.3	0.6	17.0	232.9
1949	—2.4	0.0	217.6	0.7	19.1	237.4
1950	9.1	0.0	217.4	0.7	21.7	239.8
1951	6.2	0.0	216.9	1.3	24.2	242.4
1952	—3.8	0.0	221.5	1.3	27.0	249.8
1953	—7.0	0.0	226.8	1.4	30.7	258.9
1954	—5.9	1.2	229.1	1.3	35.5	265.9
1955	4.0	—3.0	229.6	2.9	40.2	272.7
1956	5.7	4.1	224.3	2.4	44.4	271.1
1957	2.1	3.2	223.0	2.4	48.6	274.0
1958	—10.2	—2.9	231.0	2.5	53.2	286.7
1959	—1.2	—12.9	241.4	3.7	58.0	303.1
1960	3.5	0.3	239.8	3.5	63.0	306.3
1961	—3.8	—3.4	246.7	4.0	70.0	320.7
1962	—3.8	—7.1	253.6	5.3	78.1	337.0
1963	0.7	—4.8	257.5	7.2	84.7	349.4
1964	—3.0	—5.9	264.0	7.5	92.4	363.9
1965	1.2	—1.6	266.4	8.9	99.9	375.3
1966	—.2	—3.8	271.8	11.2	104.8	387.9
1967	—12.4	—8.7	286.5	9.0	113.4	408.8
1968	—6.5	—25.2	291.9	21.4	123.9	437.1
1969	8.1	3.2	289.3	30.6	132.6	452.4
1970	—12.9	—2.8	301.1	38.8	146.8	486.7
1971	—21.7	—23.0	326.9	43.2	167.7	537.8
1972	—18.5	—23.0	—	—	—	—

Defense Spending

Many would blame the problem of excessive government spending throughout the postwar period upon defense expenditures, citing the Vietnam War in particular as the cause of the most recent flood of spending and deficits as well as of the inflation. It may be argued that defense spending is too high and our priorities are wrong, but these cannot be blamed for the worsening deficits, the accelerating government spending and debt, or the inflation. To do this would imply that such spending was growing relative to other

101

spending, and this is clearly not the case.

During World War II, spending for national defense was over 40 percent of GNP, but it declined sharply to near 5 percent after the war and remained at low levels until the Korean War, whereupon it tripled and remained relatively high, declining only slightly after the war. Since 1959, there has been a steady decline. The buildup for Vietnam caused very little change in the downward trend, and the 1972 level of 6.5 percent of GNP was the lowest since 1950, the year before the Korean War.

Table 8.6 contains the record of defense spending and nondefense spending for the several years prior to the increased spending for the Vietnam War. The years following were marked by huge increases in total government spending, deficits, and an intense and stubborn inflation. It is clear that the growth in defense spending was markedly less than that of nondefense, with the rate of growth from 1966, the first year of the Vietnam War buildup, to the present being only 3.8 percent, as compared to the rate of 11.1 percent, for non-defense spending.

TABLE 8.6

Defense Versus Civilian Government Outlays
(In Billions of Dollars)

Year	National Defense Expenditures	Nondefense Expenditures
1963	50.8	63.1
1964	50.0	68.1
1965	50.1	73.4
1966	60.7	82.1
1967	72.4	91.2
1968	78.0	103.5
1969	78.4	111.1
1970	75.1	129.4
1971	71.4	149.4
1972	75.9	170.9
Annual Growth Rates (Percentage)		
1963-72	4.6%	11.7%
1966-72	3.8%	11.1%

The primary thrust in federal spending over the last decade or so has clearly come in civilian outlays, and most particularly in the field of domestic assistance, with a sharply accelerating uptrend beginning in the early 1960s during the Kennedy-Johnson years. The sharp expansion in such spending since 1964 reflected improved social-security benefits, the beginning of Medicare in 1963, and growth in direct welfare payments. The Aid to Families with Dependent Children program provided particular impetus. The trend in such transfer payments, however, has been generally upward for over forty years, beginning with legislation in the 1930s. While in 1929 the transfer payments represented barely 1 percent of disposable income, they have risen steadily—with particular acceleration, as mentioned, in recent years—and are currently around 12 percent. The increase in 1972 was the largest yearly increase of the postwar period. The 20 percent increase in social-security benefits in the fall of 1972, for example, will by itself increase spending in 1977 by $6 billion or more.

Uncontrollable Spending

A number of studies have concluded that over 70 percent of federal spending is now "uncontrollable," or locked into the budget, with the chances of reducing it rather slight without legislative changes. This makes the prospects for an early solution to the problems outlined in this book seem quite dim. The transfer payments described in the preceding section are examples of such spending. Federal domestic spending has more than tripled in real terms in the last twenty years. This increase has brought with it, as mentioned, great changes in expectations in all sectors of the economy. The government, both on the federal level and on the state and local levels, is now expected to alleviate every social ill that is brought to its attention with enough pressure. Indeed, eager congressmen and senators avidly seek out causes for political advantage. Once begun, however, federal-assistance programs tend to grow well beyond all expectations. These perpetual-motion programs grow because administrators crave more power and higher budgets, recipients demand larger benefits, and would-be beneficiaries pressure to become covered. Once covered it is only natural that the recipients should want to be protected from the ravages of inflation. It is ironic that these very programs are causing the inflation that the recipients desire protection against. Housing subsidies are an example of a program out of control. In a few short years the compounding nature of the subsidy payments had grown so rapidly that finally, in the fiscal 1974 budget, the President was forced to call a moratorium on any further commitments. Like other programs of this nature, this program was rife with scandal and with enrichment not of the needy but of builders, politicians, and others. The food-stamp program currently accounts for over 5 percent of all retail sales of groceries in the country, certainly far beyond expectations, and with such "needy" recipients as college students and striking workers. Some of the largest increases in the budget in the years ahead will be in social services, social security, medicare, welfare, and other transfer payments. The record of such payments over the postwar period is recounted in Table 8.7.

103

TABLE 8.7

Uncontrollable Government Spending

Year	Transfer Payments	Net Interest Paid
1947	10.8	4.2
1948	11.4	4.3
1949	13.8	4.4
1950	14.4	4.5
1951	11.6	4.7
1952	10.9	4.7
1953	11.4	4.9
1954	13.3	5.0
1955	14.5	4.9
1956	15.2	5.3
1957	17.5	5.7
1958	21.3	5.6
1959	21.9	6.4
1960	23.4	7.1
1961	27.0	6.6
1962	27.7	7.2
1963	29.1	7.7
1964	29.9	8.3
1965	32.5	8.7
1966	35.7	9.5
1967	42.2	10.2
1968	48.2	11.7
1969	52.4	13.1
1970	63.4	14.6
1971	75.0	13.6
1972	83.4	13.6

Interest on the Debt

Net interest paid on the outstanding debt is also detailed in Table 8.7. This expense represents another uncontrollable element of the budget, which grows not only with the size of the debt—which, we have seen, is rapidly growing—but also with the level of interest rates. This expense is another example of the long list of self-enforcing trends that we have been describing. As we will explain more fully in Chapter 9, the major effect of the government spending and deficits described in this chapter is strong upward pressure for greater credit expansion and inflation, which also leads to rising illiquidity and interest rates. These rising interest rates, in turn, are a major factor in the growth of one of the uncontrollable federal expenditures, which must be financed.

Government Employees

One important aspect of the growing government sector, which may become a more uncontrollable problem in the future, is total government payroll. Payroll expense is probably already uncontrollable to some extent, given the well-entrenched patronage aspect of political life, as well as the tendency for programs to grow once implemented as administrators build their power bases. Today, one in every five workers draws his paycheck from some level of government. Moreover, under civil service it is quite difficult to discharge workers.

Until recently, an insignificant number of government employees was unionized. Since the middle 1950s, however, the unionization of government employees has been accelerating. Between 1955 and 1968, the number of teachers organized under the AFL-CIO increased by close to 300 percent, while the total of other government employees under the AFL-CIO banner grew by nearly 400 percent. The American Federation of State, County and Municipal Employees also grew 150 percent over the same period. The saturation level is still quite low, however, and gains have been accelerating since 1968. The reader need not be reminded of the growing militancy of such public workers as garbagemen, firemen, policemen, teachers, and postmen. This huge mass of workers is only beginning to test its wings. As these groups become more militant in the future, spurred on by inflationary government spending, their wage settlements will add significantly to the uncontrollable government budgets.

Analysis and Outlook

We have seen in this chapter that the trends toward lower liquidity have their origins, in large part, in a broad change in economic and political philosophy. The seeds of this change were planted and took root in the turmoil of the 1930s, when the philosophy of small government, which had prevailed in the 1920s, began to give way to the idea of larger and more active government. The new philosophy was formalized in the Employment Act of 1946 and really took flight in the 1960s with the New Frontier and Great Society.

The new philosophy manifested itself, as we saw, in rapid growth of government spending, government deficits, and debt at all levels, which, through public expectation of even more government programs, has fed upon itself throughout the entire postwar period. Contrary to the belief of some, the main force of this spending has been in the nondefense category of spending and has come at the expense of the private sector, where the free choice of spending has been greatly restricted.

The great leap forward in government spending must be financed by higher taxes or by government debt, and both methods were liberally utilized. From 1940 to 1970, total taxes rose 1,840 percent while income rose only 926 percent. Levels of government debt also rose sharply over the entire postwar period with acceleration in recent years. Both methods of finance have led to sharply rising inflationary pressures and inflationary expectations. The higher taxes have led to higher costs, which have been passed along in the form of higher prices, while the government debt has been largely monetized, leading to inflation as well.

The steady rise in government spending, business-cycle moderation, and artificial growth has also served to create a climate in which business and individuals alike feel that the traditional penalties for economic mistakes have been eliminated or substantially reduced. This changed attitude has served as one of the cornerstones of the rapid expansion of credit and rundown in liquidity. Many government programs are directly aimed at helping individuals get into debt, while the monetization of the government debt has supplied the wherewithal to finance the expansion of credit. Much of this activity has served to eliminate many of the natural corrective forces in the economy, and the trends have now been in force so long that there may not be a painless solution.

Can Fiscal Control Be Recovered?

With over $100 billion in accumulated deficits from fiscal years 1965-73, and government spending representing over 50 percent of the total gain in national income, the question comes to mind, Does anyone have the will to reverse the stimulative spiral? Because of the size of the stimulation, it cannot be reversed quickly without huge deflationary consequences, particularly considering the depressed levels of liquidity described in earlier chapters. A steady, planned deceleration in spending would have to transcend several administrations. President Nixon began the process in 1973, but one wonders whether he has the will to continue, and whether Congress will be able to see beyond its provincial needs to the broader national need.

The present congressional mood is not encouraging. Congress has reacted to administration proposals to reduce spending by protecting its prerogatives rather than turning seriously to spending cuts. As mentioned above, only changes in many laws will enable Congress to reduce the growing uncontrollable portion of the budget, and it does not seem ready to propose the laws, let alone discuss and pass them.

Full-Employment Budget

We are in no way implying here that the administrative branch has been without guilt, for it has discovered and utilizes a tool equally as harmful to long-term stability as the philosophy of self-interest in Congress. This tool is the "full-employment budget," which was officially introduced by the Council of Economic Advisers in January 1962 and has been used ever since. It is essentially a fiscal approach whereby the budget is planned on the assumption that it would be balanced at full employment and maximum revenues. It is planned so that a balance will exist between expenditures and receipts on a national-income accounts basis only *at* full employment, not after or before. A balance before full employment (a surplus full-employment budget) would create "fiscal drag," which would stifle the growth in the economy. A fiscal plan that produces a deficit at full employment would be inflationary. This tool was hailed as the perfect systematization of the accumulated Keynesian theories. It is an automatic program to assist the economy in reaching full employment through stimulative deficits and automatically will avoid running to excesses by propitious surpluses. We cannot help wondering where all those stabilizing surpluses were in the 1960s, when the foundations for the nation's worst inflation were being set.

Anyone who has worked with the statistics of national-income accounting knows the amount of estimation involved in explaining what has already happened. The margin of error in every statistic is much larger than any official would be willing to admit. Consider, then, how much more estimation and projection is involved in planning a budget for a period several years distant. The full-employment budget takes a third step in speculation and forecasting and, despite the assertions to the contrary of many advocates, can by no stretch of the imagination be spoken of as the perfect tool.

There is a far more serious criticism of this concept than its lack of perfection as a forecasting device. It has a serious inflationary bias on two counts. First, it serves to justify the expansion of federal spending regardless of need or effectiveness. If there is a fiscal drag, the spending gap must be filled by new programs for spending. Since, as we have seen, it is extremely difficult to terminate government programs, no matter how ineffectual they may be, this concept leads to a steady encroachment of the governmental sector upon the private sector. Second, we have also seen that the Congress, by the time the fiscal year is over, has always been able to improve upon the spending plans recommended by the President's budget message. The spending recommendations in the full-employment budget, then, only represent the opening bid, setting the floor for government spending for the year. Since the full-employment budget is set to just balance the budget at full employment, the additions by Congress represent inflationary spending—assuming that the full-employment budget is accurate. Given that most administrations also have an inflationary bias in their estimates, we can see why inflation is becoming a way of life. With our graduated income tax, every inflationary increase in the GNP and personal income moves all workers gradually into higher tax brackets and furthers the trend toward aggrandizement of the public sector. It is easy to see why inflation is called a tax in every sense of the word—one that Congress and its constituents do not have a chance to vote for or even to recognize.

Solutions

Fiscal discipline has clearly broken down at both the congressional and the administrative levels of government. This is partly a problem of philosophies that must be changed and partly a problem of structure, which must also be altered. One important barrier to any solution is the lack of understanding by voters of the true origins of their problems. If they knew, they would not picket the supermarkets but would, instead, picket the Department of Agriculture. They would not complain to their congressman about taxes, they would complain about the new post office that was recently built to replace the one built five years earlier. The ordinary citizen is breaking in at the wrong link of the chain. Higher taxes and inflation are only symptoms—spending is the problem. In the short term, the government must go on a diet now to avoid a coronary later on. In the long term, structural and philosophical changes are required.

Government, in general, lacks the machinery for projecting costs and assessing results of programs. A well-organized system of cost-benefit analysis is required. Moreover, a system of weighing one interest against another is needed. Congress seems unable, within its present structure, to allocate the resources of the country and set priorities in an efficient manner. Not only the machinery but also the will is absent from the present structure. The entire system is organized in such a manner that each congressman, through compromise, is able to get *his* project for *his* constituents, but there is no overall standard of priority that must be adhered to. Only the President can afford to look at the entire picture, and even he must bow to political pressures, especially in election years. On the positive side, the Legislative Reorganization Act of 1970 makes it necessary for the administrative branch to price out the cost for new legislation for five years into the future, but as yet there is no such requirement for the many programs already in effect.

In summary, we have not yet seen the end to the burgeoning encroachment of the public sector and, therefore, we cannot yet predict an early solution to this key problem behind the long deterioration in liquidity, the rising interest rates, and the stubborn inflation. The first signs of any solution would appear in the form of changes in the machinery of Congress in terms of a central-review-of-spending procedure as well as a change in philosophy to one that is less provincial in nature. When both the Congress and the President begin to take a rifle approach to problems, instead of the shotgun approach with dollars for pellets, the path toward stability may be opened. The commitment to full employment need not be abandoned, only the tools should be changed. We mentioned above that cumulative deficits exceeding $100 billion have been amassed since 1965, yet unemployment was higher in 1973 than at the beginning of the period. Surely there must be something wrong with the approach. Until changes are apparent, it will be difficult to have much faith in the ultimate reversal of the long-term trends. Government policies of long standing usually require catastrophes before changes are effected. One can only hope that the disastrous bout with inflation and international turmoil has been enough stimulus for change. So far, however, change does not seem to be forthcoming.

Chapter 9

The Role of
the Federal Reserve

It is now time to introduce the final character in the drama, the Federal Reserve. We have mentioned how the vastly increased involvement of the government in the economic process has served in two major ways as the foundation for the postwar deterioration of liquidity. In the first place, the government's apparent success in carrying out its commitments to moderate the level of unemployment and business cycles helped to create a climate wherein the fear of economic risk was greatly reduced. This euphoria among banks, corporations, and individuals led them to feel more secure with increasingly lower levels of assets relative to liabilities. The process of liquidity deterioration resulted, and over the postwar years we witnessed the greatest expansion of credit in the nation's history and an unparalleled economic boom marred only by periodic but relatively mild economic corrections. In the second place, the government, with the help of the Federal Reserve, also supplied the money that fueled the credit expansion far beyond the point it could have reached solely on the basis of the euphoria caused by the new government paternalism. Without this massive infusion of credit the postwar expansion might have ended years ago. It is to this aspect of government spending and the resulting credit expansion that this chapter is addressed.

Financing the Federal Debt

The manner in which the increasing government expenditures are financed is crucial to the liquidity trends discussed, as well as to trends in inflation and interest rates. If the increased levels of government spending were exactly offset by rising tax revenues, the effect would have been much less pronounced. The only difference would have been that the funds were spent by the government rather than by business or private citizens. With our generally

109

graduated income taxes, one effect would have been a substantial redistribution of incomes, thereby broadening the spending base of the country. This effect, together with the government's success in moderating postwar business cycles and the high liquidity levels amassed before and during World War II, would have been sufficient to create a sizable economic expansion, credit expansion, and liquidity deterioration. As an offset, there would have occurred an even greater decline in investment incentives than has actually occurred. Overall, the expansion would have been much less pronounced. As we saw in Chapter 8, however, higher tax revenues were not sufficient to finance the explosion in government spending. Even though there occurred substantial income redistribution and a doubling of average tax rates, massive amounts of government debt have been accumulated in the postwar years.

The aims of the government might still have been accomplished with stable prices, had the deficits been financed by borrowing from the public. The effect would have been the same as that of taxation, in that spending power would have been transferred from the public to the government. The effect of financing, either by taxation or by borrowing from the public, would be merely to reallocate resources between private and government use. Unfortunately, a considerable amount of the postwar deficit financing was accomplished by creating money, the worst alternative of the three. The effects have been a much sharper credit expansion than would have been possible otherwise, with the resulting dislocations that we have been describing in this book. It could not, however, have been accomplished without the aid of the Federal Reserve.

Monetizing the Debt

The federal debt is monetized whenever the securities of the federal government, sold to finance the deficits, are purchased by the Federal Reserve. Whenever the Federal Reserve purchases a government security it supplies an equivalent amount of "high-powered money" to the banking system. This high-powered money—also called the "monetary base"—consists of bank reserves plus currency held by the public, and is so named because it has a multiplier effect within the economy. The amount of money created within the economy is many times the amount of high-powered money created by the purchase by the Federal Reserve of a Treasury security. Roughly, an increase of $1 of high-powered money will result in an increase of $2.50 in M_1, the narrowly defined money supply, which consists of demand deposits and currency in circulation. It would result in an increase of $5 in broadly defined M_2, which also includes time deposits except for large CDs.

Let us take a look at just how this is done: Suppose, first, that the Federal Reserve purchases new securities directly from the Treasury Department. The Federal Reserve, in payment, immediately creates purchasing power for the Treasury in the form of a deposit at the Federal Reserve. Since the Treasury has bills to pay, it immediately spends the acquired deposit at the Federal Reserve by writing checks on its account there, as it does for all its expenses. The recipients of the checks all around the country deposit them to their checking or savings accounts at member banks, increasing their reserves and deposits by the same amount. Only a part of the reserves so gained is needed as a legal reserve, which, in the United States, is either a deposit at the Federal Reserve or cash in the vault of the commercial bank. The balance is considered excess reserves, which can be used to make loans or invest in securities. Because of our fractional reserve system, the original deposit results in an ultimate expansion of money and credit by the multiples mentioned above.

The results are the same if the Federal Reserve purchases the Treasury securities in the open market. The Federal Open Market Committee (FOMC) would simply contact a dealer firm in Treasuries and negotiate a purchase. Payment would be made with a check drawn on the New York Federal Reserve Bank, which executes all open-market operations. The dealer would then deposit the check to his own bank and high-powered money is once again created. All things being equal, this high-powered money, and the resulting multiple expansion of money and credit in the system, is highly inflationary.

Inflationary Implications of Monetization

According to well-documented monetarist theory, there is a very close correlation between the growth in money supply in the United States and the rate of price inflation. The theory generally goes like this: If the supply of money in the economy is significantly increased, individuals find themselves with larger than desired amounts of money, which they spend on goods, stocks, bonds, and other assets until they have reduced their cash holdings to desired levels. This action raises the growth of nominal GNP after some lag and for a while may not affect prices. After another short lag, however, the increased level of income finally begins to generate price inflation. Over the very long run the effect of rapid growth in the money supply is almost entirely reflected in higher prices. The process also works in the other direction, and sharp declines in the rate of growth of money may result in recessions. The rate of growth of real GNP over the long term is determined by real factors, such as the formation of capital, the growth of population, rising productivity, and so forth. Most economists estimate the maximum long-term real growth to be somewhere between 3 and 4 percent. The compound average growth-rate of real GNP over the entire postwar period coincidently happens to be about 3.8 percent. If the money supply grows faster than this, inflation is sure to occur, and the greater the rise in the ratio of the money supply to this real growth, the faster prices may be expected to rise.

High-powered Money and the Money Supply

We have already explained how the rise in federal debt is transferred, through the Federal Reserve, into high-powered money, which is, in turn, translated into an even greater amount of money. This increased money supply, according to monetarist theory, finds its way into higher prices to the extent that its growth exceeds the growth of real production.

111

A study by Phillip Cagan in 1965 disclosed data showing that high-powered money accounted for nine-tenths of the growth in U.S. money supply over the period 1875-1960. Almost all the growth in high-powered money, moreover, came from growth in the gold supply and from growth in the credit of the Federal Reserve after it was established. Since U.S. holdings of gold fell by over 50 percent during the postwar years, we can safely say that almost all the growth in the monetary base in the postwar years came from Federal Reserve credit. Finally, we can then say that most of the change in money supply in the postwar period can be explained by growth in Federal Reserve credit.

The statistics presented in Table 9.1 would appear to substantiate the close correlation theorized above. Both reserve-bank credit and the broadly defined money supply had nearly identical compound growth-rates over the entire postwar period with almost uninterrupted rising trends. Moreover, both series accelerated growth sharply after 1960, again with similar average growth-rates over the most recent twelve-year period. Finally, both accelerated growth further after 1965. Keeping in mind that the productive capacity of the nation, by most estimates, can only grow between 3 and 4 percent, it should be no mystery to the reader why the country has been subjected to increasingly higher rates of inflation. Compare the growth-rates in Table 9.1, for all three periods for which they were computed, of money supply, real GNP, and Consumer Price Index. There can be seen a steadily accelerating upward trend in money as well as in inflation. The relatively stable performance in real GNP growth—remaining at 3 ½-4 percent—explains the inflation. If money grows faster than the production of real goods, prices must rise.

The relationship between money and prices is even more strikingly represented in Table 9.2. There we can see the relationship since 1965 among the growth in money, the growth in disposable personal income, and the growth, again, in real GNP. A summary of the percentage increase of the data in Table 9.2 from 1965 to 1972 is given in Table 9.3. Here, the problem of inflation is very vividly portrayed. With money supply up either 50 percent or 79 percent, depending upon the measure used, and population only up 8 percent, it is obvious that there are more dollars in everyone's pocket. The 62 percent increase in personal disposable income confirms this growth in spendable aftertax dollars. Yet the production of real goods and services was only able to muster an increase of 27 percent. The excess dollars will be used to bid for the relatively scarce goods and services, and prices must rise. This also demonstrates why price controls cannot work over a long period of time, and why they can work in the short term only while there is excess capacity and unemployment. As long as the excess dollars are being generated, the demand and the depreciation of the currency will also be present and controls will only cause distortions. Too often, however, misunderstanding of the basic problem of excess dollars leads politicians and individuals alike to look for other scapegoats. A perfect recent example is the national concern in early 1973 about rising food prices and, more particularly, about beef prices. The record for per capita consumption of beef in 1962-72, an increase of more than 30 percent over the whole period, is shown in Table 9.4. In 1973 controls were placed on meat-packers; supermarkets were

TABLE 9.1

(In Billions of Dollars)

Year	Federal Reserve Credit	Money Supply M$_2$ [1]
1947	23.2	146.0
1948	24.1	148.1
1949	19.5	147.5
1950	22.2	150.8
1951	25.0	156.4
1952	25.8	164.9
1953	26.9	171.1
1954	25.9	177.2
1955	26.5	183.6
1956	26.7	186.8
1957	25.8	191.9
1958	27.8	201.2
1959	28.8	210.1
1960	29.4	210.7
1961	31.4	222.4
1962	33.9	238.1
1963	36.4	256.8
1964	39.9	276.7
1965	43.3	301.4
1966	47.2	325.0
1967	51.9	351.2
1968	56.6	382.9
1969	60.8	400.6
1970	66.8	418.4
1971	75.8	485.2
1972	77.3	539.6

[1] Includes large CDs

Comparative Growth Rates

	1947-72	1960-72	1965-72
Real GNP	3.8	4.0	3.5
Federal Reserve credit	4.9	8.4	8.6
Money supply M$_1$	3.1	4.2	5.9
Money supply M$_2$	5.7	7.9	8.2
Federal spending	8.8	8.5	10.4
Consumer Price Index	2.6	3.3	4.3

boycotted and farmers maligned. The real problem was, once again, excess dollars chasing a slower-growing supply, and consumers upgrading their consumption due to higher disposable income. As long as such confusion and lack of agreement exists as to the true nature of this deeply ingrained problem, there is little hope for an orderly and painless solution.

TABLE 9.2

(In Billions of Dollars)

Year	Money Supply M_1	Money[1] Supply M_2	Real GNP	Per Capita Disposable Personal Income
1965	163.8	301.4	617.8	2,436
1966	171.0	325.0	658.1	2,604
1967	177.8	351.2	675.2	2,749
1968	190.4	382.9	706.6	2,945
1969	201.5	400.6	724.7	3,130
1970	210.0	418.4	720.0	3,366
1971	231.2	485.2	741.7	3,595
1972	255.5	539.6	789.5	3,954

[1] Includes large CDs

TABLE 9.3

Money supply (M_1)	50%
Money supply (M_2)	79%
Population growth	8%
Real GNP change	27%
Per capita DPI	62%

TABLE 9.4

Year	Pounds	Year	Pounds
1962	88.8	1968	109.7
1963	94.5	1969	110.8
1964	99.9	1970	113.7
1965	99.5	1971	113.3
1966	104.2	1972	115.5
1967	106.5		

Why Does the Federal Reserve Monetize the Debt?

Why, it might be asked, does the Federal Reserve continue to purchase government securities in the face of the overwhelming evidence of the inflationary impact? Before relating the effects of the action of the Federal Reserve upon our liquidity problem, it may be helpful to discuss this question to better understand the problem and its potential solutions.

The Federal Reserve should certainly realize that money, like any other commodity, obtains its value from its scarcity. Control over the quantity of money is mandatory if the value is not to depreciate. We have seen that the value of money cannot be maintained if the money supply is allowed to grow at a rate greater than the rate at which the supply of real goods and services can be increased. It matters little whether the currency is backed by gold, silver, or any other precious commodity. Prices will rise if the supply of money rises too fast, and Gresham's law will push gold into hiding.

Although the process of money creation takes place in the commercial banking system, most of the control rests with the Federal Reserve, for the reserves of commercial banks are primarily liabilities of the central bank and changes in them are determined by its judgments. Because demand deposits are the dominant component of the money supply, and they are determined by the level of reserves, it would seem a simple matter for the Federal Reserve to provide just the amount of money consistent with the monetary needs of the nation and price stability, since this, after all, is one of the major responsibilities with which the Federal Reserve is charged. So, we repeat, why the excessive monetary inflation?

Monetary Policy of the Federal Reserve

The original Federal Reserve system, which began operations late in 1914, bears little resemblance to the present-day system in terms of functions, operations, and philosophy. Few of the objectives that many now take for granted were in any way intended by the framers of the original act. In their own words the Federal Reserve was designed "to furnish an elastic currency, to afford a means of rediscounting commercial paper, to establish a more effective supervision of banking in the United States, and for other purposes." There was little intention of molding the powerful central authority we have today. The intent seemed to be simply to improve the banking system where it was weak. Twelve separate Federal Reserve districts were purposely set up to avoid a strong central bank. The federal government still had no formal commitment to attempt to maintain full employment or to stimulate long-term growth. The balance of payments would automatically be cured by the prevailing gold-standard system. These goals were simply not considered major problems, and certainly were not regarded as within the province of a strong central bank of the federal government. The prevailing philosophy still favored small government.

Somehow, over the years, the Federal Reserve has taken on increasing functions and objectives, some of them formally, but many merely "understood." It is, perhaps, the vagueness of some of its responsibilities and the patchwork nature of its development that has led to many of today's problems. Not to be ignored, however, is the very drastic change in philosophy regarding the proper role of the central government in our economy, which was discussed in Chapter 8.

Just as the philosophy of the role of the central government began to change during the trying period of the 1930s, so did the Federal Reserve. It was a time for trial and change. We have already detailed the experiences of monetary policy when the Federal Reserve attempted to "mop up" excess reserves and instead managed to create the recession of 1937-38. It was in the 1930s that the Federal Reserve Act was altered to give the central bank the power to manipulate reserve requirements for banks. It was also in the 1930s that the Federal Reserve was given its first selective credit-control device in the power to set margin requirements for stock purchases. Since that time, there has also been a long trend of liberalization of regulations, which has made it easier for banks and the Federal Reserve to expand credit. There has also occurred a continual liberalization in the nature of the collateral used at the discount window, making it easier for banks to borrow reserves and, of course, allowing less dependence upon portfolio buffers against deposit withdrawals. As you will now begin to see, the change in banking philosophy outlined in Chapter 3 was not spontaneous. Finally, the postwar years have witnessed a steady stream of rulings removing the last restrictions on the ability of the Federal Reserve to expand money and credit. Table 9.5 summarizes step-by-step the removal of the restrictions on Federal Reserve notes and system liabilities. As the information in the table shows, the Federal Reserve has gradually and steadily evolved into the "engine of inflation" that it is today. As such, it became a much better vehicle for carrying out the philosophy of the new economics, and its functions, restrictions, and objectives have changed to suit the new philosophy.

TABLE 9.5

Original Requirements:	Federal Reserve system must hold 40 percent in gold behind all Federal Reserve notes outstanding and 35 percent against all other system liabilities.
1945	Required holdings reduced to 25 percent for each liability.
Mar. 3, 1965	Removed gold backing requirement totally for system liabilities.
Mar. 15, 1968	All gold-holding requirements removed.
June, 1968	Silver certificates issued by Treasury no longer secured by silver bullion after this date.

Modern Objectives of the Federal Reserve

It is no simple task to neatly set forth the functions and goals of the Federal Reserve. Many have grown by custom, though with little justification, to be accepted as legitimate areas of responsibility, and most are vague and ill-defined.

The first general function encompasses most of the original tasks and conventions. It is the function of maintaining a sound money supply and an efficient banking industry. This function contains, among the more mundane tasks of check clearing and daily operations, the operation of the "discount window." The Federal Reserve serves in the role of "lender of last resort" by providing a source from which any member bank may borrow without reducing the reserves of the entire system.

In its second general function the Federal Reserve serves as a fiscal agent for the United States Treasury. Its most important service in this capacity is to aid in the sale of government securities. The Federal Reserve takes orders from dealers, banks, and other purchasers of such securities, receives payment and makes delivery, makes allotments where necessary, and performs other services to facilitate the issues. A more important service in terms of our study here, and in terms of potential problems, is the unwritten obligation to make the issue "succeed"—that is, to make sure the sale is a sell-out. It would not do for the federal government to fail in a financing. Moreover, the sale must be a success in terms of being conducted in an "orderly" market, which means that the prices must not be overly depressed by the sale. To accomplish this, the Federal Reserve must generally maintain orderly conditions in the market preceding the sale and is also obliged to "support" the market, which means buying a part of the issue itself if it does not sell, as well as purchasing securities preceding the sale to maintain orderly rates. This is, of course, where the trouble begins in terms of the expansion of money, credit, and inflationary pressures. Whenever government securities are purchased, high-powered money is supplied to the banking system in like amounts. Given the rapidly increasing federal debt and the declining liquidity of banks, which were described in previous chapters, we can now see why Federal Reserve credit is steadily growing.

The third broad function of the Federal Reserve is really a grouping of a number of social goals that it seems to have set for itself. They include: the maintenance of *full employment,* the maintenance of an equilibrium in the *balance of payments,* and the promotion of a reasonable rate of *economic growth* and *price stabilization.* Each of these goals has more or less been adopted by the Federal Reserve in a fairly informal manner. They seem to have grown out of the changing circumstances or philosophies in the government. With the adoption of Keynesian economics, the notion that the government or the Federal Reserve had no responsibility for maintaining full employment was gone, probably forever. Price stabilization has never been written into law as a goal of the Federal Reserve but is more or less understood. The goal of promoting perpetual growth developed during the middle

117

1950s, when fears of a slowdown in growth were spreading, and was enforced by the new economists of the early and middle 1960s. Finally, the need to assist in the balancing of international payments grew, of necessity, out of the continuing deficits throughout all but the very early postwar years. The pursuit of these very admirable goals, together with the problems of assisting Treasury financing, provides the answer to the question of why the Federal Reserve has continued to monetize the federal debt.

Conflicting Goals and Targets of Monetary Policy

One of the problems underlying the inflation-generating activities of the Federal Reserve is the vagueness of its commitment to the goals mentioned above and the potential conflicts among them. Not only are the obligations to pursue these goals quite informal, but no definite objectives are set in terms of *tolerable* levels of unemployment, *sustainable* rates of growth, *reasonable* rates of inflation, or *acceptable* balance-of-payments deficits. Nor are priorities stipulated among them, for they are all potentially incompatible. As we know, there is a trade-off between inflation and unemployment or the balance of payments. The low interest rates needed to stimulate economic growth may serve to worsen international flows of capital even as they lower unemployment. The list of potential trade-offs is endless, and the confusion that results from the lack of standards must certainly add to the confusion of the Federal Reserve.

Conflicting Targets of Monetary Policy

Even more basic to the problem of excessive credit creation by the Federal Reserve is its continuing inability to choose between the conflicting targets of interest rates and monetary aggregates, such as the money supply, the monetary base, or reserves. The goal of most central banks has always been to keep an even keel in the money markets—that is, to maintain "orderly markets." The Federal Reserve has always been more interested in week-to-week movements in the Fed funds rates, the prime rate, and the level of borrowings at the discount window. At the same time, it has always ignored the effects of its stabilization actions upon the level of reserves and the ability of banks to loan and invest. In effect, it concentrates on pegging the *price* of credit while it allows the *amount* of credit to be determined by the market. Since we have already seen the effects of rising reserves upon the money supply and inflation, we can see that there is a definite conflict between the Federal Reserve's approach and price stability, one of its avowed goals. This conflict would not be terribly disruptive if it were not for a number of very definite trends, some of which we have already mentioned. Because of these trends, however, the conflict of targets becomes extremely crucial, and the effects of the selection of targets are magnified.

The National Debt as an Obstacle to Price Stability

We have already mentioned the commitment of the Federal Reserve to the Treasury, which is quite definite. During World War II, to insure the successful financing of the war, the Federal Reserve agreed very specifically to peg the price of government securities at par, which amounted to providing an unlimited market for all government issues regardless of the amount of reserves that was created. This agreement finally ended in 1951 with an "accord" whereby the Federal Reserve pledged to provide "orderly" conditions in the government-securities markets, and this pledge is still in effect today, no matter how vague it may sound. It still attempts to help the government to finance on favorable terms. We have already seen the record of government spending and deficits in the postwar years. It is obvious that as long as the inexorable upward trend continues, and the Federal Reserve remains committed to insuring the success of each securities issue and to holding interest rates down, it will continue to flood the banking system with high-powered money. This high-powered money, as we have seen, has led to massive increases in money fueling the credit expansion, which has been the prime determinant of the rundown in liquidity described earlier.

Liquidity Trends

One of the major effects of the declining liquidity, we concluded, is a drastic lowering of the quality of credit in this country and a growing level of risk in all sectors of the economy. This has manifested itself in a twenty-five-year bear market in bonds and in rising interest rates. With this rising trend in interest rates, it is easy to see that the stabilizing operations of the Federal Reserve in providing orderly markets have all been onesided. The Fed has been forced to be on the buy side of securities in its open-market operations, which has, of course, served to worsen the situation. It is caught in a vicious inflationary spiral, which goes like this:

1. The federal government incurs deficits, which must be financed by selling securities.

2. The Federal Reserve is forced to buy many of the securities to stabilize the markets and to insure success of the issues.

3. In so doing, the Federal Reserve pumps reserves into the banking system, which leads to a multiplied level of money and credit in the system.

4. The excessive credit expansion has led to a long trend in declining liquidity among banks and corporations, which raises the level of risk, which together with the continuing rise in loan demand raises the level of interest rates throughout the economy.

5. The Federal Reserve must, in turn, purchase securities in open-market operations to offset the rising interest rates, but in so doing it pumps even more reserves into the economy.

So it can be seen that as long as the Federal Reserve continues to focus upon interest rates as a target, and continues to assist Treasury financing of

119

excessive federal spending, it will be caught in this upward spiral of inflation, interest rates, and illiquidity.

Still another facet of the liquidity problem exacerbates the effects of the poor choice of targets by the Federal Reserve and greatly increases its credit-expansion activities. We have already explained that in this late stage of liquidity deterioration, corporations have become less able to withstand business downturns and are less resilient on the recovery. Since the Federal Reserve is committed to the pursuit of full employment as well as to the avoidance of a complete credit collapse, it must step in, as it did in 1970, to provide the credit necessary to avoid massive credit liquidations. This infusion of high-powered money is in addition to that added to stabilize money markets and to facilitate government financing needs. As long as the liquidity trends remain in force, this problem will continue to get worse. Still another avowed goal of the Federal Reserve is to promote reasonable economic growth, which also entails holding interest rates down to reasonable levels. Because the government becomes more expansive at the time of business contractions and incurs heavy deficits, the Federal Reserve also must become automatically expansive instead of "leaning against the wind."

The Inflation Premium

The third underlying trend that serves to make the Federal Reserve's poor choice of targets much more damaging is the very trend of inflation that is caused by its activities in the money markets. The longer the inflationary trends remain intact, the more deeply ingrained inflationary expectations become. These expectations eventually lead lenders to insist upon an inflationary premium on the interest rate they charge, to protect themselves against depreciation of their dollar return. This additional impetus to rising interest-rate levels must also be offset by the open-market operations of the Federal Reserve, which, once again, leads to even further credit expansion and inflationary pressures.

The operations of the Federal Reserve generally seem to have another inflationary bias. When the financial statistics are examined it will be found that in many years, when *bank* credit has been restricted, *total* credit rises anyway. Credit-expansion trends are so deeply imbedded in the economy that there is a bias toward climbing credit throughout the system. It is not only the banking system that can supply credit. We have already seen how corporations have gradually extended increasing amounts of trade credit to keep their sales rising. Individuals may extend credit, as do savings and loan associations and other financial institutions. As inflation continues unabated and inflation expectations continue to rise, more people will learn that it is smart to borrow in such a climate. With the current liquidity condition and inflationary climate, business will continue to borrow and the Federal Reserve will have no choice but to supply the funds.

So now we have seen why the Federal Reserve continues to monetize the federal debt in spite of the obvious dislocating effects such action has upon the

120

entire economy. The role the Federal Reserve plays is critical to an understanding of the damaging trend of liquidity deterioration. The final step in comprehending the entire problem and its implications for the future is to put all the actors together to see how they each fit into this potential tragedy.

Chapter 10

A Summing Up

We have now discussed all of the ingredients necessary to recognize, analyze, and track the course of the trends that underlie our present financial problems. After so many confusing statistics, it may be helpful to briefly summarize the findings and the causes of the trends. Finally, in order to see the importance of these trends in shaping the course of the economy, we will review the financial events of the last decade in an attempt to demonstrate the key role that has been played by the phenomena discussed here.

The Liquidity Trends

As we have stated, the approach of our work is essentially one of balance-sheet concepts. Although overzealous application of Keynesian economic principles may be at the root of the entire problem, monetarist thought also revolves around money and income *flows*. It is true that the monetarists have focused correctly upon the problem of excessive volatility in creation of money by the Federal Reserve, the inflationary implications of too much money, and the effects of inflationary expectations upon interest-rate levels. They pay scant attention, however, to the cumulative damage that has been done to the national balance sheets by both government spending and inept money-supply management by the Federal Reserve. They ignore the possibility that the balance sheets may be so weakened as to be an independent inflationary force, and may be so precarious that the Federal Reserve *no longer has any choice* but to supply the money that will keep the liquidity trends in force.

Banking Liquidity

We found that the banking system, by all traditional measures of liquidity, has shown a continued deterioration since the end of World War II, and that the extent of the damage is worse than in the late 1920s, the last peak in illiquidity. The banking explanation for the disturbing relationships discovered is that the entire structure and philosophy of banking has changed to the extent that the previous levels of liquidity are no longer necessary. No longer is it necessary to wait passively for deposits, for banks can now compete aggressively for CDs and Eurodollars and can determine their own deposit levels. This philosophy, of course, is part of the false sense of confidence that the government has everything well in hand, as was explained earlier. Aggressive deposit determination is fine for one bank, but when the system as a whole is considered, what one bank gains, another loses, and all become more illiquid in the process while interest costs rise for the nation. When the level of large CDs has gone from zero to over $60 billion in a few short years, one can also conclude that this source of deposits may also be overdone.

The ill effects of the present state of banking liquidity are many. The growing aggressiveness and frenzied search for new deposit sources have created increasing volatility and therefore risk in money and capital markets as well as in the stock markets. The same aggressiveness has led to much higher interest rates than would have prevailed in the absence of the reduced state of liquidity. Finally, because the Federal Reserve must act as the lender of last resort, it must periodically rescue the system by supplying the needed reserves and thereby causes inflationary pressures, which add to higher interest rates and financial dislocations. The expectation of such rescues also serves to give the banking system the courage to continue with its bold new profit-maximization philosophy. Since the banking system is the lifeblood of the economy, its actions have a pervasive influence.

Corporate Liquidity

Corporations, in large part because of the actions of the banking system, have undergone the same long-term deterioration of liquidity. Here too the trend has progressed so far that the financial authorities may already have the proverbial tiger by the tail. Banks must provide corporations with the funds to exist, and the Federal Reserve must supply the reserves to the banking system.

The liquidity deterioration among corporations may be even more dangerous than that among banks because much of it is less apparent. It is true that the traditional and specific measures of corporate liquidity, such as the current ratio or the relationship of cash assets to current liabilities, have consistently declined over the entire postwar period. There is more cyclicality within the secular trend, however, as corporations run into periods of excessive short-term debt creation, which receives much more attention than the same problem among banks, where the analysis is perhaps more esoteric. This peak is usually reached late in the expansion phase of business, and there then follows a hectic period of issuance of long-term debt and equities to fund the short-term debt and to restore adequate working-capital levels. The fears of the financial and investment community are alleviated when they see a small cyclical improvement in the relationship of cash assets to current liabilities. They ignore the fact, however, that the short-term liabilities are not liquidated. The maturity date has merely been lengthened, and a different and less visible section of the balance sheet absorbs the deterioration. So there is not only a visual secular deterioration in the specific measures of liquidity, but there is also an even more dangerous accumulation of the results of sharp cyclical declines in liquidity that have been funded, with the result that the entire balance sheet is much weaker than a perusal of only liquidity measures would indicate.

The effects of the liquidity deterioration among corporations are the same as those caused by the banking trends. As balance sheets gradually weaken, the investment risk in the individual illiquid corporations increases. As the number of corporations with deficient balance sheets grows, the risk inherent in the entire economy increases. The volatility caused by the periodic credit squeezes, as well as the volatility caused by more highly leveraged earnings, also increases the levels of risk. The higher risk must eventually be recognized in higher levels of interest rates and in wider spreads in rates between companies with "clean" balance sheets and those in poorer financial condition. The cyclical swings in interest rates are also becoming more pronounced, particularly on the upside, because an increasing number of corporations is becoming overly dependent upon the money and capital markets, particularly in times of credit stringency. These corporations have less flexibility in the timing of their financings; they usually come to the market for funding at the very same time that the federal government is also financing. Finally, the liquidity conditions also represent the same inflationary pressure as that by the banking system. The level of corporate liquidity has reached such low levels that the Federal Reserve cannot allow a serious credit contraction to occur and must therefore step in, as it did in 1970 during the Penn Central crisis, to assure adequate funds to satisfy the financing needs of corporations through the banking system. This in turn leads to inflationary expansion of reserves and money.

Causes of Liquidity Trends

There may be a myriad of reasons, excuses, and justifications for the trends we have disclosed here. It could conceivably be that some greater good caused by these trends might justify their existence. They do exist, however, and as with most trends there are several basic causes. Although we have mentioned all of them already, we will try here to summarize them, for there are only three.

A Natural Secular Cycle

There appears to be a natural long-wave cycle in credit expansion and liquidity in most capitalistic countries that remains in force regardless of any institutional or philosophical changes. The expansionary phase of credit creation usually travels to excess and is then punctuated by a financial crisis of such proportion that it sets in motion a long period of restoration of liquidity. At some point, liquidity becomes adequate or excessive, and the base is then built for another long phase of growth and liquidity deterioration.

The last period of excessive credit creation ended with the financial crisis of 1929 and the economic collapse that followed. During the 1930s credit creation slowed and liquidity was gradually replaced. The refusal of banks to reduce the level of excess reserves, which we described earlier, is an example of the extremes that were reached in conservative banking. The duration and expense of World War II added enormously to the liquidity, for the Federal Reserve created excessive reserves by pegging government bonds at par while civilian goods were not available for purchase. The stage was thus set for the postwar economic expansion and rundown in liquidity.

A New Government Philosophy

The same economic turmoil that led to the much-improved liquidity climate also fertilized the seed of Keynesian economics, which led to the new role of government in our economic process. The belief grew that the economy did not necessarily have the ability to resurrect itself—that Adam Smith's "invisible hand" was not enough. Instead, it would be necessary to continue the sometimes massive government intervention to keep the country on its upward path. This change in philosophy, which was nurtured during World War II, formalized in 1946, and brought to its zenith in the 1960s, is the second, and perhaps most important, cause for the length and depth of the liquidity deterioration of the postwar years.

This commitment to the maintenance of full employment and to growing responsibility for the lives and fortunes of citizens led to the postwar record of enormous government spending and deficits, which has been superimposed upon the natural secular trend of liquidity deterioration. There is little doubt that, in the beginning, the present breadth and width of the encroachment on the public sector was hardly anticipated. It began with an economic concept that government intervention was needed to move the economy off the economic floor of the 1930s and the desire to insure that the same type of collapse would never happen again. Once the precedent for government intervention was set, however, it led to interference in countless areas never before even remotely considered as being within the government province. Once government spending was looked upon as the means for raising the general welfare level as well as solving most problems, it took on a momentum of its own for several reasons.

First, such spending creates rising expectation that the government will handle an increasing number of problems previously left to the private sector, which leads to *new* programs. Each new program requires more government employees and a new addition to the permanent bureaucracy. Second, established programs continue to grow far beyond original intentions. More people demand to be covered, and administrators build power bases for themselves.

Allotments must be spent or turned back, and the programs continue to grow. Old programs neither die nor fade away. Third, government spending relating to economic-stabilization policies continues to rise. As we will point out, because of the declining liquidity conditions, it requires an everincreasing amount of credit creation to increase the GNP and turn the business cycle. Finally, fixed expenses, such as the interest on the federal debt, continue to grow, especially as interest-rate levels rise.

In the early 1960s the spirit of government intervention received a strong new infusion of life with the birth of the new economists of the "New Frontier," led by Walter Heller and the Kennedy Administration. The bold new approach to governmental "fine-tuning" of the economy was extended beyond merely stabilizing the business cycle. With proper government orientation and action a steady upward growth pattern could be maintained in the economy. In the words of the chief architect, "Policy emphasis must be redirected from a corrective orientation geared to the dynamics of the cycle, to a propulsive orientation geared to the dynamics and the promise of growth." This change in orientation, and the strong rhetoric that accompanied it, removed the last vestiges of fiscal responsibility from the federal government. It embarrassed the few remaining bankers who still worried about traditional liquidity safeguards, pilloried the corporate treasurers who did not take full advantage of financial leverage, and set the stage for a drastic acceleration of the liquidity trends, government deficits, and money-supply trends that have brought the nation to its present state. It also gave corporations and security analysts the inspiration to concentrate upon growth in earnings per share at any cost. It justified the "funny money" used during the years of "creeping conglomeration" among corporations. It pushed the balance sheet out of the limelight until the Penn Central put it back on center stage in 1970.

The effects of the government's philosophy and spending actions throughout the postwar years are much the same as those of the liquidity trends for which they are responsible. The superimposition of government spending upon the natural trend toward a liquidity rundown served to extend the trends further by supplying the means to extend credit and to modify the natural corrective forces of the business cycle upon debt creation. The government has, in effect, created an artificial growth-rate in the economy much higher than would have occurred. This rate has been made possible by the overextension of credit and a complete change in the credit ethic among business and individuals alike. It has permitted the deterioration of liquidity to go far beyond what would have been possible and perhaps too far to be reversed comfortably.

The Federal Reserve

The third and final cause of the financial trends discussed here is the Federal Reserve, which makes it all possible by supplying the money to create the credit needed. There is a basic flaw in the operations of the Federal Reserve in that it cannot chart the path of the price of credit at the same time as the quantity of credit. In the past, it always chose to regulate the price of credit and lost control of the quantity of money. This made the postwar liquidity trends possible. Even with this said, however, the nomination for best actor must still go to the federal government, whose spending has created the interest-rate pressures and credit demand that have caused the Federal Reserve to issue the reserves in order to moderate the price of credit. With the natural cycle of liquidity deterioration, the Federal Reserve's policies would have still been inflationary, but not nearly to the extent made possible by its obligation to help to finance the federal debt. The Federal Reserve must settle for best supporting actor.

The Age of the New Economists

We have now presented evidence of pronounced secular trends of liquidity deterioration among both banks and corporations, which have persisted with little relief throughout the postwar years and up to the present day. We have also presented an explanation of the probable major causes of these trends as well as brief descriptions of some of the major effects resulting from them. We would now present a more detailed description of the dozen years since 1960, with the intention of showing the entire process in action. We hope to be able to explain the events of this period in terms of the interactions of the four basic destabilizing forces at work in the economy: banking liquidity, corporate liquidity, government spending, and the credit-creating activities of the Federal Reserve. The reader will see that the trends described above were not only in force throughout the period but are also accelerating measurably. Their effects of inflationary pressures, increasing volatility, risk, and upward interest-rate pressures combine to form a violently self-enforcing upward spiral of accelerating instability, as evidenced by increasingly intensive credit crunches. We have selected this particular period for intensive study because it also marks the beginning of the reign of the new economists—when, for the first time, they were granted full leave to put into practice the policies they were developing during their near hiatus of the Eisenhower years. It also marks the beginning of the period where the liquidity trends reached more normal levels from the excessively liquid condition at the end of World War II. This truly Keynesian coronation marked the beginning of the rapid acceleration in the trends that have brought the nation to its present state.

The Accelerating Sixties

In the 1960s, the new "perpetual economic growth by government tuning" theory of the new economists finally got its test. On the surface, it seemed entitled to passing grades, for the country was treated to a record 105-month economic expansion, and the feeling spread that the business cycle was beaten. With the governmental emphasis upon growth, it is no small wonder that the feeling spread to banks, corporations, security analysts, and investors. Just as growth in earnings per share was pushed into the financial limelight, the balance sheet began to ride the bench. If economic growth was perpetual, why shouldn't financial leverage be used to perpetuate earnings? If cash sales restricted growth, why not extend more credit to customers? If payments were slow and business slowed, why not extend the payment terms? The banks were there to finance the receivables, and the Federal Reserve was there to supply the reserves. If the current federal budget did not balance, use the new full-employment budget and avoid the fiscal drag. The answer to all questions of perpetual growth was credit, and as the answer became manifest to more people, credit began to accelerate; with this acceleration, the seeds of destruction were being sown.

Table 10.1 summarizes the record of credit growth in the 1960s, leading up to the recession of 1969-70 and the recovery following. By every measure in the table it can be seen that the trends, beginning from the 1950s, were not only upward but accelerating in each period. The period 1961-65 covers the early expansion activities of the new economists and ends with the determination by the government and the Federal Reserve to attempt to bring the economy under control. This attempt led to the monetary crunch of 1966 and the minirecession. Once again, the expansion of credit was allowed to accelerate even though war pressures were building. Finally, as the nation became engulfed in the worst inflation in fifty years, an attempt was once again made to cool the economy, which was boiling over the fires of excessive money and credit as well as growing inflationary expectations. Once again, the extremely low levels of

TABLE 10.1

Money and Credit Acceleration

| | Compound Annual Growth Rates (Percentage) | | | |
	1950-60	1961-65	1966-69	1970-72
Monetary base	1.6	4.3	5.3	6.2
Money supply, M_1	2.2	2.2	5.6	8.4
Money supply, M_2	3.4	7.9	7.3	16.5
Bank loans	8.5	12.5	10.3	13.6
Total bank credit	4.5	8.9	9.1	12.7
Federal Reserve credit	2.8	6.6	8.0	7.7
Total private debt	8.6	9.3	10.5 [1]	
	(In Billions of Dollars)			
Federal budget NIA (Deficit)	(2.5)	(8.7)	(11.0)	(51.3)
Unified Budget (Deficit)	(10.0) [2]	(22.8)	(34.5)	(48.8)

[1] 1966-71
[2] 1954-60

liquidity to which corporations and banks had declined made it impossible for monetary constraint to be continued long enough, and in the summer of 1970, in the midst of the worst credit crunch of the postwar period, the Federal Reserve floodgates were opened and lifesaving reserves were poured into the banking system to allow banks, corporations, and the government to finance their debts. A third round of credit expansion is now underway. Each round brings greater amounts of debt creation, lower levels of liquidity, higher interest rates, and greater volatility. Each round also increases the chances of a massive liquidation of the accumulated credit of the entire postwar period. It is for this reason that every attempt to curb inflationary pressures was stopped short of its goal, with the Federal Reserve forced to halt the decline and turn the economy upward once again. Each time, however, the increasingly debt-burdened corporate sector required a larger credit transfusion to move again. Since each succeeding transfusion had to be larger, however, the foundation for the next credit expansion also grew.

At the heart of the problem each time were the burgeoning federal expenditures. A record of the cumulative deficit in each period of the sixties and early seventies is also included in Table 10.1. The drastic acceleration is even more alarming when one notices that each succeeding period contains a smaller number of years. The two-year deficit in the unified budget of 1970-72 is over four times as large as the deficit accumulated in the six years of 1954-60, and 50 percent greater than the three-year cumulative deficit of 1966-69, which included the high-water spending mark of the Vietnam War. Despite the extremely high level of both monetary and fiscal stimulation, the growth in real GNP continued at a leisurely pace, illustrating the tinsellike illusory growth of the 1960s.

The Process of Acceleration

There are actually two forces behind the acceleration of the trends in the 1960s. One is the obvious acceleration in federal deficits, which, as we have explained, becomes monetized. The other is the internal, self-sustaining interrelationships of all the effects of the liquidity trends. It may be possible to decelerate the rate of federal spending, but, as shown in Chapter 8, this might be difficult. Moreover, it is problematical whether the spending could be reduced enough, without a crisis, to reverse the self-enforcing internal nature of the process of liquidity deterioration that took hold in the 1960s. Shortly, we will try to show these interrelationships in an anatomy of the two credit crunches of the period. First, however, we will clarify the problem through a review of the entire period from 1960 up to the more serious credit crunch and the first recession.

The period began after fifteen years of deterioration in both corporate liquidity and banking liquidity in which the levels were already down substantially from the excessively liquid 1940s and had reached a state somewhat below adequate by previous standards. Added to this accumulation of debt was a budget deficit totaling well over $60 billion for the entire period, and volumes of rhetoric extolling the New Frontier, the Great Society, and the demise of the dreaded business cycle. Given the diminished liquidity and the newfound aggressiveness and courage of investors, businessmen, and bankers, who were emboldened by the promise of continuing growth, what use was there for relatively sterile investment in government securities? In stepped our fourth character, the Federal Reserve, to the rescue. Over the period from 1960 to 1969, Federal Reserve holdings of government securities more than doubled from $27 billion to over $57 billion, while other governmental agencies also stepped up to the counter. The first mistake, obviously was incurring deficits instead of raising taxes or holding down spending. The second mistake was that less than 20 percent of the entire accumulated deficit for the period was financed by selling debt to private individuals. In fact, the percentage of marketable federal debt held by individuals actually declined. Now the entire process of self-enforcing acceleration can be seen.

The irresponsible fiscal policy has led to rising government debt, which is monetized and ends up as a multiple expansion of money and credit, which begins a process of inflation and an acceleration of the liquidity trends as the increased money flows through the system. Now, let us see how the forces and their effects interact to sustain the accelerating trends.

Banking System

As the reserves flow into the banking system, the profit-maximizing philosophy of banking dictates that they be used for the higher-earning loans at the expense of more liquid investments. The decline in loan-deposit ratios and other banking liquidity indicators leads to increasing risk and higher bank-loan rates, which permeate the economy. The inflationary pressures of the debt monetization also add an inflation premium to interest rates. The rising interest rates serve to sustain the trend of an increase in time deposits at the expense of demand deposits. This trend, in itself, releases more excess reserves to help to fuel the entire process of credit expansion. The growing loan content of bank credit, and the growing inflationary pressures, combine to raise the velocity of money, which further fuels the liquidity trends. As the ratio of government securities to total bank credit declines, the banking system loses a source of liquid funds with which to meet the rising loan demand during periods of tight money. This very lack of liquidity helped to mold the new cult of liabilities management, which has been presented as a bold and aggressive new banking technique. Actually, it appears to be more of a rear-guard action born of necessity. This technique brought forth all the innovative banking talent in the system to the task of imaginatively seeking out new funds. We mentioned the rapid growth of large negotiable Certificates of Deposit as an invention of this period. Prior to 1960, there were no CDs (see Table 10.2). Later in the period, during the credit crunches of 1966 and 1969, these CDs became the prime source of trouble, as we will explain. The credit crunch of 1969-70 also saw the widespread introduction of Eurodollars as a source of funds as liabilities management went international. The record of such Eurodollar borrowing is also presented in Table 10.2

TABLE 10.2

Year	(In Billions of Dollars) Large Negotiable CDs	Eurodollars	Paper Issues
1960	1.1	0.9	0.0
1961	3.2	1.0	0.0
1962	6.2	0.8	0.0
1963	9.9	1.0	0.0
1964	12.6	1.1	0.0
1965	16.3	1.4	0.0
1966	15.7	4.0	0.0
1967	20.3	4.2	0.0
1968	23.5	6.0	0.0
1969	10.9	12.8	4.2
1970	26.1	7.7	2.4
1971	34.0	0.9	2.0
1972	44.9	1.4	2.6

We discussed in an earlier chapter the use of bank-holding-company commercial paper and many other techniques or loopholes that the banking system resorted to in its frantic search for deposits during the crunch of 1970. Nor did the system show the least reluctance about utilizing more fully the federal-funds market or the discount window. All these techniques have one important thing in common, however. They all served to substantially raise the *cost* of the banking system's liabilities.

Profit-maximization philosophies do not work if the cost of borrowed money is less than the return on loaned money. Given the higher costs of aggressive liabilities management, government securities, in spite of their superior liquidity, were certainly not suitable investments. Thus, we see the self-enforcing circle coming around again. The lower liquidity of a diminished government-securities-to-bank credit relationship works through the entire process into higher levels of interest rates and costs of deposits, which leads to a further diminution of government-securities holdings. If banks require higher-yielding loans and investments, they must take higher risks, which they did throughout the 1960s. First, banks turned to higher-yielding municipal bonds, which they bought in longer and longer maturities. Not only did they move to less liquid municipals from governments, but they then purposely lengthened the average life of the municipal portfolio to get even higher returns and, naturally, even less liquidity. As we will describe later, when loan demand accelerated and interest returns rose, the banks attempted to trade their municipals for loans and found that there was no market for the bonds. Back they went to their portfolio of government securities and reduced it further. By now the circular process of acceleration is probably becoming quite familiar to the reader.

The next method of obtaining the needed return on loans to offset the rising cost of deposits was the lengthening of the maturity on loans. Historically, banking theory and practice revolved around the short, self-liquidating business loan, which was, of course, suited to the short-term nature of bank liabilities. Now, the new banking theory condones a trend of gradually lengthening bank loans until many corporations become so deeply in debt to some banks that the lines of credit must gradually grow just to keep the prior loans safe. This is happening at the same time that the source of banking liabilities is becoming more short-term in nature and more volatile. So we have an increasing amount of long-term loans by banks, and their investment portfolios have come to be dominated by municipal bonds with fairly long average lives. As interest rates continue to rise as a part of the entire process, they come back again in the circular process to strike at the portfolios, and paper losses mount within the municipal portfolios. This, of course, renders the municipal portfolio even more illiquid, for banks dislike turning paper losses into actual losses on their statements.

Just to keep the circular process going, it is time to bring the Federal Reserve back into the picture. Not only is the Federal Reserve playing a continuing part in the process by monetizing the federal debt as it becomes necessary, but it also enters the chain of liquidity deterioration in several other roles. Since it has assumed the role of maintaining orderly money markets and stable interest rates, and since one major effect of this entire process is higher interest rates, the Federal Reserve has, of necessity, been continually on the net-buy side in its open-market operations, thereby supplying even more reserves to the market. As maintenance of full employment is also one of its unstated goals, it has fallen upon the Federal Reserve to supply increasingly larger reserves to turn the economy upward after each business slowdown. Finally, its goal of fostering continuing economic growth also necessitates holding interest rates at low levels to stimulate investment. The Federal Reserve has always believed that the way to accomplish this is to increase the money supply, although monetarists declare that the opposite tactic is needed. We have seen that the result *is* just the opposite. The Federal Reserve activity, combined with the declining bank liquidity, serves to raise interest-rate levels throughout the economy. The rising bank credit, of course, represents someone's debts, and so, into the spiraling interaction of the Federal Reserve, government spending, and the banking system, enter the effects of declining corporate liquidity.

Corporate Liquidity

By 1960, the deterioration in corporate liquidity was already far along. Cash as a percentage of current liabilities had already been cut in half since the end of the war, as were coverage ratios. Interest expense as a percentage of profits had tripled. It was on top of this record that the massive credit expansion of the 1960s was added.

From this shaky base the growth cult began to spread among corporations, investors, and security analysts. The primary aim for every corporation became a record of steadily growing earnings per share. The job of security analysts and the joy of investors was to find such companies. The quality of the earnings did not matter. Depreciation schedules could be lengthened, expenses deferred, and acquisitions overstated. This was all in keeping with the growth-at-any-cost philosophy of the new economists. In the early 1960s, investors bought any stock that showed an unbroken record of earnings, no matter how contrived they may have been, no matter how small the yearly gains, and no matter what business they were in. Utilities, for example, were given price-earnings multiples as high as thirty or forty for those in fast-growing areas. No attention was paid to the growing need for capital or to the declining condition of the balance sheets of these utilities.

The Magic of Leverage

With the growing faith in never-ending economic growth without serious business corrections and in the cult of earnings growth, it was only natural that corporations would turn increasingly to financial leverage to raise their rates of growth or to revitalize sagging growth. Little attention was being paid to the relatively static balance sheet—or to its footnotes, for that matter. If the company could grow on its own capital, couldn't it grow even faster on others' money? Just as the Federal Reserve found a banking system ready and willing to expand the reserves it received into multiple expansions of credit, the banks found corporations ready and willing to borrow. Liquidity and the overall corporate balance sheet continued to decline.

Creeping Conglomeration

It was only natural that corporations then began to utilize their borrowing power, as well as their inflated common stock, to acquire other corporations to enhance their own earning power and to continue their growth. Thus, the age of the conglomerates was born, in which corporations competed feverishly with each other to acquire any companies with assets, earning power, patents, trained personnel, or simply liquid assets. The justification was "synergism," or the simple formula that $1 + 1 = 3$. As corporations were acquired and brought under the guidance of the "superior" management of the conglomerate, the earnings of the whole, it was claimed, would be greater than the sum of the parts. It did not matter that the conglomerates, as their name implies, were combinations of scores of dissimilar operations. In fact, acquisition of totally unrelated businesses was the loophole by which these companies escaped anti-trust actions, for there were no legal precedents for attacking mergers of unrelated companies.

The real reason for the conglomeration craze was to buy growth through the leveraging of the assets of the conglomerate and by using every accounting trick that could possibly be invented. As creeping conglomeration continued, illiquidity among corporate balance sheets accelerated. The trend finally ended when the balance sheets caught up with the conglomerates, and the intelligent security analysts who were able to see the trouble in time were the very few who remembered that such a thing as a balance sheet existed. Indeed, only a handful were able to cut through the multiple layers of debt, preferred stock, warrants, convertibles, and all the "funny money" to see that the growth was illusory. When the balance sheet was discovered by analysts once again, the financial empires began to tumble.

Interaction of Corporate
and Banking Liquidity

It was not only among conglomerates that balance sheets were run down but throughout the entire corporate sector. The same general liquidity trends of the 1950s continued, but they accelerated measurably with the aid of government spending, monetary inflation by the Federal Reserve, and the aggressive lending policies of the banking system. Cash positions and current ratios continued to decline as corporations avidly pursued sales. A significant portion of the sales growth, however, was generated through the extension of trade credit, which was also considerably lengthened. Here, of course, an aggressive, risk-taking banking system was required to provide the credit to corporations. Hence, the entire growth of the 1960s was marked by rising sales but an even faster growth rate of credit granted by corporations and borrowed by corporations, a situation to be abhorred by any security analyst. As short-term credit rose, liquidity fell, and as inflationary pressures began to build from the excessive credit creation of the mid-1960s, the Federal Reserve attempted to restrict the growth of credit and the rapidly building inflationary pressures. Every attempt was abandoned prematurely as the Federal Reserve's policy precipitated credit crunches. While many reasons are given for the failure of monetary policy, there is only one overriding reason— liquidity. Because bank liquidity was extremely low, any monetary constraints quickly led to drastic rationing of bank credit. Because corporations had also accumulated huge amounts of short-term debt and were vitally dependent upon bank loans, the situation quickly became dangerous. The danger was that a domino-type credit liquidation might begin, and the massive amount of accumulated debt made this intolerable. Money and reserves were quickly thrown into the system to avert the liquidation, and the process of deterioration was able to resume. The shock of each crunch, however, was enough to frighten corporations into funding the short-term debt and improving their liquidity enough to calm the fears of investors.

Going to Market

In recent years corporations have found increasingly less flexibility in their long-term financing. During expansionary periods, they have relied excessively upon increased short-term debt and then, as mentioned above, have been frightened into quickly funding their short-term debt with little opportunity to choose their timing. An earlier table summarized the postwar record of corporate financings. It was pointed out that after each credit crunch during the 1960s there occurred a bulge of long-term financing, which eased the liquidity pressures but served only to worsen other sections of the balance sheet. Here, once again, we see the circular, reinforcing nature of all the forces at work. Fiscal and monetary stimulus leads to excessive creation of bank debt and short-term corporate debt. The debt is funded, which increases the debt load of the corporation and lowers its interest-coverage figures. This increases the risk and thus lowers the ratings of the bonds of the corporation, which leads to higher interest rates. The sudden stampede of many corporations in the postcrunch funding also serves to push interest rates higher, just as the increasing inflation premium adds to the rates. The Federal Reserve, in helping the corporate sector through the funding period by supplying reserves to the banking system, increases inflationary pressures still further. As interest rates rise, the debt-service load of the corporations becomes still heavier and ratings

TABLE 10.3

Total Government Securities Issued
(Federal, State, & Local)
(Billions of Dollars)

Year	Total Non-corporate	U.S. Government	State & Municipal
1947	13.4	10.6	2.3
1948	13.2	10.3	2.7
1949	15.1	11.8	2.9
1950	13.5	9.7	3.5
1951	13.5	9.8	3.2
1952	17.7	12.6	4.4
1953	19.9	13.9	5.6
1954	20.2	12.5	7.0
1955	16.5	9.6	6.0
1956	11.5	5.5	5.5
1957	17.7	9.6	7.0
1958	22.9	12.1	7.5
1959	21.3	12.3	7.7
1960	17.4	7.9	7.2
1961	22.4	12.3	8.4
1962	19.3	8.6	8.6
1963	22.9	10.8	10.1
1964	23.2	10.7	10.5
1965	24.1	9.4	11.2
1966	26.9	8.2	11.1
1967	43.7	19.4	14.3
1968	43.6	18.0	16.4
1969	26.1	4.8	11.5
1970	49.7	14.8	17.8
1971	60.4	17.3	24.4
1972	54.5	17.1	23.0

drop even more. The rising rates also serve to create further paper losses in bank portfolios of tax-exempts, thus further decreasing banking liquidity.

As if the financing problems described above were not enough, it is usually at the very same time that corporations are vying for long-term capital that the federal government is also in the market to finance the deficits incurred in restimulating the economy. Table 10.3 discloses the same postcrunch bulges in financing in 1967, the year after the crunch of 1966, and the same acceleration after the crunch of 1969-70. As the Federal Reserve again is forced to monetize a large part of this debt, the base is set for the next round of credit creation and inflation. It is interesting that in 1970, all federally sponsored financings, both inside and outside the budget, accounted for well over 40 percent of all the funds available in the private credit markets that year. It would appear that governmental "fine-tuning" leads to a number of discordant notes.

Credit and the Business Cycle

The postwar record certainly leads one to ask whether the government and the Federal Reserve have acted as forces of stability or instability. A more important question is whether the economy is becoming increasingly unstable due to their efforts. The intuitive answer, in the light of the extremely volatile nature of the stock market, the money markets, the capital markets, and the credit growth in recent years, would seem to be in the affimative. The evidence tends to confirm this conclusion.

We mentioned earlier that the credit-creation activities of the Federal Reserve tended to have an inflationary bias since, when Federal Reserve bank credit did decline, total credit in the economy continued to rise. A record of all postwar business contractions is given in Table 10.4 It can be seen there

TABLE 10.4

Cyclical Credit Expansion

Economic Contractions	Growth in Bank Loans
Nov. 1948-Oct. 1949	No Change
July 1953-Aug. 1954	+ 1.1%
July 1957-Apr. 1958	+ 1.3%
May 1960-Feb. 1961	+ 3.9%
Nov. 1969-Nov. 1970	+ 4.5%

that in each successive contraction in business, the continuing expansion in credit was larger, tending to confirm that the monetary authorities' control over the process of credit growth is dimishing. We saw in an earlier chapter how an overly aggressive banking system was able for quite some time to avoid much of the restraint placed on it by the central bank. The sharper slow-down in credit growth in earlier recessions helped also to slow the decline in corporate liquidity. The more rapid growth in later years explains why the cyclical improvements in corporate and banking liquidity have been smaller. There was, in fact, no liquidity improvement among banks after the 1970 crunch. Thus, it may be seen that because of the internally reinforcing nature of the credit expansion and liquidity trends, the Federal Reserve may no longer have complete control over the entire process. The natural corrective forces of the business cycle are no longer operative, due to the advanced stage of the liquidity deterioration. This becomes even more apparent when the credit expansion of the recovery stage of recent cycles is examined in Table 10.5, which shows the expansion of total bank credit in each twenty-four-

TABLE 10.5

Expansion of Total Bank Credit Over the
24 Month Period Following the Recession Through

Apr. 1958-Apr. 1960	+ 7.2%
Feb. 1961-Feb. 1963	+ 16.8%
Nov. 1970-Nov. 1972	+ 28.3%

month period following the business trough. The amount of credit expansion required to effect the economic recovery accelerated markedly in the post-1960 period. The expansion following the most recent recession was nearly four times the amount in earlier recoveries. The record seems even more dramatic when looked at in terms of dollars and cents, as in Table 10.6. When the dollar-change in real GNP in each economic recovery is related to the dollar-change in bank credit over the same period, the result is an indication of the credit expansion required to buy each dollar of real GNP expansion. In the recovery of 1949-53 it required 28¢ of bank credit to produce an additional dollar of real GNP. By the recovery of 1970-72 every dollar of recovery cost exactly $1.75 of credit. From the peak preceding the recession of 1969-70 to the end of the first year of recovery, it required $3.00 of credit for every $1.00 of GNP expansion. Given the declining state of liquidity throughout the economy, one wonders just how much will be required to bail out the economy next time. These statistics demonstrate two very important aspects of the liquidity problem. The first, we mentioned in Chapter 5 in our discussion of corporate liquidity. As corporations become increasingly illiquid they become much less resilient. Many do not survive the recession, many more do not have sufficient funds to bounce back quickly from a depressed period as

TABLE 10.6

Financing Economic Recovery
(In Billions of Dollars)

Expansion Period	Change in Real GNP	Change in Total Bank Credit	Bank Credit/ GNP
Oct. 1949-July 1953	90.3	25.0	0.28
Aug. 1954-July 1957	46.0	15.5	0.34
Apr. 1958-May 1960	52.2	12.9	0.25
Feb. 1961-Nov. 1969	242.6	203.2	0.84
Nov. 1970-Dec. 1972	67.4	118.3	1.75
Nov. 1969-Dec. 1971	26.1	84.5	3.24

their debt loads become too heavy, and the scare becomes greater with each more intense credit crunch. Second, the aggregate illiquidity represents a growing deflationary force within the economy, which must be offset by the monetary authorities. As liquidity worsens, the potential of a spreading credit liquidation becomes more real, and the Federal Reserve and the federal government are gradually being painted into the proverbial corner. The growing inflationary pressure from the excessive credit expansion is becoming intolerable, but the risk of an uncontrollable credit liquidation is becoming even more dangerous. To prevent the liquidation, the system must be flooded with inflationary high-powered money, and, as the statistics indicate, the cost in terms of potential inflation becomes more expensive with each cycle. Each time the credit liquidation is avoided, the basis for the next crisis is laid. These crises, or crunches as they have come to be called, are occurring with both increasing frequency and intensity. A closer examination of the two crunches of the 1960s will reveal that they are only manifestations of the underlying liquidity trends described here.

The Credit Crunch of 1966

The first five years of the age of the new economists under Kennedy and then Johnson looked successful on the surface. The rate of real GNP growth averaged 4.8 percent during the years 1961-65, a full percentage point above the entire postwar average of 3.8 percent, but the price in terms of future stability was high. Over the same years, bank loans rose at nearly three times the rate of GNP, total private debt more than twice the rate, budget deficits totaled nearly $25 billion, and money grew at nearly twice the rate of GNP. Moreover, much of the real growth was only possible because of excess capacity and unemployment at the beginning of the new era. By the end of 1965, the nation was approaching full capacity, and unemployment had reached a low 4 percent. Clearly it was now time to pay the piper. With inflationary pressures beginning to mount and heavy new demands for Vietnam spending, the time for monetary restraint had arrived. The Federal Reserve began to tighten money in December 1965. The new policy of constraint was relatively ineffective throughout the early months of 1966, as money continued to rise during the first quarter and bank credit continued to rise strongly throughout almost the entire first half of the year.

One of the Federal Reserve's problems was the lack of cooperation by the federal government. Just at the time that fiscal restraint was clearly needed, it was not forthcoming. The government failed to raise taxes or impose an excess-profits tax, as in previous wars, or to invoke wartime controls. Even as Vietnam spending rose significantly, there was no cutback in the civilian programs of the New Frontier and the Great Society. Contrary to the belief of many that defense spending was the cause of the inflation of the 1960s, nondefense spending rose much more significantly. It was primarily this guns *and* butter approach that negated the attempts of the Federal Reserve to curb the inflationary pressures. One of the causal factors in the stubbornly rising loan demand was the attempt of the government to finance the war by means other than higher taxation. One method used was an acceleration of corporate tax payments, forcing corporations to pay taxes more frequently. With the growing inflationary pressures and full capacity, corporations did not wish to reduce their capital spending and instead ran down their liquid assets and incurred short-term debt. As a result, corporate liquidity declined precipitously in early 1966. Interest rates were also rising strongly as a result. Once again, government financing coincided with private, and the competition pushed interest rates to new postwar records in 1966. After a tax cut in March 1964, on top of a budget deficit for fiscal 1964, federal deficits began to accelerate. The Federal Reserve recorded record purchases of government securities in the open market to help finance the deficits in 1965. This addition of high-powered money was one of the major obstacles to Federal Reserve restraint in the following year. The expansion in money in early 1966, in spite of policy intentions, was due to the continued Treasury financings through the first quarter of 1966. Great pressure also came from financings by federal agencies during early 1966, which totaled amounts three times as great as the year-before period. Remember, this was all on top of huge demands from the private sector.

The second major obstacle to the Federal Reserve's attempts to bring inflation under control was, once again, the continuing liquidity trends among corporations and the banking system. To understand the problems in the banking system during the 1966 credit-crunch year, it is necessary to travel back again to the early 1960s. As banks were already experiencing rising loan-deposit ratios and disintermediation, larger banks began to pursue CD money, aggressively competing with both commercial paper and Treasury bills. In 1959, there were no CDs outstanding, but by the peak in 1966, the amount outstanding had risen to over $17 billion. Close to 50 percent of all new time deposits over the period came from large CDs, and the number of banks utilizing this deposit source rose substantially. Predictably, the rising cost of deposits for banks necessitated higher-yielding investments by the banks. Since liquidity and yield are not compatible, the declining liquidity trends were reinforced. Because loan demand was not sufficient in the early 1960s, banks generally turned to higher-yielding municipal bonds, and uncomfortably large percentages of all new deposits moved into municipals, particularly those with longer maturities and correspondingly higher yields. When loan demand finally began to accelerate in 1965 and 1966, with resulting higher interest rates, banks attempted to reduce their municipal portfolios. They found that the markets for their municipals were extremely thin, which was due to the large amounts banks had for sale, plus the tight banking-credit conditions that had led many dealers to reduce inventories. It was quickly confirmed that U.S. government securities were the only true source of liquidity for banks. These were sold in large amounts to support loan demand. Excess reserves, which were already at low levels from the long liquidity deterioration, were reduced even further. Banks continued to sell CDs vigorously in 1966 until, in the third quarter, the Regulation Q interest-rate ceilings were reached for the first time; the Federal Reserve refused to raise the ceilings.

With Treasury financing needs subsiding, the Federal Reserve was finally able to implement an effective restrictive program after the first quarter, and the final three quarters of 1966 showed very little money growth. The stage was thus set for the credit crunch of 1966.

Both federal agencies and corporations were still borrowing heavily in August, the Federal Reserve was still tightening money, and interest rates competitive with CDs were beyond the CD ceilings. The banking system faced its first CD runoff. Nearly $4 billion of CDs matured in August, with over twice that amount scheduled to mature in the following two months. A liquidity scare followed among banks as they rushed to restore liquidity, first by borrowing heavily and by continuing their attempts to reduce municipal holdings, which could only be done at substantial discounts. Substantial government securities were also liquidated as the percentage of total bank credit represented by such securities fell from over 22 percent to 17 percent in slightly over one year. Finally, there was no choice but to begin to liquidate loans. By the first quarter of 1967, this led to a substantial decline in the rate of GNP growth, which was later dubbed a minirecession. By early fall, the Federal Reserve began to ease monetary conditions, and interest rates reached their peak in August of 1966. The first credit crunch of the period was over, and the Consumer Price Index temporarily peaked in 1966. The following year, as we saw in previous tables, corporations, wary from the credit crunch, funded much of their excessive short-term debt, and as a result corporate liquidity improved slightly.

The Credit Crunch of 1969-70

The Federal Reserve shifted toward a massive easing of money in early 1967, and by mid-year total spending was once again rising rapidly. Many economists have suggested that the Federal Reserve, by this action, missed an opportunity to finally bring inflation under control. In its defense, it may be said that there was very little choice in the matter. The state of liquidity in the banking system and among corporations did not really allow a continuation of sharp monetary constraint. As to maintaining only moderate growth in money and credit after the 1966 crunch, there was also little choice. Throughout 1967 and 1968, a high rate of government spending continued and budget deficits mounted. Because the economy was still at full employment, the rate of inflation resumed its upward climb even more intensely. Even though interest rates were falling early in 1967, the Federal Reserve was forced to continue to monetize the debt. By June of 1967, when interest rates turned upward from rising credit demand, the Federal Reserve moved to prevent them from rising by adding even more reserves to the system. Any improvements in liquidity in 1966 and early 1967 were short-lived, for the trends toward lower liquidity resumed with renewed vigor. It was pointed out in a previous table that total credit, bank loans, Federal Reserve credit, and money supply all grew at accelerated rates after the brief slowdown in 1966. The Federal Reserve was still also fighting these inexorable trends.

In early 1968 it was quite obvious that inflationary pressures were building and that monetary restraint was clearly appropriate, but debate was in progress on the tax surcharge and the Federal Reserve awaited the outcome. When the tax surcharge was finally passed in June 1968, fears of "overkill" pervaded the Federal Reserve. Just as the fiscal year ended with the largest budget deficit of the 1960s, with the nation at full employment and inflationary pressures everywhere, another overt move toward monetary ease was taken. As 1968 drew to a close, it became evident that the fiscal policy was not restrictive and that inflation was being fanned by the monetary policy. Early in 1969, the Federal Reserve turned strongly toward restraint, as did fiscal policy, and the stage was set for the coming credit crunch.

Many financial analysts and economists tend to consider periods of credit stringency as independent and unique events. However, they are really periodic manifestations of the underlying problems and trends discussed in this book, and they will continue to occur with increasing frequency and with greater intensity as long as the current liquidity trends remain intact and there is little or no change in governmental and Federal Reserve policies and philosophies. It is possible that new events or structural changes might alter the appearance of future credit crunches, but the event of 1969-70 was a replica of the 1966 crunch, though much more intense and potentially more dangerous. Since we have already discussed the 1970 period several times in this book, we will limit our discussion here to the similarities between the two credit crunches of the 1960s.

Both events were preceded by cyclical declines in the long-term liquidity trends brought about by the same forces. Both crunches were preceded by massive federal deficits, large increases in Federal Reserve credit, and growth in bank loans and total credit. Corporations accumulated excessive amounts of short-term credit and, in each case, the banking system cooperated by running down its liquidity. Government securities as a percentage of total bank credit had reached a new postwar low in 1969 (13 percent), as did all other measurements of banking liquidity. After the runoff of CDs in 1966 from the peak of over $17 billion, banks continued to pursue this source of funds aggressively, and they reached a new peak over $23 billion at the beginning of the monetary constraint. The result was once again new record levels of interest rates and inflationary pressures and expectations that threatened to erupt into runaway inflation.

Once again, the Federal Reserve, and this time the federal government as well, attempted to halt the climb in prices. This time the monetary constraint was seriously pursued, leading many monetarist economists to claim it was excessive and to predict a recession. The first half of 1969 saw money growth of less than 2 percent, but the Consumer Price Index was also rising in excess of 5 percent. As in 1966, the Federal Reserve again attacked business loans, which were rising dangerously as the plant and equipment boom continued unabated despite the new restrictive policies. Businessmen probably believed the constraint would be as short-lived as that of 1966. Because interest rates were already quite high, long-term financing was delayed; liquid assets were run down instead and short-term debt increased, just as happened in the 1966 period. To slow the growth in business loans, it was necessary for the Federal Reserve to once again attack the large banks that made most of these large business loans. Once again, the Regulation Q ceilings were used as prime tools. The Federal Reserve refused to raise the interest-rate ceilings, and banks suffered their second CD runoff. This one was of much greater proportions since the decline began from the record level above $23 billion and fell well below $10 billion. We earlier detailed the frantic scrambling of the banking system as it utilized Eurodollars extensively, sold commercial paper through holding companies, and attempted to utilize a number of other loopholes to stem the tie of declining reserves.

A second demonstration of the unsuitability of municipal bonds as liquid buffer assets was given as the market for such bonds in 1969 disappeared and a number of respected dealers were wiped out. It was the government securities that were liquidated, just as in 1966, while the level of municipal bonds remained stable in the aggregate. With the rising interest rates during the period, banks undoubtedly suffered huge paper losses in their portfolios. If the portfolios were "marked to the market" to show the true asset values at current prices, it would have been seen just how close the nation came to financial disaster.

With the already low levels of corporate liquidity, the massive increases in short-term debt once again left corporations at the mercy first of the banks and money markets and later of the capital markets. As the monetary restraint wore on into 1969 and corporations finally felt the pressure of decreased availaibility of bank loans, issues of commercial paper increased substantially. Many corporations were also being forced to the long-term capital markets and began to pay record long-term interest rates.

Finally, in the second quarter of 1970, a large Treasury financing forced more reserves into the system; money supply rose, but it was almost too late and was only temporary. In June 1970, the Penn Central filed for bankruptcy. A full-scale crisis developed that could have grown into an extended, self-enforcing credit liquidation. The worthless commercial paper of the Penn Central led the financial community to suspect many commercial-paper issues. Because of the extensive use made of the commercial-paper markets in the credit-restraint period, a gaping hole would have been left in short-term corporate financing if this market were removed. It could only have been filled by an immediate transfusion of reserves, and the Federal Reserve, to its credit, saw the problem and acted quickly. Monetary conditions were eased considerably and the ceilings were removed from CDs with maturities of 30-89 days. The level of CDs began to rise once again, and the crisis was past—for a while.

In the two years that followed, the level of long-term corporate financing and government financing exceeded by far any levels in the history of the country. The fear and consternation suffered in the 1970 crisis were still in evidence as late as 1973. The financings left corporate liquidity improved from the record low levels set in 1970. The only differences between the credit crunches of 1966 and 1969-70 were those of length and intensity.

The Next Credit Crunch

Although we will save the predictions for Chapter 13, it may be helpful in the way of a preliminary summary to discuss the possibility of another credit crunch occurring soon. We have seen that the credit crunches are not separate, unique experiences but merely symptoms of a continuing problem. Both crunches had a similar pattern and the causal forces were the same. At the root of each crisis is the continuing trend of declining liquidity, sustained by the policies and actions of the federal government and the Federal Reserve and by its own circular process of reinforcement—that is, its own momentum. Periodically, short-term debt creation and the inflationary pressures resulting from excessive credit become so intense that the government attempts to slow the process. Because liquidity is so low, monetary restraint must be curbed in order to avoid a significant credit liquidation, which, because of the size of the total debt, would be too disastrous. The restraint is ended too soon to completely eliminate the inflation, and the expansion of reserves that results from the attempt to turn the economy around again lays the foundation for another period of cyclical credit expansion and the next crisis. The funding of short-term debt that follows brings a measure of cyclical recovery in corporate liquidity, which supplies the confidence for the corporate sector to renew the deterioration of its balance sheets in the search for higher profits and continued growth. Throughout the entire period, including the credit crunches, total credit in the economy continues to grow at rates far in excess of the capacity for real growth of goods and services. As long as this continues, inflationary pressures will continue to grow, though they may be bottled up from time to time.

To predict that there will not be another credit crunch of even greater proportions, one must be able to say that the basic causal factors have been eliminated. This is not the case. In the years since the 1970 crisis, government spending continued to grow at its postwar rate of roughly 9 percent, and all measures of credit and monetary aggregates continued to grow in excess of the real growth of the economy. Banking liquidity in 1973 was far worse than it was at the depths of the 1970 crisis. Corporate liquidity was only slightly improved, considering the record business expansion of the preceding two years. In 1973, the banking system's holdings of government securities reached a point below 10 percent of all assets and below 6 percent for the large banks. The low mark in 1970 was 13 percent. Since it was the remaining holdings of government securities that finally proved to be the only source of liquidity for banks at a reasonable cost, one wonders where they will get relief the next time, considering the extremely low levels of holdings currently. When the next crunch occurs, the government will once again have to provide the final relief. Every time this happens, as pointed out previously, an increasingly larger amount of credit is required to accomplish the mission. The government is, in effect, trapped into perpetuating the downward trend in liquidity and the rising trend in prices and interest rates. To refuse the relief is to invite a potentially uncontrollable credit liquidation. The problem is too much credit, but the government must supply even more. Credit is needed to bridge the gap between the production of one period and the consumption of the next. Too much credit provides funds in excess of the amount needed to clear the previous period's production. This leads to growth in speculation and ultimately to inflation.

Chances of a Financial Panic

Throughout history, all extensive economic corrections have come as a result of the liquidation of large private debt. The larger the level of debt, the greater the liquidation and recession. Most panics of the past were caused by overextension of credit related to periods of high speculation, and the corrections were short but quite intensive. Because the base upon which the speculation was built was also quite small, the government did not interfere to moderate the correction.

The postwar years under study in this book differ from past periods only in terms of the length and the nature of the speculation. Many of the new government safeguards against such panics and deep recessions could conceivably *make* one possible. The relatively greater activist role that the government has taken since World War II, together with the inventiveness of the banking system, served to remove many of the natural corrective forces that were once present in the economy, and has allowed the excessive credit expansion to last much longer than it ever could have in the past. Thus, the situation has reached such proportions that it may soon be out of control. One well-known economist was noted to remark that the government has learned to control the business cycle but in so doing has lost control of the economy.

Another reason for the length and the amount of credit creation may lie in the nature of the speculation that characterizes the present period. Spurred by the pervading feeling that the government had legislated away the business cycle, business slowly but steadily learned to take more risk in the form of lower levels of liquidity and higher debt structures and interest-service load. Unlike the South Sea Bubble or the Mississippi Bubble of the past, this speculation has been a more respectable type of business speculation, fostered and encouraged

145

by the government, which is interested in maintaining a continuing growth pattern in the economy. The government has been a partner in the process in the name of business stability and growth and at the expense of the balance sheet. The government has succeeded in changing the entire credit ethic of the nation, so that debt, in the name of growth and full employment, is no longer considered evil. Hence, the credit expansion, allowed and encouraged to continue, has attained a size unequaled in history.

Even if one were to conclude that these secular trends will culminate in a credit liquidation or financial panic of great proportions, he would be hard-pressed to time the happening of the event. It is difficult to assess just how long the government can delay such an event, for as we have seen from the credit crunches of the past, infusion of more reserves can end a panic. The cost of such delay, however, is manifested in many of the effects we have described, such as inflation, higher interest rates, increased risk, and greater volatility in financial markets. As long as the liquidity trends remain in force, it is safe to say, their effects will continue to be present and will intensify in time. By tracking these effects one can also predict a little more exactly just when the trends have gone so far that the risk of remaining in certain investments may be too great. We will discuss each of these effects in more detail in the chapters that follow.

Chapter 11

The Continuing Effects of Deficient Liquidity

Although it should now be abundantly clear that an unmistakably accelerating trend of excessive credit expansion has existed in the United States since the end of World War II, one might still argue that an economic armageddon is not necessarily imminent—that liquidity is a state of mind. There is some truth in this argument, in light of the power and the willingness of the government and the Federal Reserve to extend the trend. As we have seen, a credit crunch can be ended quickly with a transfusion of sufficient new reserves into the banking system. Even a heroin addict can be kept "high" indefinitely, but the damage to his system must eventually be recognized and the cure taken. Similarly, the costs of maintaining the unhealthy liquidity trends are also high. We have mentioned the major costs as being inflation, rising interest rates, accelerating risk, and increased volatility, and in this chapter we will explore them in more detail. As these effects are allowed to exist for extended periods of time, however, they begin to permeate the entire economic system and emerge in many different forms. Gradually, these secondary effects become a permanent part of the system. We are speaking here of such secondary effects as rising levels of speculation and shorter investment horizons, growing militancy among unions, strikes, boycotts, ecology problems, balance-of-payments deficits, rising international speculative flows of money, disruptions of international trade, devaluations, trade and capital restrictions, and eventually, even wars. These, and many other phenomena, are the direct results of inflation and the artificially high rates of growth made possible by excessive credit growth. Many are mistakenly thought of as causes of inflation problems rather than as results of inflation. Though we may not be able to exactly date the ultimate credit collapse, we can make many useful observations as to the climate in which the end can be expected to occur, and we can track the progress of the liquidity trends through a continuing study of their major effects.

Inflation

In addition to the complete confusion among the general populace regarding the causes of inflation, there is extensive disagreement among professional economists and financial analysts. Though many blamed the disastrous inflation of the late 1960s upon the Vietnam War, the same inflation plagued the nation in 1973, with monthly advances reaching new post-World War II records even though the Vietnam War had ended. Even worse inflation plagued nations that had not been at war. Many, who despondently predict continuing inflation, base their fears upon such things as the world energy crisis, the growing service component of the GNP, irresponsible militant unionism, and a world food shortage. All, of course, ignore the underlying and fundamental reason for the past inflation and its anticipated continuation into the future. This reason is the monetization of the burgeoning federal deficits and the resulting trends in excessive credit expansion, illiquidity, and artificial economic growth that we have discussed in this book. We have already shown the unmistakable line of causation between excessive money-supply growth and inflation. We know that increased money supply can come from only two sources: inflow of gold or expansion of bank credit. Since the nation's gold supply has been sharply reduced during the postwar years, there remains only excessive expansion of bank credit to explain the massive money and credit growth. Because banks can only expand those reserves that are given them by the Federal Reserve system, and because we know that the primary tool of the central bank for supplying reserves is the open-market purchase of government securities, we can further narrow the blame to the excessive purchases of government securities by the Federal Reserve. Although many of these purchases were made in continuing open-market operations to stabilize interest rates or to keep them low to either stimulate the economy or maintain its growth, the bulk of the impetus came from aiding the financing of the federal deficits, which lie at the root of the problem.

Secondary Effects of
Continuing Inflation

The economic and social ramifications and dislocations of continuing inflation within an economy are too numerous to be treated in detail here. However, we will discuss briefly the interrelationships among inflation and the other major effects of the credit trends. We will also discuss a few of the so-called structural causes of continuing inflation, many of which are merely additional manifestations of the basic liquidity and credit trends.

Labor and Inflation

A shift in the balance of bargaining power between labor and management in favor of large, militant unions is often given as one of the important structural changes in the economy that makes complete control over inflation impossible. It is true that important legislation, particularly in the 1930s, helped to pave the way for stronger unions. It is not true, however, that union actions are primary causal factors in inflation. There have been many periods when there was no inflation to speak of even though strong unions were in existence, and there have been extreme cases of inflation in countries where no unions existed. There is no doubt that strong and militant unions can make it more difficult to control an inflation that has already started, but this would be a case of workers "reacting" rather than "acting." The workers are usually reacting to extended periods of rising prices that have shrunk their real pay. The inflation from which they attempt to find relief through strikes and tough bargaining stems from the forces we have already described. The causal factor of inflation is, in short, excessive demand stemming from excessive money and credit creation. This overstimulated demand leads the businessman to bid up the prices of labor to fill his orders. His increased costs, passed on as higher prices, eventually force labor to go to the bargaining table with a resolve to "get theirs." As most wage demands are patterned after those received by other unions, the settlements tend to spread. As inflation becomes built into the system, union members tend to expect large settlements and escalation clauses. With their more militant stance, and with the aid of the government, unions have become stronger relative to business. All this has led to an inflationary structural bias with wage levels seldom declining and rising strongly in inflationary periods.

Many other government programs strengthen the inflationary bias. In many states, striking workers are eligible for unemployment compensation, food stamps, and welfare payments, all of which make strikes more attractive. Business, in effect, subsidizes employees while it is being struck. The minimum wage keeps many potential workers out of the market, which helps to keep the labor market tighter for those working and serves to increase inflationary pressures. The fact that more unemployed unskilled workers exist at any given time, as a result of the minimum wage, also leads to more fiscal-stimulation policies to decrease unemployment, which also, as we have explained above, increase inflationary pressures in the form of monetized federal debt. Once working, many of those potential workers, who are now barred from employment, might seek to move up into skilled trades. It is small wonder that unions are strongly behind the minimum wage. It not only helps to keep the labor market tight but also raises the wage floor for future bargaining. All of these programs induce workers to offer less work at a given wage, which, through lower productivity, leads once again to higher rates of inflation. It is important to remember, however, that the labor militancy was not spontaneous. Though it may have been fostered by a benevolent government, it is primarily a reaction to strong demand-pull inflationary pressures resulting from excessive credit creation.

Corporate Profits

Continuing inflation is not good for any corporation, although some are more able to adjust to it than others. Inflation always squeezes profits because prices are "spot" by nature and fluctuate with demand, while costs are gen-

149

erally contractual and long-term in nature. Short spurts of inflation are not too troublesome, because in the early stages of inflation, prices rise faster than costs. Later, however, higher costs are gradually locked in and, as mentioned above, labor becomes more militant in light of its declining real wage. We showed in an earlier chapter that profit margins and returns on capital have generally been declining in the postwar years. With rising fixed costs, business gradually becomes less likely to cut prices and clear inventories when sales decline, preferring instead to let sales decline. Thus, prices become as "sticky" on the downside as wages. We have a double structural problem in that both prices and wages are responsive to fiscal and monetary expansion but not to monetary contraction, which leads to accelerating money growth just to keep the economy growing. Yet they are structural only in the sense that they result from continuous overexpansion of credit. With the rhetoric of various pressure groups and politics, the basic underlying cause gets lost. Blame is instead cast upon unfair international competition, a declining work ethic, controls, a growing service economy, or any other handy scapegoat.

The confusion caused by the proliferation of many such secondary effects of inflation and declining liquidity serves to disguise the real causes of inflation or to distract attention from them. We saw earlier how the excessive credit creation that spawns inflation has also caused the long decline in liquidity, which has now reached the stage where it is also a prime cause of inflation as even more credit creation is needed to offset the growing deflationary implications of an overloaded debt structure. We have continually striven here to show that from the one basic source of trouble many secondary effects grow, which then interact to gradually form a self-sustaining additional source of inflation so great that even if the problem were attacked at the source, the momentum might be difficult to halt. The declining profit margins worsen the liquidity problem, which continues to grow on its own anyway. Add to this the problems of militant and powerful unions partially spawned by the same liquidity and inflation problems, and the long-term profit potential in many industries is substantially reduced. Since risk and interest-rate levels are also growing, there is generally less incentive to commit capital investments to these industries. This, of course, reduces the total productive capacity and lowers possibilities of productivity improvement, both of which increase inflationary pressures. As we will see a little further on, capital formation and productivity gains in the United States have been increasingly disappointing.

The Phillips Curve

The Phillips curve (after A. W. Phillips) illustrates the cost of the government commitment to full employment. The trade-off between lower unemployment rates and the rate of inflation can be seen in Figure 11.1. In former years, if the government reached its goal of full employment at a 4 percent unemployment rate, it would expect a rate of inflation of roughly 4 percent as a cost of its policy. In other words, the government was able to "buy" more jobs by inflating the economy and injuring those who were already employed. This deliberate policy decision is, of course, one of the primary sources of our inflation

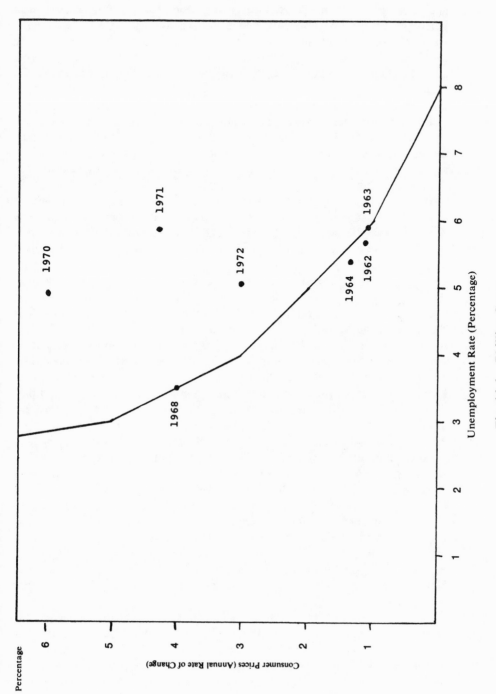

Fig. 11.1—Phillips Curve

problems in the postwar years. There is, no doubt, a value judgment involved here, and it is not up to the author to decide whether the right one was made. Nevertheless, two brief points should be made on this question. First, it is quite clear that the public has not been made sufficiently aware of the fact that such a trade-off does in fact exist. If it were, the government might not have had the same free hand it has had in the postwar years. Second, there may be many alternative ways in which to accomplish the same purposes without releasing the inflationary pressures that we have suffered from. With more challenge by an enlightened public, the government might have been forced to develop better retraining policies and to improve the mobility of labor, and, most important, it would not have been so successful in promoting the minimum wage, which has destroyed millions of jobs.

It is particularly important to reexamine this trade-off today because the cost of full employment in terms of inflation seems to be rising considerably. In Figure 11.1, it can be seen that for 1970 and 1971 the rate of inflation for a given unemployment rate more than doubled—that is, the entire Phillips curve shifted to the right. Although it appeared to have shifted back to the left in 1972, the acceleration of prices in early 1973 with unemployment still at 5 percent would indicate a sharp swing to the right once again. This is the result of the continuing decline in liquidity and the imbedded inflationary pressures and expectations that follow. More specifically, it is the result of many of the secondary effects we have already discussed—that is, the growing power and militancy of organized labor, a changed composition of unemployment helped by minimum-wage laws, and the resulting "sticky" wages and prices on the downside of the cycle. Even the growing participation of women in the work force can be at least partially explained by the declining family liquidity. What we have termed the growing militancy of organized labor is, in reality, a growing education of organized labor—education regarding the realities of the effects of embedded inflation. Workers have learned that it is not the dollar amount of their raise that is important. It is their "real" wage—that is, what their pay buys in terms of actual goods and services—that is important. The government can no longer buy off organized labor with price increases. The raise labor has learned to ask for in dollar amounts will be large enough to insure that the real wage will rise also—that is, the dollar raise will more than offset what labor feels the rate of inflation will be over the life of a contract. These increased wage settlements will be passed along by business in the form of price increases, which will be even higher than the increased wage cost as business will also anticipate even further cost increase

We have t .ed to demonstrate throughout this book that the sources of our inflationary problems are demand-oriented, and that the effects of continuing excessive credit creation react upon each other to form an independent force with growing self-enforcing momentum, which it will take years of concerted effort to reverse. The relationships above very succinctly demonstrate the problem. Growing illiquidity will continue to force the government to utilize increasingly greater inflationary forces to reverse every economic downturn, while at the same time the Phillips curve will continue to shift to the right as citizens learn to protect themselves against the effects of embedded inflationary pressures. This will require greater amounts of inflation to reduce unemployment, and so the upward spiral will continue. Underlying the more militant action of labor are the increased reliefs of higher unemployment compensation, welfare payments, and food stamps mentioned above, which all serve to create less hardship for the striker. The net result is that price and cost pressures become stronger at any given level of capacity utilization.

Government Share of GNP

We have demonstrated that the government share of the nation's GNP has been steadily increasing throughout the postwar period. This must be considered an additional structural change in the economy that helps to insure continuance of inflation. Though this factor need not be inflationary, history shows that it has led to chronic deficits in all other countries. Governments have a terrible record of failing to resist political pressures that lead to inflation. It has always been more popular to spend money and provide services than to raise taxes or cut spending. It has always been easier for governments to rely upon the invisible tax of inflation than upon overt forms of taxation. This is another lesson that must be learned by the public before the present government-spending philosophy can be altered. Inflation is the cruelest and most unfair of all taxes. It is also the most regressive, in that it falls most heavily on the poor and the elderly on fixed incomes, who cannot protect themselves through ownership of property and other assets that would appreciate along with other prices. Inflation, as mentioned earlier, also works to increase government tax revenues as individuals are gradually moved into higher tax brackets. This serves to enforce the trend of growing government share.

Like all the other effects we have discussed, the growing share of government spending permeates the entire system, interrelates with other effects, and causes secondary effects of its own, which all combine to strengthen the internal momentum of imbedded inflation. The greater government share and higher taxation that results gradually weaken incentives in the system, which together with rising levels of risk and interest rates work toward lower capital investment and eventually lower growth and productivity levels. Individuals lose incentives to produce as the aftertax share of their paycheck declines. These actions lead to lower levels of production of real goods and services, which, when combined with artificially induced levels of demand, strongly enforce the inflationary spiral.

Restraints upon Inflationary Policies

We pointed out in Chapter 9 that all restraints upon the freedom of the Federal Reserve to create credit have been systematically removed. The absence of those restraints must also be considered a structural change. The original Federal Reserve Act provided a number of safeguards to prevent the central bank from acting as an engine of inflation. Originally, the Federal Reserve was prevented from monetizing the federal debt, but later amendments permitted the Treasury to sell debt to the system. It was not intelligent, positive, forward planning that led to the changes in restraints. The changes were a necessity and took the place of discipline in federal spending.

Before the final restraints were lifted from the Federal Reserve, it was necessary to assume that individual citizens would not be able to discipline the government by converting their paper money to gold. In November 1960, the prohibition against the holding of gold by Americans was broadened to include the whole world rather than the continental United States only. Lest one believe that the huge government deficits of the late 1960s were unplanned, he should examine the conditions in 1965 very carefully. As we detailed earlier, the nation was approaching full employment in 1965 with inflationary pressures beginning to build and necessary Vietnam expenditures looming ahead. A deliberate decision was made to both increase Vietnam expenditures *and* maintain a high level of domestic spending with no unpopular tax hike planned. Federal deficits were clearly ahead, and it would be necessary for the Federal Reserve to monetize them. But the Federal Reserve was approaching the legal limits of debt creation. Therefore, the remaining gold-cover requirements were removed in March 1965. In the three years that followed, Federal Reserve credit rose by over 50 percent, and currency in circulation rose nearly 20 percent. Finally, in March 1968, the remaining 25 percent gold backing behind Federal Reserve notes in circulation was removed, making the dollar a full fiat currency and removing the last constraint on monetary inflation. There now exist no legal restraints on the overissue of either Federal Reserve credit or currency.

When one dwells upon these seemingly harmless removals of restraints, he runs the risk of being labeled a "gold bug" by today's sophisticated financial analysts. We will, instead of recommending gold stocks, merely leave this to the reader as one more indication of the underlying trends of inflation and debasement of the dollar (if one did not already surmise this from the massive dollar outflows of recent years). It is peculiar how, despite a sophisticated new banking philosophy that scoffs at traditional measures of banking liquidity, old economic laws stubbornly remain in force. One of the oldest is Gresham's law, named after Sir Thomas Gresham (1519-79). The law simply states that newly debased money will drive older and more valuable money out of circulation. People will hoard the old money and use new and less valuable money to pay their debts. The disbeliever in this law should ask himself where are all the old silver dollars, the silver Kennedy half-dollars, and all the other old silver coins. If gold were freely circulated in the United States, it too would soon disappear.

Future Inflation

It would indeed be pleasant to conclude than an end to the inflationary problems is near, but there is clearly no evidence to support such a conclusion. As long as there is so little recognition of the basic source of the problem and no structural and philosophical changes are evident, this story

154

cannot have a happy ending.

The end of the current inflation will not be signaled by reasonable labor-contract settlements within wage-control guidelines, as many hope, for labor is not primarily responsible for the inflationary trend. There would not be any inflationary wage settlements if the supply of money were not increased—increased money supply is a necessary condition for inflationary wage settlements. The growing militancy of organized labor will soon spread to unorganized labor. Labor organizing drives will be more successful in the years ahead. Only recently have the huge armies of government employees learned the power of the strike. As the inflation continues, paralyzing strikes of public employees will occur nationwide. Though this will all add to inflationary pressures, it is still only the effect and not the cause of inflation.

The problem is simply too much monetary growth and credit. Until there is a change in the government's machinery and philosophy for dealing with inflation, plus the will for a sustained effort, the problem will continue. As we have seen, the problem cannot be contained with monetary policy as long as government spending continues to rise. President Nixon was making a strong attempt to reverse the process of government spending, but it will require full cooperation over several terms to accomplish the solutions in an orderly manner. There is little evidence as yet that this is forthcoming.

Many feel that a reasonable amount of controlled inflation is possible and even desirable since people can adjust to it. This is simply not possible. No country has ever attempted to sustain a steady but moderate rate of inflation without it getting out of control. We have already demonstrated how continued inflation builds its own self-perpetuating secondary effects, which lead to a spiraling and accelerating inflation. We have shown how trends of declining liquidity have been accelerating, how volatility has been growing, and how the Federal Reserve is gradually losing all flexibility to use restrictive monetary policy. Every attempt to curb inflation through monetary policy will lead to increasingly serious credit crunches. Every crunch will require a larger dose of inflationary monetary expansion to turn it. Each such expansion will help to sustain the continuing trend of liquidity deterioration, which builds in an increasing potential for deflation. The inflation will only end when the trend of liquidity deterioration is ended. Considering the length of the trend, the end to the upward spiral in inflation will be followed by a period of deflation as a cumulative contraction of credit ensues and a search for liquidity occurs.

The government, the Federal Reserve, and the banking system have already demonstrated considerable innovative ability to keep the trends intact, and perhaps they will succeed for a while longer. However, because of the accelerating nature of the effects of their policies, it may be that their options are running out.

Interest Rates

A glance at the postwar history of interest rates, as depicted in Figure 11.2, leaves little doubt as to the direction of interest rates, the magnitude of the change since World War II, and the accelerating nature of the trend. The action of interest rates is perhaps the best indicator of the underlying decline of liquidity in the United States, for interest rates have historically correlated closely with all the measures of liquidity discussed.

Cause of Higher Interest Rates

The basic cause behind the postwar rise in interest rates is the continuing decline in liquidity among corporations and banks. This trend, and its secondary effects, has already been described in detail, but a brief review of its specific relationship with interest rates may be helpful.

Risk and Interest Rates

The most direct effect of declining liquidity is a rise in the level of risk in both individual securities and loans. This higher level of risk must be reflected in the level of interest rates and is, in a number of ways. Among corporations there are two different types of risk.

The first is the risk of default on the bonds or short-term loans of the individual corporation. The most important measure of this risk is found in the interest-coverage figures of the individual corporations. In the discussion of corporate liquidity in Chapters 5 and 6 we noted the dramatic and continuing decline in aggregate coverage ratios. These coverage ratios are the key factors used by financial rating services in identifying the level of risk in the securities of the individual corporation. The higher the level of risk, the lower the rating placed upon the security of the corporation. We also offered, as qualitative evidence of rising levels of risk, the increasing number of rating reductions in recent years by the financial services. The rising debt ratios among corporations, as well as the serious deterioration in the current section of the balance sheets, indicate growing levels of risk in the corporate sector.

The second risk in the corporate sector is related to the aggregate illiquidity that exists in the entire economy as a result of aggregate corporate illiquidity. Every period of extreme credit stringency, such as those in 1966 and in 1969-70, raises the risk of the entire economy tripping off into an extended period of spreading credit liquidation and a rush for liquidity, as occurred in the 1930s. As the trends in liquidity continue unabated, the probability of this happening becomes increasingly stronger. This risk, as indicated in Figure 11.2, must be reflected in a rising level of general interest rates.

There is also the growing risk in the banking system, which is reflected in higher interest rates. We have demonstrated that banking liquidity, by any measure, is at record lows. As liquidity for a bank declines, there is a heightened risk of sudden deposit withdrawals leading to unprofitable liquidation of loans or investments. This must be covered in the rate of interest charged by banks. As a secondary effect, the declining bank liquidity, combined with the aggressive new profit-maximization philosophy, has led to an aggressive search for deposits at any cost. With a resulting higher cost of money, banks

Percentage

Monthly Averages of Daily Figures

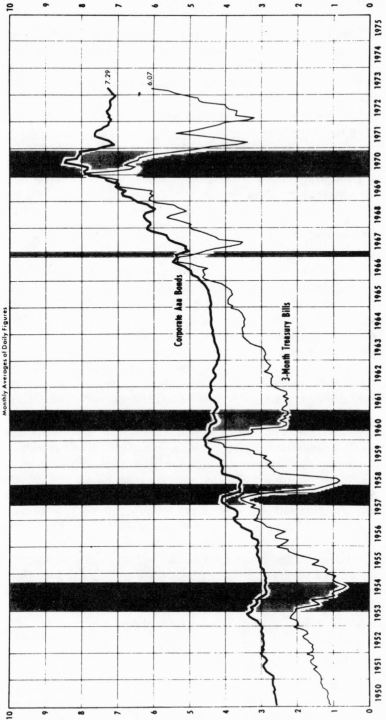

Corporate Aaa Bonds

3-Month Treasury Bills

7.29

6.07

Note: The shaded areas shown in 1953-54, 1957-58, 1960-61, and 1969-70 represent periods of business recessions as defined by the National Bureau of Economic Research. The shaded area in 1966-67 represents an "unofficial minirecession."
Latest data plotted: March estimated

Source: Federal Reserve Bank of St. Louis

Fig. 11.2—Interest Rates

have been forced to seek out higher-yielding and consequently less liquid investments, which include long-term municipal bonds and a loan portfolio that includes a much longer average maturity. This results in both higher risk investments and a policy of lending long but borrowing increasingly shorter. The more volatile sources of funds also run the risk of CD runoffs, as in 1966 and 1969. This obviously higher risk must also be recognized in higher interest returns on investments and loans.

The final aspect of risk that can be listed as a cause of the rising level of interest rates is the risk to portfolios that results from the growing volatility in both money and capital markets. This problem has been discussed at several points in this book, and will be treated in greater detail in the following section.

Cyclical Demand for Funds

A second cause of the rising interest-rate levels can be found in the cyclical demand for funds typical of every business expansion. In the heat of a business expansion, the demand for short-term funds usually gets temporarily out of balance with the supply. This, however, would not explain the new record-high interest rates in each expansion unless there has been a change in the nature of business expansions. This is certainly the case.

We have shown that the rate of credit expansion has accelerated in each succeeding postwar business expansion, which, all things being equal, should explain higher peak interest rates. We have also described how the low levels of corporate liquidity, particularly at the cyclical lows, left corporations entirely at the mercy of the capital markets when they rushed to fund their excessive short-term debt. The banking system also becomes increasingly illiquid during business expansions, which helps to make every credit crunch more serious and to intensify the scramble for funds by both banks and corporations. An excellent illustration of the growing intensity of each cyclical expansion of loan demand and the following crunch is found in Figure 11.2 It depicts the postwar record of the gap between short-term and long-term interest rates represented by Treasury bills and corporate Aaa bond yields. Normally, short-term rates rise relative to long-term rates during economic expansions and then fall to the more normal level well below long-term interest rates. It is fair to assume that the more intense the credit expansion, the narrower the spread will become at the peak before each recession. It is easy to see that in each succeeding business expansion the spread also reached a postwar high after the crunch of 1969-70, illustrating the growing volatility in capital and money markets.

Government Demand for Funds

Closely related to the cyclical corporate demand for funds is the need for government financing of deficits. We have remarked that increasingly larger doses of monetary expansion are needed with each credit squeeze. It is precisely at the same time that corporations, frightened by the credit squeeze, are rushing to the long-term capital markets, that the federal government is financing the deficits it incurred to reverse the economic contraction that resulted from the crunch. Just as corporations are rushing to the long end of the interest-rate market, lenders, concerned about inflation, rising interest rates, and consequent declining bond portfolios, are rushing out of the long end, causing extreme dislocations in the markets. Because both government deficits and corporate external-financing needs are growing, interest rates make new record highs at each peak.

The Inflation Premium

The final ingredient of rising interest rates is the premium added to interest rates, due to the rising rate of inflation, to compensate the lender for any losses of capital due to depreciation of the dollar. Considerable empirical evidence compiled by monetarists substantiates this phenomenon. Since we have concluded that inflation will continue to be a companion to the liquidity trends we have discussed, a brief explanation of the relationship between inflation and interest rates is in order.

Monetarists generally feel that changes in the supply of money affect interest rates in three ways: The first reaction is called the *liquidity effect* because the increase in money supply causes the individual to have larger cash balances (liquidity) than he desires—assuming that the amount he held prior to the change was just sufficient to meet his everyday cash needs. He will then reduce his cash balance by either spending it or purchasing financial assets, which has the effect of lowering interest rates in the very short term. The effect does not stop here, however, for within less than a year the increase in money supply will have induced a rise in income. Rising income increases the demand for money and credit, which begins to move interest rates back up until they reach higher levels than those before the injection of additional money. This is called the *income effect*. Finally, after another short lag, the rising income leads to inflation as full employment is reached. If people expect the inflation to continue, the rate of inflation is added to interest rates, causing a further rise. Thus, by this theory, there are two parts to each interest rate: the "natural" rate of interest, which is determined by the forces of supply and demand and is relatively stable, and a premium equal to the expected rate of inflation. For example, if the natural rate of interest for corporate Aaa bonds happens to be 4 percent and the expected rate of inflation is 3 percent, lenders will ask for a rate of 7 percent to compensate them for any expected loss of purchasing power. Is this so much different from the wage demands of organized labor in periods of inflation?

A number of interesting monetarist studies of the 1960s demonstrate the structural changes and dislocations that result from an extended period of inflation and excessive credit creation. Investors act in one way when the nation experiences only short and periodic bouts with inflation followed by periods of stability. They act in quite a different way when inflation stubbornly persists. Inflation expectations become fully absorbed into their investment thinking. Several empirical studies concluded that the inflation premium accounted for almost all of the increase in interest rates during the 1960s, while another found that the time lag in adjusting interest rates to the change in rates of inflation was considerably shortened. This conclusion could have been reached intuitively, for it is quite similar to the labor-negotiation situation discussed above. Once someone becomes aware that his real return, or his real wage, is declining in spite of the seeming prosperity, and once he learns how to protect himself, it would be illogical, in the light of the long inflation the nation has suffered, to assume that he would not become increasingly alert to changes in prices. This simply demonstrates once again that the longer the inflation is allowed to persist, the more difficult it will be to contain it, even if the true causes are finally recognized. The extremely low levels of liquidity in the economy constitute one of the chief obstacles to containing the inflation. Such institutional changes as the much improved flow of information on economic statistics and conditions also help to shorten the lags. Because of the persistent nature of the inflation and the growing volatility in the capital and stock markets, the news media have also become much more aware of economic and financial terms and help to publicize the news more than in previous times. The lower liquidity, higher risk, and greater volatility all make it necessary for the investor to move quickly, thus shortening all lags.

Conclusions

From the preceding discussion, it is easy to see that the postwar rise in interest rates stems, in one way or another, from the underlying trends in liquidity and the money-creation process that allows them to continue. The rising interest rates are both a major effect of these trends as well as the best indicator of the progress of the trends. Admittedly, it is difficult to discuss any of the major effects of the liquidity trends separately, as we are doing in this chapter, without also touching upon the others. The rising level of risk in the economy, for example, is a major determinant of interest rates; nonetheless, we will treat this subject separately in Chapter 12.

We have attempted to show that there are strong interrelationships among the effects, and that each major effect leads to other problems. The final results may be lower capital expansion, growth, and productivity. We must not lose sight of the fact, however, that all the problems emanate from a common cause.

Future Prospects for Interest Rates

There is little doubt as to the direction interest rates will take if the underlying liquidity trends remain in force. The long-term bear market in bonds is not over. We will continue to see periodic credit crunches, and new highs will be made for all interest rates. The volatility of capital and money markets will become greater with each crunch as the Federal Reserve is forced to supply more reserves each time to reverse the contraction. Each crunch will be featured by larger amounts of loan liquidations because government securities will not be available to meet requirements. Municipal-bond markets will suffer larger declines since banks will be forced to sell into this illiquid market, which will be made worse by liquidation of dealer loans from banks, which are callable on demand and the first loans to be liquidated. Between the crunches, the troughs of interest rates will remain high due to the increasing inflation premium that will be added and also to reflect the rising level of risk and lower ratings. The gap between corporate Aaa bonds and corporate Baa bonds will continue to widen as the most illiquid firms find it increasingly difficult to find financing. More demand will be placed on short-term financing as investment and speculative horizons are shortened. Finally, one of the credit contractions will get out of control, and the trends will be reversed—but at considerable cost.

Volatility and Risk

The rising volatility described in this book has many implications. It is certainly one of the major effects of the long-standing decline in liquidity and, therefore, is also a good indicator of the trend. We have already examined the role of rising levels of risk in the trend of rising interest rates from the point of view of higher risk of default among individual corporations and the overall risk of a total financial collapse as the accumulated debt is liquidated and a search for liquidity follows. We touched only briefly upon the role of greater volatility in the level of risk. This we would like to rectify now.

Evidence of Volatility

Even a casual reading of the financial and economic news of recent years would uncover a considerable amount of surface evidence of growing volatility. It would be very difficult not to notice the wild gyrations of recent years in the bond and stock markets, the news-making credit crunches and Penn Central failure, the gigantic international speculative dollar flows, and the history-making devaluations and floats of the dollar. Upon closer examination, the wildly fluctuating spread between short- and long-term rates mentioned in a previous section lends some documentation to the volatility. The deposit-turnover data given in a previous chapter is further confirming evidence of the hectic pace that is developing in money markets. The turnover figures for New York continue to show a steadily accelerating trend upward.

The frantic nature of the search among banks, which was detailed in Chapter 3, gives the reader some notion of the reasons behind the growing volatility. With two credit crunches still fresh in their minds, every suspected movement by the Federal Reserve toward tightening of the money supply is greeted by extreme nervousness among all money managers. With the low levels of liquidity, the reaction time must be quicker than ever. In Table 11.1 we present a record of the behavior of interest rates during each official postwar recession. The periods covered include the months of the official recession plus an additional year before and after. We have measured the change in "basis points" for both triple-A corporate bonds and Treasury-bill rates for new issues from the beginning yield for each period to the high rate

161

TABLE 11.1

Interest-Rate Volatility

[1] Recessionary Period	Basis Point Corporate Aaa	Fluctuation Treasury Bills	Change in Bank Credit (Percentage)
1948-49	9	41	9.1
1953-54	45	41	13.8
1957-58	95	126	15.5
1960-61	21	172	14.8
1969-70	229	241	25.7

[1] Actual Periods Used

Nov. 1947-Oct. 1950	May 1959-Feb. 1962
July 1952-Aug. 1955	Nov. 1968-Nov. 1971
July 1956-Apr. 1959	

reached within each period. The results show growing volatility in each period, with the final recessionary period of 1969-70 demonstrating the largest fluctuation in rates for the entire postwar period.

As of this writing, we have not suffered another recession or credit crunch since 1970. We have demonstrated, however, that the credit expansion following the last credit crunch set another postwar record and that the liquidity trends are still intact. One would expect even greater volatility, therefore, at the next credit crunch. A glance at Table 11.2 will show that we need not wait that long. In the latest full year available at the time of this writing, it can be seen that record movements have already been recorded in every measure of short-term interest rates in only one year, as compared to the three years required to set the last record upward fluctuation. We can only wonder what the new record will be when the cyclical peak is finally made.

Ramifications of Growing Volatility and Risk

Like the other major effects of the liquidity trends, the growing volatility, and the added risk it entails, permeates the entire economy, leading to many other secondary effects. Many of these effects may seem so far removed from the primary causes that the connection is not recognized. This, of course, makes the identification of the major problems more difficult.

The Performance Cult

One such side-effect of volatility is the growing concentration of institutional investors upon the very short term. The higher levels of risk resulting from growing volatility explain a large part of this fascination for short-term per-

TABLE 11.2

Money Market Volatility

	Interest Rates		
	Week Ending 3/23/73	**Week Ending 3/14/72**	**Change in Basis Points**
Treasury Bills, 90 days	6.26	3.81	245
Federal Funds	7.13	3.93	320
Eurodollars, 90 days	8.63	5.61	301
CDs, 30-59 days	6¾-7	3¾-3⅞	300-313
Commercial Paper, 30-59 days	6¾	3¾	300
Treasury Bills, 180 days	6.66	4.27	239

formance. Whenever the level of risk is high, time horizons for investment and speculation are short. The same process of investment selection that leads foreign investors in underdeveloped and politically unstable countries to insist upon short payoff periods for their investments, applies to purchasing a stock or a bond in the organized markets of the United States. If volatility of interest rates is growing, possibilities of large bond-portfolio losses are greater and time horizons become shorter. Qualitative evidence of this phenomenon is the growing popularity of *bond* trading among financial institutions, as opposed to the former preoccupation with simply buying and holding to maturity. The entire process leads to much more aggressive management of portfolios, which, of course, further adds to the volatility.

Interest-Rate Spreads

Another indication of the growing risk in the economy is the spread between high-quality and lower-quality bonds. Whether it is the risk from low liquidity levels or that resulting from volatility, the tendency for investors to seek out the higher-quality investments will continue to grow. If the volatility is great enough on high-quality bonds to successfully trade, why should the investor be satisfied with lower-quality bonds where the added risk of default is evident? This feeling should be manifested in a steadily widening spread between lower-quality and higher-quality bonds. Table 11.3 indicates that this has been the situation. Although the long-term trend is not smoothly in one direction, it is not coincidental that in recent years the spread has been at its highest.

During periods of financial constraint, the interest rates on the lowest-rated bonds rise the most. When funds are extremely tight and rationing is necessary, it is always the least creditworthy who are refused loans. Here we see another reason why the financial stimulation the Federal Reserve must exercise to alleviate credit squeezes becomes greater with each credit crunch. As the inexorable process of liquidity deterioration relegates more firms to the undesirable-credit-risk category, and as banking liquidity becomes worse, the difficulty of getting the necessary funds to those who need them the most increases. In a similar light, the fiscal policy of a tax cut is also fine, but it too does not help the firm that has no profits.

The interest-rate spreads recorded in Table 11.3 reflect this problem. In each period of credit stringency during the postwar years the spread rose substantially. In 1970, the spread moved past 100 basis points for the first time, reflecting the perceived credit risk in the markets of that year. Over eighteen months after the bottom of the credit crunch of 1970 the spread set a new postwar high.

Other Implications of Rising Volatility

The rising volatility of interest rates has implications beyond the increased risk of bond-portfolio losses. Since the stock market represents alternative investments, there is some level of interest rates that makes bonds more attractive than common stocks on the long-term total-return basis. Indeed, a University of Chicago study demonstrated that the long-term return on common stocks has proven to be roughly 9 percent. Thus, the greater risk and volatility in bond and money markets is translated to the stock market. Many institutional investors attribute much of the 1970 bear market in stocks to higher interest-rate levels of alternative fixed-income investments.

The volatility in interest rates is also translated, through disintermediation, to dislocations in the rate of savings in banks, savings and loan associations, and other financial institutions. Since the availability of mortgage money is the most important variable in the level of building expenditures, the fluctuations in savings flow in savings and loans, caused by the volatility of interest rates, lead to sizable cyclicality in one of the largest industries in the country. So we see that the implications of rising volatility extend well beyond the capital and stock markets. It is not totally unlikely that this entire process of increasing risk and volatility, coupled with declining corporate profits, will lead to a relatively lower level of capital formation in the long run. We will examine this possibility in the next section.

Future Prospects

Since the origins of the growing volatility described above are the same as those for the other effects of inflation, interest rates and risk, the same discouraging predictions must also be made for volatility trends. Unless there is some slowing in the rate of credit creation, we will witness even greater volatility in the future. The record so far is not encouraging, as we have demonstrated throughout this book. For example, bank credit has not declined in any year during the entire postwar period, and more importantly, increases

TABLE 11.3

Spread Between Aaa & Baa Corporate Bonds

Year	Corporate Bonds Aaa	Corporate Bonds Baa	Spread
1947	2.61	3.24	0.63
1948	2.82	3.47	0.65
1949	2.66	3.42	0.76
1950	2.62	3.24	0.62
1951	2.86	3.41	0.55
1952	2.96	3.52	0.56
1953	3.20	3.74	0.54
1954	2.90	3.51	0.61
1955	3.06	3.53	0.47
1956	3.36	3.88	0.52
1957	3.89	4.71	0.82
1958	3.79	4.73	0.94
1959	4.38	5.05	0.67
1960	4.41	5.19	0.78
1961	4.35	5.08	0.73
1962	4.33	5.02	0.69
1963	4.26	4.86	0.60
1964	4.40	4.83	0.43
1965	4.49	4.87	0.38
1966	5.13	5.67	0.54
1967	5.51	6.23	0.72
1968	6.18	6.94	0.76
1969	7.03	7.81	0.78
1970	8.04	9.10	1.06
1971	7.39	8.56	1.17
1972	7.08	7.93	0.85

Source: *Moody's Investors Service.*

have become larger in recent years. Even if bank credit were slowed, there is no guarantee that total credit creation would also slow immediately, for the credit ethic is well entrenched. Table 11.4 summarizes the entire credit picture. Debt creation has been growing at well over twice the growth of production of real goods and services. When the trend is broken down into subperiods, a steady acceleration is evident. The problem is getting worse, not better. It must be noted that the rapid gains of recent years are percentage changes on top of a base that has been growing rapidly for the entire postwar

TABLE 11.4

Comparative Average Growth Records
(Percentage)

A. 1949-71

GNP (constant dollars)	3.8
Total bank credit	6.9
Total net public & private debt	7.3
Total private debt	9.7
Total corporate debt	9.7
Total individual & noncorporate debt	9.9

B.	1949-60	1960-71	1965-71
GNP (constant dollars)	3.80	3.85	3.0
Total bank credit	4.6	8.6	16.4
Money Supply (M$_2$)	3.3	7.6	8.1

Source:
Survey of Current Business, U.S. Dept. of Commerce.
Business Statistics, 1971, U.S. Dept. of Commerce.

period. Despite the rapid acceleration of credit, the growth in production of real goods has been stable. The result must be continued inflation, rising volatility, and increasingly serious credit crunches each time the government attempts to halt the trend.

Capital Formation and Productivity

The major effects of the postwar liquidity trends discussed so far have been quite direct and easy to see. We have shown how the several major effects are not only interrelated and self-enforcing but also lead to many secondary effects, such as increased labor militancy. Still other important effects may be traced to the liquidity trends, although the connections are not as clear and other causative factors exist as well. It is these effects to which this section is devoted.

Capital Formation

Many different factors enter into the corporate decision to add to productive capacity. Many of these factors are directly or indirectly related to the financial trends already discussed.

Profits

Rising capital expenditures have always been considered a reliable lagging-economic indicator for the simple reason that businessmen always respond strongly to profit levels. Rising profits and profit margins have always emboldened business to expand in order to gain an even larger share of the market. Consequently, just when interest costs are the highest and the business expansion is mature, competitive-capacity building occurs. When profits have been declining and building costs are lower, capital expenditures are at their low. We have already demonstrated that profit margins and returns on equity for corporations have been in a decided downtrend throughout the postwar period. Growing corporate illiquidity has played a major role in this decline in profitability, for reasons that we have already discussed. Illiquid firms generally suffer under heavy debt-service loads, which have grown worse in recent years with rising interest rates. With heavy debt loads and management preoccupation with financing problems, firms move from one crisis to another. They fall prey to militant unions and suffer higher wage costs. They have little time for long-range planning and competitive capital expansion. As a result, they lose both domestic and international market share.

Rising Tax Levels

Rising levels of corporate taxation, particularly on the local level, are also deleterious to capital spending in several ways. Since business is never able to completely pass on all higher costs, rising taxes must be considered as one more cost and therefore an additional pressure upon corporate profit margins. Declining aftertax returns should also, all things being equal, lead to lower incentives to commit capital to marginal plant additions. Inflation is also a hidden tax upon all of us that must somehow be included with the already rising tax rates. To the illiquid corporation, which already has trouble remaining price-competitive, inflation becomes ruinous. It is a pressure upon the margins of all corporations as it results in higher wage and material costs that cannot always be fully passed on. The illiquid firm is least able to pass along the costs. Thus, through its effect upon profit margins and upon general incentive levels, the increased tax burden of corporations should result in lower levels of capital expenditures.

Risk-Reward Ratios

Basic to any decision to invest is a comparison of the potential return to the cost and the risk of loss. We have demonstrated a combination of postwar developments that should make it obvious that the risk-reward ratios of capital investment have tipped strongly to the unfavorable side. Rates of return on investment have generally declined over the entire postwar period, while levels of risk are strongly rising. Highly leveraged firms have the additional risk of being increasingly vulnerable to adverse swings in the business cycle as well as to other crises. Volatility in capital and stock markets adds considerably to the risk and uncertainty, while periodic credit crunches leave firms uncertain as to future bank lines of credit to see them through liquidity problems. Add to this the continually rising cost of borrowed funds, which must enter into the investment equation, and the overall incentives for capital formation are greatly reduced.

Wage and price controls, which are a direct result of inflationary pressures and an indirect result of the trends in liquidity, add another strong note of uncertainty to the investment equation. Since controls also indicate the increasing encroachment of the government sector upon the private sector, they represent a further disincentive to invest on the part of business and individuals alike.

International Competition

In a world that is growing smaller by the year, the adverse financial trends described here cannot be considered as simply a domestic problem of the corporate sector. Growing illiquidity, inflation, and the rising power of unions and government all work to the disadvantage of U.S. corporations. Without engaging in a lengthy discussion of international economics, we can simply offer the performance of the dollar in recent years as a test of the success of our domestic financial policies.

To add to the corporate woes, neither the tax rate nor the manner in which corporations are taxed encourages capital investment. The value-added tax, used widely overseas, generally allows purchases of new capital equipment to be exempted from the tax, which is the same as allowing the full cost of the capital to be deducted in the first year. Other laws are generally unfavorable to capital formation, as compared with other industrialized countries. Treasury Department estimates showing the cost of acquiring new plant and equipment in the United States and other countries in 1970 appear in Table 11.5. For every $1 of cost for a new plant or new capital equipment to a U.S. firm, a foreign manufacturer's cost would have been that given in the table. The table clearly shows the disadvantage suffered by U.S. corporations in the ultimate cost of their products. It also points out the reasons for overseas investment by U.S. firms. Even this method of avoiding the disadvantage has been diminished by the two interim devaluations of the dollar.

The figures in Table 11.5 do not take into consideration the growing proportion of every dollar of domestic capital spending that must be devoted to pollution abatement. Because this expenditure results in no additional product or efficiency, it reduces the overall return on invested capital even though much of the additional cost can be passed along to the final consumer. McGraw-Hill estimated that in 1971 manufacturers allocated nearly 8 percent of their capital budgets to air- and water-pollution controls. The percentage will probably rise in future years.

Evidence of Deficient Capital Formation

So far we have given a number of reasons why capital formation can be expected to be lower, as a result of the postwar financial trends, than it might otherwise have been. It is difficult to say exactly what would be the ideal rate of capital growth or what would be sufficient. Table 11.5 gives the report card for

TABLE 11.5

Capital Formation

**Cost of New Plant and Equipment Relative to
Each One Dollar of Cost for a U.S. Corporation, 1970**

Canada	$0.97
Netherlands	0.94
France	0.90
Belgium	0.85
Sweden	0.83
West Germany	0.83
Italy	0.82
Japan	0.81
United Kingdom	0.79

Capital Investment as Percentage of GNP, 1960-69

Japan	27
Netherlands	20
Germany	20
Sweden	18
France	18
Italy	14
United Kingdom	14
United States	13

the United States relative to other major industrialized countries for the years 1960-69. The results are anything but encouraging. Since the period covered begins fifteen years after the end of World War II, the excuse that other countries were replacing capital destroyed by the ravages of the war cannot be used. Nor can the excuse be used that the U.S. GNP grew faster than that of the other countries, for this is not the case. The evidence clearly suggests that capital formation in the United States has not been keeping pace with the growth of the economy, confirming what one might intuitively conclude from the incentive-reducing trends enumerated above.

Thus, we see an example of one more adverse circular, or self-enforcing, trend in the United States. Inflation and liquidity deterioration, and their secondary effects, help to reduce the level of capital formation. The lower rate of capital formation reduces the level of goods that might have helped to reduce inflation. Higher capital investment would also have produced greater gains in productivity, which would have been extremely helpful in slowing inflationary pressures.

Productivity

Until the trends of government spending and liquidity deterioration can be reversed, one of the best hopes for bringing inflation under control without inducing an uncontrollable credit liquidation rests with rapid productivity gains. Real incomes can only be raised by increasing the quantity of goods and services produced by a given labor force. As noted above, one of the primary sources of productivity gains, capital investment, is sadly deficient. Additionally, the invisible and confiscatory tax of inflation falls most heavily upon the workers of the middle class, who contribute most to the productivity of the nation.

The Postwar Record

As one might have predicted on the basis of the capital-formation trends discussed above, the trends in productivity have been equally disappointing. The record of productivity gains for the years 1965-70 is presented in Table 11.6. In a comparison of productivity gains for some major industrial countries, including several that were examined in Table 11.5 for capital formation, the United States finished in the same position. In fact, there is a remarkable correlation between capital-formation trends and productivity trends. The productivity record for the United States for the entire postwar period is presented in Table 11.6, and the trend is equally dismal. Productivity gains have become progressively lower throughout the postwar years, paralleling the deteriorating financial trends with their deleterious effects upon capital formation. Although

TABLE 11.6

PRODUCTIVITY

Output Per Man-Hour Yearly Gain, 1965-1970

Japan	14.2%
Netherlands	8.5
Sweden	7.9
France	6.6
Germany	5.3
Italy	5.1
United Kingdom	3.6
United States	2.1

Output Per Man-Hour Increase U.S.

1948-1955	3.11
1955-1965	2.51
1965-1970	2.1
1968-1970	0.8

capital formation has a major effect upon productivity, a number of other factors also play a role. A full discussion of all the determinants of productivity and the influence of liquidity trends upon them should prove quite enlightening.

Sources of Productivity Growth

Underlying both capital formation and productivity is the basic profitability of the corporate sector. Continuing additions to the nation's stock of capital and efficiency gains simply do not come, in the long run, from unhealthy companies. Total corporate profits, as a percentage of total gross corporate product, have deteriorated over the entire postwar period, with a new low being made at 10 percent in 1970. This compares to an average of nearly 16 percent for the 1960s and close to an 18 percent average for the 1950s. In addition to this declining return on capital, we have already indicated the record of deteriorating profit margins of manufacturing firms. Since, as we have demonstrated, the twin effects of declining liquidity and inflation have had a major impact upon corporate profits, we can say that these trends also contribute to the disappointing productivity record.

On the other hand, productivity is also an important contributor to corporate profits, since unit-labor costs are basic to the profitability of the firm. To the extent that compensation per man-hour is allowed to grow at a greater rate than output per man-hour (productivity), unit-labor costs will rise. To the extent that rising unit-labor costs cannot be completely offset by rising prices, profits will decline. Thus, to reverse the decline in profits, corporations must either stem the rise in compensation per man-hour or accelerate the rise in productivity. We have already seen how the interrelated effects of inflation and declining liquidity have influenced the growing militancy of labor. Other factors, such as the rising minimum wage, which places a rising floor under wages, also contribute to the growing inability of corporations to resist rising wage demands. Therefore, the task of reducing the very critical unit-labor cost falls heavily upon increasing the output per man-hour. Let us see how good the chances are of accomplishing this task. That is, what are the sources of productivity improvement?

The level of labor skills, or changes in the quality of labor, is one important source of productivity improvement. The shift in the mix of the labor force in the direction of more youth and women is a negative factor here. At least one reason for the increased participation in the work force by women is the much lower liquidity among individuals and families, for individuals in the postwar period, though we have not discussed this in detail, have acted in substantially the same way as banks and corporations. The liquidity of the individual has deteriorated considerably over the same years and due to the same stimulus. The growing restrictiveness of trade unions has also served as a limiting factor in this source of productivity gains.

Changes in the state of technology are also important determinants of productivity changes. Meaningful improvements in techniques and technology can lead to a much more efficient use of labor input. Once again, the prospects are not good, for there has been a pronounced slowdown in research-and-development spending. With the reduction in such spending, the hope for significant ad-

171

vances in the knowledge needed for the development of new production techniques is considerably dimmed.

We have already mentioned that total capital investment, or the real value of capital employed per worker, is one of the best hopes for improving productivity. We have also seen the disappointing record of capital formation.

The availability of resources, including labor, and the extent to which they are fully and efficiently utilized, is also a significant element in productivity progress. With the exception, perhaps, of farm products, there seems to be little cheering news as to improving availability of resources. The energy crisis is but one example, though the most dramatic, of the growing dependence of the United States upon outside sources of raw materials. As to the efficient utilization of our human resources, there are also several disturbing problems. The restrictiveness of labor unions has greatly impeded the growth of a skilled labor force while at the same time extorting huge relative wage gains that add to inflationary pressures. The minimum wage limits the entry of unskilled workers into fields of gainful employment. Finally, there has been scant progress in improvement of labor mobility and organized retraining programs. Thus, there is little evidence that improvements in future productivity will come from this source.

A final category of sources of productivity growth is much less susceptible to accurate measurement. It includes all the sociological, political, and cultural factors that form the overall climate of the economy. It would be almost impossible to list all of these ingredients, but a few unfavorable ones definitely stand out. There seems to have been a definite change in the work ethic of this nation, as evidenced by the many "dropouts" from the system, the discontent with assembly-line work, the decline in pride of workmanship, and other manifestations of disenchantment with work. We have mentioned the higher levels of taxation and the greater percentage of each dollar being spent by the government as sources of declining incentives to produce or to take financial risks. This may also be a partial explanation of the growing disenchantment of small investors for stock investment and speculation. The effects of increasing government controls must also be factored in as an explanation of declining incentives. Finally, there is little argument that the nation is rapidly growing into a service-oriented economy, in which improvements in productivity are naturally much more difficult to effect than in a production-dominated economy.

As we reflect on the ingredients of productivity growth mentioned above, there seems to be little basis for predictions of a reversal in the productivity downtrend that has been in effect throughout the postwar years. In fact, there is considerable evidence to support an expectation of steadily worsening productivity gains. Since improvements in productivity are a key to containing inflation, there is little hope for an early solution to our inflationary pressures, at least from this source.

Conclusions

We have attempted in this chapter to separate the causes of our postwar financial problems from their major and secondary effects, which, by confusing the issue, serve to divert attention from the real problems and thus to forestall their solution. We have also tried to show that once the major effects have been set into motion, they tend to interact to form a self-sustaining momentum of their own, making the solution even more difficult. Finally, we have attempted to briefly assess the future direction of the trends that have been set into motion.

We have seen that the basic and underlying cause is the continuing overextension of credit, which has led to a growing illiquidity that permeates the entire economy. Though the liquidity trends have a momentum all their own, they have been sustained and extended by the actions of the federal government and the Federal Reserve, which have inhibited the natural correction of the trends by their own inherent deflationary buildup.

The interaction of these three major forces has led in turn, to the major trends in inflation, rising interest rates, rising levels of risk, and volatility. These effects continue to interact over the years and lead to lower capital formation and declining rates of productivity improvement, as well as to many more less measurable effects, such as declining incentives, labor discontent, and various institutional changes.

Once we can successfully differentiate the true causes of our problems from the effects, we should be in a much better position to determine whether the government's policies are offering true solutions or merely palliatives that will only serve to extend the trends. The longer the true solutions are avoided, the more painful will be the final resolution. If the basic causes are not attacked, the ill effects that we have described in this chapter will continue to worsen in an accelerating fashion, and you should prepare yourself for them. From the assessment of the future prospects of each of these effects individually, there seems little doubt that they will continue to worsen without any improvement in the underlying causes. Because of their own momentum, there is even a question of whether a mild slowdown in the rate of credit growth will be enough to reverse the trends. In Chapters 12 and 13 we attempt to put it all together and to assess the future prospects for the economy and for investments.

Chapter 12

Update 1980

As we reflect back over the span of nearly six years since the publication of the first eleven chapters, it is incredible and just a little frightening to realize how little our government policy-makers have learned. They are still making most of the same predictable mistakes and the nation is still suffering from the same equally predictable adverse effects. The only difference is that they are becoming increasingly painful.

Trends and Cycles

What have we learned in the interim? Our assumption that the government would not willingly change its spots proved to be valid. Our other assumption that, in the absence of such change, economic conditions will steadily worsen was also confirmed. In fact, this is almost axiomatic, so there is little predictive skill involved.

The underlying long-term trends of excessive government spending and credit creation that we documented earlier are still very much in force. The growth of both, in fact, has even accelerated. The resulting steady financial deterioration in all sectors of the economy—banking, nonfinancial corporations, and consumers—has continued. The inevitable adverse effects that must accompany these trends—price inflation, rising interest rates, declining productivity, volatility, and growing risk—have also predictably worsened.

We described earlier how these long-term trends did not proceed in a smooth manner but came, instead, in waves, each wave worse than the preceding ones. In fact, the last few years have clearly confirmed a well-defined and highly predictable credit cycle. The cycle starts with accelerating credit growth and financial deterioration accompanied by rising prices, interest rates, and volatility. This is followed by a credit crunch as the last of the liquidity is rationed out, and then by a recession. Consequently, prices and interest rates recede as private credit is liquidated, and balance sheets are temporarily improved as we move down toward the trough of the cycle. The government, however, never allows the economy to completely restore the balance sheets. Afraid of a serious credit collapse, the government invariably reinflates the economy and sets the stage for the next cycle. Because distortions always remain from the previous cycle, it requires more new credit each cycle for the economy to recover.

Thus, we are left with a series of steadily worsening credit cycles. Each credit expansion is greater and each recession is more severe, including more bank failures, more loan losses, and more bankruptcies. We also have successively higher peak and trough rates of inflation and interest rates. Since the first edition, this pattern has been confirmed by new cyclical peaks in 1974, higher trough rates in the following period, and still new higher postwar peaks as this is written.

So, the overall picture has continued to darken over the past six years. As we now update each step in the process of economic deterioration in each sector, the picture is also the same. Most of the important statistics from the original work have been updated here, so the reader may update our tables. Not every number has been brought up to the present but, rest assured, our situation has continued to deteriorate by every measure.

The Government Sector

The growth of government spending—the first step on our way to trouble— has continued to accelerate since 1974. Happily, our earlier criticism of Keynesian economics has become a much more widely held view in the intervening years. Unfortunately, there is still little agreement yet as to a theory to take its place. Consequently, the Employment Act of 1946 is still the law of the land for government policy-making. The economic ideas underlying the Great Society are defunct but the institutions created during that time still require financing and, like all bureaucracies, continue to grow on their own.

Total Government Spending

The growth of overall federal spending has compounded at an annual rate of over 11 percent from 1972 through 1979. This is higher than the excessive growth of 10.5 percent from 1965–1972, indicated in Table 8.3, which set the stage for the previous inflationary surge and bust of 1974–1975. The story is told even more clearly by the comparative accumulated federal deficits of the two periods. During each of the postwar recessions the government, unwilling to resist the political pressures to restimulate the economy, has laid the groundwork for the following private credit expansion. In the five years preceding the publication of our original edition, the accumulated federal deficit (1970–1974) was approximately $78 billion. The result was a record credit expansion, balance sheet deterioration, inflation, interest rate surge, and credit crunch. In the five years since (1975–1979),

176

the accumulated federal budget deficit has been approximately $235 billion. Not coincidentally, we have again witnessed new postwar records in all the same measures.

The Growing Government Influence

The greater the proportion of the Gross National Product represented by government spending, the greater the proclivity for price inflation and all the other deleterious conditions it creates. The prospects for the efficient operation of the free market, as well as for personal individual freedom, are equally bad. Concern was expressed in Chapter 8 with the steady growth of government from 10 percent of the GNP in 1929 to 33 percent in 1972, the last year of our Table 8.1. The record since that time is displayed below:

TABLE 12.1

Government Spending as a Percentage of GNP

1973	34.0%
1974	35.5%
1975	38.4%
1976	37.0%
1977	36.4%
1978	36.0%
1979	37.0%
1980	40.0% Est.

The proportion of government spending has thus been showing the same uneven growth. It leaps in each recession but never quite recedes to the previous level before the recession. Our estimate for 1980 is based upon an expectation of a serious recession in that year.

A Government Budget Still Out of Control

In the first edition, despair was expressed that the federal budget could not politically be brought under control notwithstanding any good intentions. At that time, nearly 75 percent of the budget was considered uncontrollable. It was not the Vietnam War, as many thought at the time, that was the cause of the burgeoning government deficits. It was the War on Poverty plus the extension of the New Deal, the Fair Deal, and all the other Welfare State–Big Brother schemes. This politically charged spending, once commenced, is impossible to stop. These "transfer payments" represented the fastest growing segment of the budget. From 1966–1972, they grew at the astronomical rate of 15 percent, or nearly four times the ability of the economy to increase its production of real goods and services. Such spending has accelerated still further in recent years, growing at an annual rate of 17.1 percent from 1972–1978. The data from Table 8.7 are updated in the table below:

TABLE 12.2

Federal Transfer
Payments

(In Billions of Dollars)

1973	118.9
1974	140.8
1975	176.8
1976	192.8
1977	208.8
1978	226.0

One can easily see the inexorable climb of such spending. Each recession brings a great leap forward but no receding afterward. Few legislators have the political courage to vote against such spending even when it's no longer needed. The Social Security System, for example, is trillions of dollars underfunded, using the same rules that the government so stringently applies against private pension plans. Even using the unrealistic actuarial assumptions of the federal government regarding future inflation, birthrates, and growth in the real wage, there is no way the government can make good on its promises of future benefits short of hyperinflation and a complete destruction of private savings. Yet, benefits have been steadily increased since 1974 to the extent that Social Security benefit recipients have been one of the few groups who have kept ahead of inflation.

Even a much less controversial segment of the budget, the interest payments on the government debt, illustrates further the growing uncontrollability of the budget. Look at the figures on the next page, which bring the rest of Table 8.7 up to date.

Here one can see the worsening pattern of the budget as the growth of the debt service of the government has doubled since our last edition. It also demonstrates one of the many self-enforcing aspects of our problems. The growth of government debt and its financing raises the level of interest rates. They, in turn, raise the cost of servicing the debt, necessitating even more debt. And so it goes.

TABLE 12.3

Net Interest Paid on
the Federal Debt

(In Billions of Dollars)

1972	14.6
1973	18.2
1974	20.9
1975	23.3
1976	27.2
1977	29.1
1978	35.5

This review of government spending is sufficient evidence to see that the very root cause of our economic ills has not improved, but has, instead, worsened. For further indications, one can examine the accelerating defense budget, the creation of several new giant government agencies over the past few years, burgeoning growth-killing government regulation at all levels, and expansion of government presence at the federal, state, and local levels. We could almost stop our update of the thesis of the coming credit collapse right here. Until this fundamental flaw in our economic system is addressed, it is easy to predict a continuation of all the economic problems we listed over six years ago.

The Federal Reserve

Have we seen any encouraging news at the Federal Reserve, the partner-in-crime of the government in the inflation process? Monetary targets were set by the Federal Reserve since our first edition, but the money supply has grown even faster. Each new Fed chief talks about fighting inflation but keeps the printing presses going. More recently, the Fed announced that it would begin to manage the money supply directly instead of concentrating on interest rates. Monetarists were elated and immediately declared the War on Inflation to be ended. Though this should allow the Fed to come closer to its monetary targets in the short run, it says nothing about what those targets will be. The reader must continue to remind himself just how deeply embedded our problems are and that minor palliatives or changes in procedures will not change things much. Remember the new Congressional budget procedure enacted in 1976? Supposedly it too would make the Congress more efficient in controlling spending and holding down taxes. Since that time, the overall tax burden has risen three full percentage points.

No, neither the government nor the "independent" Federal Reserve has changed. Government intervention is greater than ever and even more difficult to bring under control. So, the first step in the process has not changed over the past six years.

Credit Update

The next step in the inflation process is the translation of the government deficits into money and credit—the monetization of the federal debt. The uneven spread of this excessive credit creation throughout the economy is the cause of most of the economic distortions the country has suffered. Since the basic cause of our adverse financial trends has continued unabated since our first edition, we should expect the credit creation process to also have intensified. Indeed, this has been the case. A glance at the table below will confirm this:

TABLE 12.4

Growth Rates

	Federal Reserve Credit	Monetary Base	M_1
1969–1972	7.9%	6.9%	5.8%
1972–1975	9.3%	8.4%	5.8%
1975–1978	9.6%	8.7%	6.8%
1977–1978	11.2%	9.4%	7.8%

A brief review of the process by which federal deficits are turned into credit inflation may be in order. The first step in the process is the sale of government securities by the government to finance the deficits. The next step is the purchase of some of the securities by the Federal Reserve Bank paid for with a check written by the Fed. This process is measured by Federal Reserve credit in Table 12.4. Table 9.1 is also updated below:

TABLE 12.5

Federal Reserve Credit
(In Billions of Dollars)

1973	84.7
1974	89.0
1975	107.7
1976	116.3
1977	123.5
1978	135.0

The Federal Reserve check is eventually deposited in a commercial bank, becoming reserves for the banking system to loan. Money is already created at this point since the Federal Reserve check itself was drawn from an account of thin air. In the third step, these increased reserves, together with currency in circulation (also printed by the Fed), comprise the monetary base. As you can see from Table 12.4, this too has been accelerating. As this "raw material" for the banking system enters the loan markets, it becomes multiplied many times over into the money supply—in our table measured by M_1. As you can see, the original increase in government deficits did indeed work its way through to accelerating monetary growth.

Credit Growth

As the reader knows, the process does not stop here. The impact of the creation of the narrow M_1 money input is magnified even further by all forms of credit growth. This process has also accelerated.

TABLE 12.6

	Total Funds Raised by the Nonfinancial Sector	Total Bank Loans
1965–1972	8.6%	10.2%
1972–1978	14.2%	11.1%
1975–1978	23.0%	12.9%

It is clear that the growing government involvement in the private economy has been translated to an increase in total credit growth as well. But that does not even begin to tell the entire story because the credit growth figures are only aggregates. That credit is distributed throughout the economy in a very uneven fashion. Some borrowers are far more overextended than others. Many new credit vehicles were created in recent years to help them get into even deeper trouble. Second mortgages on homes, for example, have been created in growing numbers, leveraging up new-found, and perhaps precarious, equity in homes brought about by price inflation and housing speculation. Commercial paper outstanding has increased at an annual rate of 16.6 percent from 1966 through 1979 and at an annual rate of nearly 22 percent since 1972. Whenever bank credit becomes too tight or too expensive, many corporations aggressively turn directly to the credit markets. We have already had one major commercial paper scare with the Penn Central as well as a more recent one with Chrysler before a government bailout.

As we know, the other side of credit is debt. Accompanying the accelerating growth of credit is continuing deterioration in the aggregate balance sheets of each economic sector. By now it should not be surprising that the deterioration has also continued to worsen since our first edition. We review each sector below.

The Banking Sector

Despite steadily weakening balance sheets, bank failures, and the highly volatile and risky financial environment, the aggressive contemporary liabilities management approach by bankers has continued. Bankers have become more aggressive than ever in their lending policies and have relied even more on purchased liabilities. The rule of the day is still maximization of earnings through large and increasingly risky loan portfolios. The approach is still to get the loan first and worry about the funds to meet it later. Competition in the industry for loans is more intense than ever and so is the competition for funds. Competition from outside the industry for bank funds is also growing much more intense. Money market funds, for example, are burgeoning, taking billions of dollars away from the commercial banking system.

Purchased Liabilities

Rather than cutting back on loans in the new competitive environment for funds, banks have become more aggressive and innovative than ever in their search for funds to loan out. This is true especially toward the end of the credit cycle when funds are tight. Unfortunately, these sources of funds are usually very short-term in nature, highly volatile and expensive.

Repurchase agreements have become much more popular in the past few years. Here, banks temporarily sell their Treasury securities to corporations with the stipulation that they will buy them back. Banks get funds to meet loan demands and the corporations earn interest on their excess funds. The problem is that in the late stages of the credit cycle, exactly when banks are most likely to turn to this kind of loan financing, corporate liquidity is also beginning its last sharp deterioration. As the excess corporate funds dry up, banks are forced to scramble to replace this source of funds just when money is most tight. The result is a sharp intensification of the final credit crunch. A related problem is the confusion that such activity causes in monetary policy. In effect, corporations are earning interest on their demand deposits and the funds represented by these repurchase agreements should rightly be counted as part of the money supply. But they are not, and this has the tendency to make the Fed overshoot its monetary targets.

Eurodollar borrowing by our banks also continues to be a big source of funds for lending very late in the credit cycle when domestic sources of funds are being squeezed. This high-cost and volatile source of funds also helps to add to the hectic final stages of the credit cycle. In the most recent credit cycle expansion, there was a huge Eurodollar inflow which helped to extend the cycle long enough to add substantially to the balance sheet deterioration. This shifting of such vast amounts of funds across borders only serves to add to the uncertainty and volatility of the final stage of each credit cycle and ultimately to the credit collapse that follows.

Fed Funds and discount window borrowing also continues to reach new record magnitudes near the peak of each credit cycle. Large money-center banks especially have relied upon borrowings from smaller, more conservatively financed banks in the Fed Funds markets when credit becomes tight. But this is in for a drastic change soon. In the most recent credit cycle, smaller banks have run down their balance sheets much more than in prior cycles. For the first time, they have been borrowing in the Fed Funds market themselves. If this continues, as I think it will, this portends even more problems. Late in each credit cycle, borrowing at banks by business always accelerates strongly relative to other sources of credit demand. By this time, corporate liquidity levels have become quite low on a cyclical basis. Because large money-center bank loan portfolios are substantially business loans, they usually suffer a much greater liquidity deterioration at this time than smaller banks. With small bank balance sheets now as equally strained as their big city counterparts, this means there will be even more volatility and even higher interest rates at each peak. It also means a much larger number of small bank failures in the years ahead, as we will discuss in the next chapter. With recent changes in Federal Reserve policy allowing the Fed Funds rate to fluctuate more, this means much higher Fed Funds rates at the top of each credit cycle.

Worsening Bank Balance Sheets

Bank balance sheets have continued to deteriorate in quality almost unabated since the first edition. The industry is entering the decade of the 1980s in unquestionably the worst financial condition in modern history. The stage is set for what will be a new postwar record correction in terms of bank failures and loan losses. A glance at Table 12.7 clearly shows that the steadily worsening pattern of such indicators as the loan ratio, loan/deposit ratios, and governments/total bank credit is still intact. The data there update information in Tables 2.2, 2.5, and 4.2.

The loan ratio, for example, reached a new postwar high, as one would expect, during the height of the credit crunch in 1974 along with the record interest rates reached in the same year. The ratio receded with the debt liquidation in the recession and economic recovery that followed, again the same as the historical

TABLE 12.7

(All Commercial Banks)

	Loan Ratio	Governments/ Bank Credit	Loans/ Demand Deposits	Loans/Demand + Time Deposits	Deposit Turnover N.Y.
1973	.70	.090	2.45	.82	297.5
1974	.72	.073	2.35	.82	290.9
1975	.69	.111	2.27	.76	335.0
1976	.68	.125	2.33	.76	391.9
1977	.71	.110	2.54	.81	503.0
1978	.73	.091	2.75	.85	541.9

pattern. Once again, it began to rise until reaching a new postwar high in 1978 and again in 1979. The same pattern was evident in the loan/deposit ratios. The ratio of government securities to total bank credit had still not reached new postwar lows yet but the longer-term pattern has been roughly in line with the other indicators. There were also technical reasons for its lag. Deposit turnover has also continued to accelerate dramatically.

So, on the surface, there is no question that the long-term decline in banking liquidity is not yet over. Beneath the surface, the financial condition of the banking system is even worse.

Loan Portfolios

Not only has the proportion of bank assets devoted to private sector loans continued to rise, but the quality of the loans in the aggregate has also continued to deteriorate. Since both corporate and individual balance sheets have continued to deteriorate in quality, we can really say that, by definition, the loans of banks in general must also be of lower quality since these are their loan clients.

While the source of bank funds continues to become increasingly short-term and volatile, the average maturity of the loan portfolio is steadily lengthening. Many companies use bank credit lines like permanent capital. Others, unable to reach the capital markets, are dependent upon bank credit.

There is also the problem of prior bad or questionable loans that remain on the books of many banks. The bad tanker loans that received so much publicity during the credit crunch of 1974–1975 are still on the books in most cases. The bad real estate paper of the REIT's of the same cycle is also still being carried. In many cases, the banks have foreclosed on the real estate and are now servicing it. Billions of dollars of loans to Third World countries, which have little chance of repayment, are also carried on the books at full value. Defaults by Iran and Pakistan in 1979 may have been harbingers of future troubles.

Banks have also been much more aggressive during recent years in consumer lending. Bank credit cards, for example, have proliferated substantially since our original work. The consumer, as we will discuss shortly, has also been changing saving and borrowing habits over the same period in the face of continued high rates of price inflation. As a result, consumer borrowing has been at far higher relative levels than during past cycles. Bankers, either to cash in on the loan demand bonanza or to avoid turning down their depositors, have met the loan demand by increasing their consumer loan portfolios substantially. Such loans are generally considered to be of lower quality relative to business loans. So, to the extent that the proportion of loan portfolios devoted to consumer loans has expanded, the quality of the entire portfolio has declined. Since consumer balance sheets are also at their lowest quality in modern history, the credit-worthiness of consumer loans is lower than usual.

Putting all this together, we must conclude that a double-barreled problem exists in banking balance sheets as far as loans are concerned. Not only is the average loan portfolio too large relative to the overall asset structure of the bank, and still rising, but the quality of the loans within the portfolios is much lower than at the time of my original work.

Bank Capital Structure

One aspect of the banking industry problems not discussed in depth in our original work was the question of the capital position of the industry. A lack of liquidity, whether in banks, individuals, or corporations, is one thing. Given time and perhaps some restructuring of the balance sheet, it can be cured. A deficient long-term capital position is quite another problem. Here it is a question of solvency. That is, after all the debts are paid, is there any capital remaining?

Banking is a highly leveraged industry to begin with, as large amounts of liabilities are resting upon a fairly small equity investment. But the equity base has not grown in pace with the enormous growth in total bank credit over the years. With the aggressive philosophy of banking that we have described, it should not be surprising that bankers would also attempt to maximize their return on equity as well. As a result, they had not been raising much equity during the earlier advent of liabilities management. In more recent years, with bank stocks selling under book value, they have not been able to raise money this way without seriously diluting shareholder equity. It has also been difficult and costly in recent years for most banks to sell long-term debt to bolster the capital position. Consequently, long-term capital positions of banks in general are even more precarious than the liquidity positions.

When you look further below the surface, the situation is potentially more ominous. Bank investments are carried on the books at cost. But we know that any municipal bonds purchased for the bank portfolio a number of years ago when interest rates were 2 percent–3 percent are worth much less today. There are substantial paper losses in the average bank portfolio as a result. There are billions of dollars of bad loans on the books of banks where interest is not being paid or paid at below market rates. They should be written down in value to reflect this, but are not. Should all the investments and questionable loans be written down to reflect realistic current market values, there would be no equity capital in the entire banking industry. Given the importance of the banking industry and its prime role in the implementation of monetary policy, this is not a comforting thought to those who feel that the government can handle any crisis. It is certainly difficult for me to muster more confidence in this area than I could a few years ago.

The Corporate Sector

Financial trends in the nonfinancial corporate sector over the past six years are not unlike those in banking. Despite the increased awareness of the problem of deteriorating corporate balance sheets over the period and two credit crunches, corporations continue to grow more illiquid.

All the measures of balance sheet strength discussed earlier reached new postwar low readings during the crunch of 1974–1975. After recovering from the crunch, they again began to deteriorate. By the end of 1978, the current ratio of all manufacturing firms was already below the recession trough of 1975. The quick ratio also reached new postwar lows by early 1979. Table 12.8 updates these readings contained in Tables 6.2 and 6.5.

185

TABLE 12.8

Year End	Current Ratio	Quick Ratio
1972	2.27	.24
1973	2.05	.29
1974	1.95	.25
1975	2.02	.31
1976	2.01	.33
1977	1.96	.28
1978	1.84	.26
1979*	1.79	.22

*Second quarter.

It is clear that corporate liquidity trends are unchanged. There are cyclical repairs done periodically but on a longer-term basis the deterioration continues unabated. The table below shows still another indication of the trend, liquid assets as a percentage of total short-term liabilities for all nonfinancial corporations.

TABLE 12.9

Liquid Assets as a
Percentage of Short-Term Debt

1967	103.0%
1968	97.4%
1969	83.3%
1970	78.2%
1971	84.5%
1972	81.4%
1973	74.5%
1974	63.0%
1975	77.5%
1976	82.6%
1977	71.3%
1978	65.3%
1979*	57.1%

*First quarter.

The common explanation for this deterioration is that corporations have learned how to economize on cash balances, but it is not a good one. Liquidity, like insurance, is only needed in emergencies. With growing volatility and risk in our economic environment, liquidity should be growing.

All these readings are particularly ominous since there is generally a last sharp

186

decline in corporate liquidity as the country moves into the corrective recession. During this period, corporate liquidity indicators have all reached their new postwar record lows. The sharp decline in corporate profits and the surge in involuntary inventories are the last straws that frighten corporations into their periodic balance sheet repairs. At this writing, the sharp decline in corporate profits and the inventory buildup have not even begun and liquidity readings are already well into new low ground. There is, therefore, no question that the financial deterioration in the most recent credit cycle will be the worst on record. This confirms the long-term pattern of steadily worsening credit cycles.

Funding the Liquidity Problems

As we know, the liquidity problems do not really disappear when corporations perform their temporary balance sheet repairs. The excessive short-term debt is simply moved over into the long-term section of the balance sheet through the process of selling long-term bonds to pay it off. Excessive inventories are also liquidated and other cost-cutting measures are temporarily instituted. There is no great conservative enlightenment among businessmen, as analysts usually say during this rebuilding period. There is only a little temporary fear and the realities of the business cycle. By this process of funding the liquidity problem, however, it is gradually being changed to a solvency problem. After the funding, the base is then set for the next cyclical rundown in the short end of the balance sheet.

This process can be monitored by watching the new security sales. Following each crunch, there is a period of roughly two years when the dollar value of new corporate bond issues reaches new record proportions. This is an integral part of the continuing credit trends. Records were once again set following the 1974–1975 crunch. This can be seen in Table 12.10 which updates Table 7.1. As we saw, balance sheets again became heavy with short-term debt following the funding. By the end of 1979, the corporate calendar was again beginning to build. The more things change, the more they remain the same.

TABLE 12.10

New Security Issues
(In Billions of Dollars)

	Bonds & Notes	Common Stock	Preferred Stock	Total
1973	20.7	7.6	3.3	31.6
1974	31.5	4.0	2.3	37.8
1975	41.7	7.4	3.5	52.6
1976	41.0	8.3	2.8	52.1
1977	39.9	8.1	3.9	51.9
1978	36.0	8.0	2.8	46.8

When the total financial condition of aggregate corporate balance sheets is viewed against the need for capital spending in the 1980s, the situation looks even more disturbing. A key determinant of productivity gains, and, therefore, real economic growth, is the capital-labor ratio or the amount of capital invested per worker. A look at the average productivity gains for the periods below will demonstrate our growing problem:

TABLE 12.11

Productivity Gains

1947–1965	3.2%
1965–1973	2.3%
1973–1978	1.0%
1979*	−1.7%

*First nine months.

The explanation of this poor performance lies in the capital-labor ratio. From about the mid-1950s to 1967, the ratio grew at 2.7 percent. From 1967 through 1979, however, it was less than 1.5 percent. Business fixed investment in the 1970s averaged about 10 percent of the GNP. This will have to be raised several percentage points if the economy is to grow at even 3 percent. Wharton recently published its estimates for the capital requirements for the U.S. in the 1980s. Its estimate of $1.8 trillion of new capital spending would require $846 billion of additional corporate debt and $97 billion of new equity. This means approximately $77 billion of new corporate debt annually in the 1980s compared to $50 billion in the 1970s. All this presumes that corporate profits will not slip further, causing even more external financing needs. Given the current shape of corporate balance sheets and continuing government intervention, the reader will understand why my best case assumption for the 1980s is continuing stagflation.

The Enlightened Consumer

If there were an area deserving of more extensive treatment in the first edition, it would have been the consumer sector. We simply made broad references to personal balance sheet deterioration that had roughly followed the same long-term and cyclical patterns in the other sectors. We believed there would have been double-counting of the debt and perhaps "over-kill" in the presentation since the same financial deterioration elsewhere was obviously confirmed. We also looked upon the consumer as playing a more or less passive role in the process. He too was caught up in the same credit syndrome. His balance sheet also displayed the same progression of higher cyclical peaks and troughs of quality. He too ran into cyclical limits to the debt he could service and periodic fears which led him to temporarily clean up his finances.

Changing Consumer Attitudes

Though the consumer has played the credit game like everyone else, until recently he has been a stabilizing force in the economy relative to the other sectors. It has been from the consumer sector that the savings were generated to keep the economy going. The consumer has generally pulled in his horns voluntarily on a cyclical basis when his balance sheet become too overburdened with debt. He also raised his saving rate when confronted with an unanticipated increase in price inflation. In so doing, he helped to let a little steam out of the credit expansion by releasing funds for credit-starved businessmen near the peak of the credit cycle.

But when the consumer's basic currency has been severely and persistently depreciated over a long period of time, he eventually learns how to cope with it. He learns to spend more, save less, and go even further in debt than before. That is exactly what has been happening over the past few years. The consumer has now learned to react to sudden spurts in price inflation by spending more, not less. He has become more tolerant of debt in his balance sheet. As a consequence, he will be adding to the intensity of each credit cycle rather than acting as a moderating force. In the most recent credit expansion he continually confounded the economic experts who kept expecting him to reduce his spending and borrowing. For this reason most economists expected a recession first in 1977, then in 1978, and finally in 1979. Each time they were fooled as the consumer kept right on spending and borrowing. As a result, in the most recent credit expansion ending in late 1979, the consumer ran down his balance sheet to a much greater extent than in any prior cycle. His saving rate was the lowest of all the postwar cycles. He went on a house-buying spree. For the first time, there was a pronounced "buy ahead" psychology at work among consumers and an incipient general retreat from currency on the part of consumers—a rush to get out of money and into "things."

The Recent Record

There are as many balance sheet measures to track the progress of the consumer as there are for the other sectors. I've tracked many of them for years in my monthly economic letter. The pattern in all of them is similar to the other sectors, as mentioned above. The measures of balance sheet quality are similar to those used to track other sectors: Relating accumulated debt to some income measure or asset measure relating debt service (loan repayment plus interest) to a measure of income, or indicators of payment problems.

The deterioration in the consumer sector, measured in many ways, has closely paralleled other sectors. It also comes in broad waves like the other sectors. By the end of 1978, all measures were again at postwar lows. A summary of several appears at top of page 190.

Consumer Installment Debt to Disposable Income	A new postwar high as early as 1977 with further deterioration in 1978 and 1979.
Total Consumer Credit as a Percentage of Income	At a record 21 percent by the end of 1978 compared to a peak of 20 percent in 1973.
Mortgage Debt Service as a Percentage of Disposable Income	Reached a new record level by the end of 1978 at 52 percent compared to the previous 1973 peak of 47.5 percent. More deterioration since.
Total Consumer Liabilities as a Percentage of Liquid Assets ·	A new postwar record high at the end of 1978.
Delinquency Rates on Consumer Loans	Generally a lagging indicator, the rates were already in excess of the 1973 peak of 2 percent at the 1978 level of 2.4 percent.

Space will not be taken here to duplicate the tables for these indicators for the entire postwar period. The pattern is disturbingly similar to the other sectors. One is duplicated below, however, to give you a flavor of the rest.

TABLE 12.12

Ratio of Consumer Installment Debt to Personal Income

1946	2.16	1963	11.41
1947	3.26	1964	11.98
1948	4.18	1965	12.41
1949	5.48	1966	12.37
1950	5.96	1967	11.96
1951	5.72	1968	12.04
1952	6.78	1969	12.27
1953	7.87	1970	12.16
1954	7.83	1971	12.14
1955	8.87	1972	12.49
1956	9.15	1973	13.01
1957	9.47	1974	12.69
1958	8.92	1975	12.18
1959	9.79	1976	12.24
1960	10.55	1977	13.84
1961	10.05	1978	14.67
1962	10.60	1979*	15.15

*June.

With the obvious continued financial deterioration in the consumer sector and elsewhere and the changing consumer attitudes, we may expect the consumer to continue to add to the volatility of the economy. Because of this change, recessions will be worse as well. An even more harmful aspect of the changing consumer relates to long-term economic growth. As mentioned, the consumer has been the chief source of savings for investment.

Adverse Effects of Continuing Deterioration

At this stage in the update the next step should be obvious. If government spending has not abated, total credit creation continues to accelerate, and balance sheets continue to deteriorate, then all the adverse effects predicted in our original work should worsen.

Some of the major direct effects, like price inflation and interest rates, have ebbed and flowed in steadily intensifying waves, paralleling the waves in balance sheet deterioration. In late 1974, new postwar records were set for most interest rates and price inflation crested at double-digit rates, both confirming the series of higher cyclical peaks. Late in 1979, most of these records were again broken.

Other adverse effects slowly and steadily worsened over the past six years. Not only has the government flooded the economy with credit to finance its growth in spending, but the tax burden on the average American family has increased sharply as well. Volatility and risk in all financial markets have also increased steadily. In one week in October 1979, interest rates exploded in the greatest one-week advance in history. One underwriting syndicate lost as much as $12 million in a matter of days and several small bond firms went out of business. In the desperate search for funds that characterizes the credit crunch near the end of each credit cycle, the interest rates charged to marginal borrowers rise so fast that the quality spreads between rates charged to high- and low-quality borrowers widens each cycle to new postwar highs. This widening drives borrowers out of the market and often out of business.

Stagnating Economic Growth

A number of secondary social and economic effects naturally result from the major direct effects of excessive credit growth. They are often long-lasting and have a direct impact upon future economic growth.

The continued depreciation of our currency, for example, makes business calculations and planning extremely difficult because currency is our economic measuring device. Even *real* profits are difficult to calculate. Add to this growing volatility and direct government intervention into business decision-making, and planning problems mount. Such direct government intervention has increased substantially since our original work. Between OSHA (Occupational Safety and Health Agency) and the EPA (Environmental Protection Agency) uncertainty and delays in building new plants have been increased substantially. The additional cost is also significant. Additionally, a substantial proportion of investment funds has been diverted by government edict to meet OSHA and EPA requirements. The result is much less productive investment by business.

Labor militancy is also on the increase. Aided by special favors granted by the government, organized labor has succeeded in winning wage increases far in excess of productivity gains. This has put pressure on the government to stimulate the economy in order to offset the unemployment that would result.

Putting all this together, we find an extremely adverse climate for capital investment. The result is deficient capital formation and disappointing productivity gains. Much of what capital investment there has been has been aimed toward shoring up declining profit margins rather than adding to the aggregate total of productive capacity. In recent years business has also been utilizing excess funds to buy existing capacity from other companies. This makes good sense to individual businessmen. In such an era of uncertainty, it is better to buy completed plants rather than build a new plant and run the risks of costly delays and arbitrary government edicts. But again, this does not add to total productive capacity.

The net result of these trends is increased inflationary pressures because of a slowing in supply. It also means that the country will continue to live off its capital, promising years of economic stagnation.

Credit Cycle Updates

In completing the update of the first edition, it is disturbingly clear that nothing has really changed. The long-term trends are becoming more firmly entrenched and the nation is adjusting to them rather than attacking them. But this is a losing battle. The individual credit cycles around the underlying trends have also become a financial phenomenon that must be considered in any investment planning. Since we had an anatomy of earlier cycles in the first edition, we are ending this chapter with a similar summary of the most recent two cycles.

The 1974–1975 Crunch

Not too long after the publication of the first edition, the cyclical credit expansion ended. The overall growth of credit in that upswing surpassed all previous ones during the postwar years. All the other adverse effects caused by credit growth also reached new records.

Price inflation, as measured by the Consumer Price Index, finally reached its peak in December 1974 but not before reaching the first double-digit rates in peacetime. The nation's experiment with controls was a complete fiasco. Though consumer prices subsided in the period following the cyclical peak, the trough rate was higher than that of the previous cycle. Not only did we confirm the pattern of progressively higher peak rates in prices but we were also not able to wring out inflation and bring it back to the starting point for the cycle.

The story was the same for interest rates, another very sensitive barometer of the declining financial health of the nation. In the final credit crunch, which has come to mark the end of each credit cycle, interest rates rose to a level never seen during the postwar years. Again, the long-term pattern of progressively higher cyclical peaks was confirmed. The rates, after peaking for the cycle in late summer and fall of 1974, also began their cyclical decline. Like consumer prices, however, they too troughed at a higher level than during the previous cycle.

In the final drastic rundown of liquidity in the economy, balance sheets became more severely strained than at any time in history. In the final crunch, when money was not available at any price for some, the stage was set for the recession during which many of the distortions and overextended balance sheets would come to light.

Our personal theory of the business cycle is that recessions are caused by the credit expansion that immediately precedes them. The intensity of the recession is a direct function of the magnitude of the credit expansion. The greater the credit expansion, the greater the resulting economic and financial distortions that must be cleansed by the recession. Credit expansions have been growing with each upswing in credit growth, and recessions have been growing more intense as well. Predictably, the 1974–1975 recession was the worst of the postwar period, just as the credit expansion that preceded it was also the greatest.

By the spring of 1975, the recession had hit bottom when the government and monetary authorities engaged in massive restimulation. Again, the pattern was the same. The authorities, afraid to let natural forces correct the financial damage of prior government behavior, stepped in to reliquefy the economy. The private debt liquidation which had set in was replaced by new government debt. As quickly as private bank loans were paid off, banks were given government securities to replace them. In so doing, the government set the stage for the next credit boom/bust. The recession was arrested before it had cleansed the economy of all economic distortions. Balance sheets stopped deteriorating by the spring of 1975 and began to improve.

The pattern of government intervention continued to be the key to the steadily worsening cycles. Each credit surge creates economic distortions throughout the economy that constitute a "deflationary drag." The recession begins to correct them by liquidating bad investments, questionable loans and overextended companies. But the government is afraid to allow the complete collapse of the debt accumulated over the past few decades and steps in to bail out many individuals and companies. Many of the distortions are simply carried over into the next cycle rather than being liquidated. This means that even more credit is required in the next cycle to get the economy moving again while carrying much of the deadwood of the prior cycle. But the larger bailout each time means that even more distortions are created and an even bigger bust is preordained.

It all happened again in 1975. We did survive another bone-rattling credit crunch but at the cost of another even bigger surge of new credit which set the stage for the next credit cycle.

Sure enough, by late 1976 the period of balance sheet improvement was over and the long-term financial deterioration resumed. Importantly, balance sheet improvement fell well short of restoring them back to the levels that preceded the previous declining stage. After the crunch there was the usual rhetoric about bankers, individuals, and corporate treasurers having learned their lessons. Never again would they run down their balance sheets as they did before. Not much!

The 1979–1980 Crunch

As this is written, another long credit expansion is ending and an inevitable bust lies directly ahead. The magnitude of the credit expansion already far exceeded the previous cycle. Record highs in most interest rates have again been set. Price inflation has once again reached new postwar record levels and has still not peaked. The stability in financial markets has already exceeded all previous cycles and a credit crunch has already begun. After the crunch, record bankruptcies, bank failures, and loan losses may be expected.

Was this all preordained again? Or was it the fault of OPEC, gold speculators, greedy consumers, aggressive businessmen and bankers, or any of a number of other scapegoats that have been offered up? The answer must be clear by now.

Following the Script

From the time in late 1976 when balance sheets resumed their cyclical decline, the die was already cast for all the events of late 1979 and those to follow in 1980. From that time forward, the credit cycle script was followed faithfully. Early in 1977, we remarked in our economic letter that the burden of proof was on those who maintained that we would not once again see new record postwar highs in interest rates. Though this was a decidedly minor viewpoint at the time, it did not even faintly resemble a fearless prediction.

Even before balance sheets resumed their deterioration, the magnitude of the eventual move in prices and interest rates was fairly clear. The foundation was already laid with government deficits that dwarfed those in the same "take-off stage" in the previous cycle. The government literally deluged the economy with government securities to replace the debt being liquidated during the recession by the private sector. With money being pumped into the economy during the recession, falling loan demand, and a huge inventory liquidation, banks had nowhere to put their money to work except in Treasury securities. The banks were then poised and ready to meet the inevitable loan demand recovery. When it started, the banking system multiplied the original infusion of money many times over.

Monetary Base Growth

The next step in the credit creation process also faithfully followed the script. The expansion of the monetary base from the trough of each postwar recession to the following peak has been larger with each cycle. The expansion preceding the 1974–1975 crunch far exceeded all prior cycles, and so did the interest rate rise. From the business trough in March 1975, the growth in the monetary base was considerably larger. From the vantage point of early 1977, then, it was not difficult to hypothesize still worse inflation and interest rates.

194

Money Growth

The money supply growth eventually mirrors the growth in the monetary base. By early 1977 it was already clear that the growth in the money supply was at least as great as that preceding the prior crunch. The standard measures of money, moreover, were also understating the true money growth. Given sustained experience with inflation, savers were already finding new ways to earn more interest on their money. Money market funds literally exploded in popularity as individuals moved their money from bank accounts in search of higher returns. These handy funds have all the advantages of bank accounts, including checking privileges, and should be counted in with the money supply. If they were, the more accurate measure of money would have revealed a much higher growth than reported for the narrower definitions of money. The expanded use by corporations of repurchase agreements further understated the growth of money during the period. So, this next step in the credit creation process also confirmed the record magnitude of the most recent credit cycle.

Total Credit Growth

The best measure of the ultimate expansion of the original government deficits can be found in the examination of the trends in total credit. With total credit growing at 9 percent–10 percent over the postwar period, compared to the roughly 3 percent that the economy is able to increase the production of real goods, it is no wonder why prices have risen. Within that compound rate of growth, however, there has been a pattern of acceleration in each upward wave of credit growth. Since 1973, there has been only one year where the growth in total credit was less than the long-term growth rate. That year was 1975, the worst recession year of the postwar period. In that year, the growth of total credit only slowed to an 8.2 percent rate. Since 1975, every year has been far over the long-term rate, with both 1977 and 1978 showing growth over 13 percent. The growth in the most recent credit cycle has been roughly 25 percent higher than that in the two years preceding the last recession. Remember also that those earlier growth rates were computed on a much smaller base.

So, by the best measure of credit it was easy to expect record high interest rates in the most recent cycle. It was also easy to predict that all the other adverse effects of the credit cycle would also reach record proportions.

A Perfect Timetable

When you examine more closely the last credit cycle, you begin to appreciate the regularity of the timetable of events for each cycle. Earlier than usual in the most recent cycle, the consumer accelerated his credit buying. On schedule, he found bankers willing to extend loans on favorable terms, even though, only a short time before, financial literature was replete with claims that bankers had learned their lesson the last time around. Banking liquidity began to decline on schedule. Later, bankers predictably began to liquidate government securities to trade them for higher yielding municipals and to meet loan demand. Toward the end of the cycle, when deposit inflows began to slow and the supply of government securities to liquidate began to shrink, bankers once again aggressively sought "purchased liabilities" in the form of Eurodollars, repurchase agreements, Fed Funds, and discount window borrowing.

The same pattern was followed in corporate finance. The liquidity that corporate treasurers restored to balance sheets was soon dissipated despite earlier claims that they too had learned their lessons well. The plain fact is that when the government combines with the Federal Reserve and the banking system to make credit available, corporations will find a use for it.

On schedule, by the end of 1979 the string was running out. Liquidity was disappearing and balance sheets had been thoroughly exhausted. Corporations were already beginning the process of funding their liquidity problems. And the economy had been so thoroughly distorted by years of excessive credit growth that a recession was inevitable. The Federal Reserve by late 1979, just to nail the coffin shut, was again slowing the money supply growth. Once again, its timing was too late to avoid price inflation and other distortions, but was just in time to make the recession even worse. If the pattern holds, it will step in during the ensuing recession to reliquefy the economy in time to ensure another even worse credit cycle in the 1980s.

Chapter 13

Future Trends

We saw in the previous chapter that the long-standing financial abuse visited upon the economy by the government has been continuing up to the present day. The big question is: Where do we go from here? How long can the economy continue to survive in its present form before complete control is lost in one way or another? Has six years of additional experience with credit trends given us any new insights? The answer is yes, and no.

Can we now say with more certainty exactly when and how it will all end? The answer to that question is still no. But we have learned much more about coping with the continuing adverse economic environment until we find the answer. There is, as we described, a fairly predictable recurring credit cycle that can be utilized for investment timing. But which one will be the last cycle is still open to question.

We reasoned in 1974 that the future course of the economy would be more "business as usual," as far as the government was concerned. The basic cause would not be removed by the government, for that cause was the government itself. Government spending, we concluded, would remain high, credit creation to finance it would remain excessive, and the resulting economic distortions would spread. But, through crisis economics and patchwork policies, the government would control the economy and avoid a collapse in the foreseeable future. All we could do, we suggested, was to take one cycle at a time. That is still the best advice.

In the meantime, there will continue to be violent economic swings and high volatility in all financial markets. There will also appear to be many false "solutions" to the problems that will gain popularity, born out of wishful thinking. The key to avoiding mistakes as a result will be in keeping the long-term picture in mind at all times. Use a proper time horizon that can fit the cycle and the short-term vagaries of the markets into the broader perspective we have talked about here.

Hopefully, the reader can now sense the deeply embedded nature of our current economic problems. Excessive credit growth and the resulting financial deterioration we have measured are only the *proximate* cause of price inflation and all the other economic problems. One has to step back at all times to ask the reason for the excessive creation of money and credit, and whether that is truly changing. Of course, we have shown it to be government spending and the growth of government influence generally. But that activity rests upon strong political and public acceptance of the welfare state and a belief in the government as ultimate fixer. What's more, after decades of such beliefs, sturdy institutions have been built upon them that cannot be changed overnight without considerable pain. Millions of workers, for example, did not prepare for their retirement, but relied instead on Social Security benefits. There would have to be serious basic changes made, and powerful forces behind them, before these long-standing habits and policies could be changed. Temporary slowing of money growth or a few minor legislative changes are not sufficient changes. Keep this in mind when some minor event is hailed as some great watershed.

The Next Cyclical Bust

Taking our own advice of worrying about one cycle at a time, our first problem is the corrective phase of the most recent credit expansion—the recession. As this is written, the next postwar recession is imminent, preordained by the expansion of credit. Why do I say that? Economists, of course, have been debating the origin and timing of business cycles as long as the science of economics has existed. Even today there are many theories of the business cycle.

My view of the business cycle and the cause of recessions is a simple one and is based upon the role of money and credit in the economy. It is also strongly based on theories of the Austrian school of economics, so named because its key early thinkers were Austrian. Today, this school is the leading school of free market economics and one which rests heavily on individual decision-making as the key to understanding how the economy and markets work. Judging by economic policies proposed by governments over the past few decades, it is probably the only school of economics which still gives a rightful high recognition to free markets. Though this is not the place for a full exposition of this economic theory, a brief summary of its approach to business cycles is important for understanding why a recession is imminent and why recessions have become increasingly severe.

Recessions are not the symptoms of an unstable free market, as interventionists so often claim. And they do not result from sudden tightening of the money supply. They are the inevitable reaction to a preceding overexpansion of credit by the government and the central bank. As each cyclical expansion of credit proceeds to permeate the entire economy, it also creates serious economic distortions throughout the economy that have deflationary implications. Eventually, these distortions overwhelm even government policy-makers and the nation suffers a recession. The recession eases the pressures in the economy by at least partially curing some of the distortions. Huge artificial expansions of credit create the economic distortions by sending thousands of false signals through the economy which in turn cause resources of the economy to be sent where the free market would not.

Malinvestment

The interest rate, as we have mentioned many times throughout the book, is an extremely sensitive economic signal. When it is artificially altered by government activities, even temporarily, it sends out many false signals to all sectors of the economy. Because the interest rate is a particularly important signal in the investment process for business, serious distortions have serious consequences. Capital investment is not some big glob, as most conventional economists seem to believe, but a delicate interrelated series of productive stages from the original raw material source to the final consumer product. At each stage in the production process, whether it is a mine, a smelter, a fabricating plant, railroad or department store, businessmen must decide how much to invest in productive facilities. And the interest rate, as an important cost of investment, is an important part of the decision.

Conventional economists have always been fascinated with low interest rates. There is nothing wrong with that, since low interest rates are a sign of an economy with plenty of savings and an attractive investment climate. But our policy-makers have persistently tried to create artificially low interest rates by overexpanding the money supply. When they succeed, this false signal leads business to overexpand investments particularly in long-range projects. The delicate balance of capital investment is thus thrown out of kilter with too much invested at certain early stages of production and not enough at later stages closer to the consumer. Late in the expansion phase of the business cycle, businessmen sadly discover that there was not nearly as much saving as the false interest rate signaled to them, and they are left with unprofitable new and partially completed projects. On the other hand, raging consumer prices tell us that there is a serious shortage of consumer goods because too much money and too many resources have been invested in other places.

Though our explanation is an oversimplication of a complex process, the true problem is that the economy suffers from *malinvestment*. It's not that we have too much investment. It's just that the government has so thoroughly confused businessmen with its credit policies that the investment that has been made is poorly distributed. That's why we are seeing so many instances of spot shortages at the end of every business cycle expansion. Businesses must fail, some investment projects must be abandoned or converted to other uses, profits must decline for some investors, and unemployment must rise as the labor force is redirected. The corrective phase, in short, contributes significantly to the recession.

Distributing the Government Favors

Unfortunately, this is not the end of the distortions caused by government credit policies. As we know, overexpansion of money leads to price inflation, but that is only part of the damage. The new money created by the government is distributed throughout the economy not by efficient economic signals, but through an essentially political and arbitrary process. Whoever gets the money first, whether it is a defense contractor, the recipient of a housing subsidy, someone on the welfare rolls, or a retired worker on Social Security, spends the money first and gets full value before any prices rise. As the new money goes from hand to hand, more and more prices rise, and each succeeding recipient receives less real value until the ones at the end of the process are left holding the bag. Incomes and wealth are arbitrarily redistributed. Some are left richer, not because of producing real wealth, but because they have more political clout. Others, though they are hard-working producers, become poorer.

In the same way, industries that are favored by government policies benefit temporarily. The government may create new millionaires in housing by funneling subsidy money into the industry or in the defense industry by awarding contracts. With the new money, these industries can bid up wages and prices and attract resources into their industries and increase profits. But as the expansion increases, other industries also expand and try to bid the resources away from the originally favored industries. It's a funny thing about the free market—it usually gets its way. The resources that were bid away with the government money will go back to where they would have gone naturally unless the government sends even more money into the original industries. In fact, it requires more and more government injections of new money to maintain the artificial profits of the industries, as the free market is always pulling the resources back. With a particularly large credit expansion, there are many of these "most-favored" industries throughout the economy, all enjoying artificial profits and all requiring ever increasing credit "fixes" to keep them. Eventually, the government cannot or dares not create the amount of money needed to hold it all together, and the free market wins out. In the transition process, however, there are sharply declining profits in some industries, increased unemployment as workers look for other jobs, and other deflationary forces. Thus, we have another source of recession.

Balance Sheet Deterioration

The third source of the recession is the uneven distribution of the debt that is created during the credit expansion. Spurred on by the easy money climate of the credit expansion, large numbers of marginal borrowers eventually find their balance sheets so strained that they are forced to liquidate their debt and cut back spending. As we discussed, there are also billions of dollars of loan losses for lenders, personal bankruptcies, and business failures.

The Final Crunch

These credit-related economic distortions eventually combine to cause the correction phase of the credit cycle. All the problems come to a head at roughly the same time in one big credit crunch followed by a recession.

Businesses that unwittingly invested in unprofitable long-term projects because of false interest rate signals struggle in the final crunch to find funds to keep them going. Industries short of capacity because of malinvestment also compete for funds to expand. Industries dependent upon more government funds to maintain their artificial profits desperately search for alternate sources of funds to keep going. Shortages that led to overaccumulation of inventories must be financed at now spiraling prices and with record interest rates. By this time, bankers are also short of funds to meet loan demand and are also competing for the dwindling supply of funds. Consumers as well are struggling under a heavy debt load and are borrowing simply to meet their obligations. Others, driven by expectations of inflation, are borrowing to buy before prices go even higher. By now, the government is just a little frightened by the inflation it has wrought, and it usually tightens the money supply too late to help, but just in time to worsen the imminent recession. Worse yet, it is also in the credit markets to finance its own deficit and is adding to the credit problem.

During this final phase of the credit expansion, interest rates are rising feverishly, thus rationing out the remaining funds to the most urgent borrowers. In the process, not everyone is able to obtain financing, and all the bad investments of the prior expansion are liquidated in the months following the crunch. A massive liquidation of private debt follows. Marginal borrowers go bankrupt. Others, frightened by the crunch, start repairing their balance sheets by paying down debt and reducing spending. All this, of course, adds to the recession.

This is the credit crunch that has marked the top of each of the credit cycles we have described. The recession that follows is predetermined by the government credit policies during the expansion phase.

The greater the preceding credit expansion, the greater are the economic distortions and, therefore, the greater is the recession required to correct them. Each credit expansion in the past several decades has been greater than the preceding one. Predictably, each recession in the past two decades has been more severe than the prior one. As this is written, we are moving rapidly to the end of another credit expansion that has confirmed the pattern of progressively greater increases of credit. The expansion, in fact, has been approximately 25 percent greater than the last. And that expansion brought us the worst recession of the postwar period. We must expect an extremely serious correction of the most recent credit expansion.

The *timing* of our postwar recessions is also explained by a close study of credit trends. In our view, the recession develops when the balance sheet quality of each of the major economic sectors reaches new postwar lows and the economy runs out of liquidity. The credit crunch we described, as well as the final increase in interest rates, is a good indication that a recession is to follow. The poorly timed and belated tightening of money by the Federal Reserve is also another indicator that the top of the cycle has been reached.

By late 1979, all the ingredients were present to suggest a recessionary correction. Balance sheet quality was at a record low by nearly every measure. There was very little residual liquidity left in the economy. On schedule, the Federal Reserve was finally tightening the financial noose.

The Shape of the Next Recession

So, another postwar credit expansion is ending and it now remains to be seen how bad the corrective phase will be and whether it will confirm the pattern of steadily worsening recessions. Given the magnitude of the expansionary phase of the credit cycle, record interest rates, and unprecedented volatility in the financial markets, a serious recession is to be expected. That is, a substantial correction is needed to offset the distortions in the economy.

A serious correction is called for, but the exact shape of the recession is not quite clear. It could be long and drawn out, or it could be shorter but more painful. The last recession was both. It was also characterized by a once-in-a-lifetime increase and then liquidation of business inventories. Given the climate of the last credit cycle, this was not surprising. The long bout with wage and price controls starting in 1971 created shortages throughout the economy, just as all controls in the past have done. At the same time, the nation and the world also suffered a period of farm product shortages due to extremely bad weather. On top of all this, the Arab oil embargo and oil price hike occurred. This, combined with the normal cyclical shortages associated with increased capacity utilization at the peak of business, created a shortage hysteria with double and triple ordering by business to make sure it had the needed raw materials for production. On top of this voluntary and speculative inventory hoarding was piled the involuntary build-up of inventories at the retail level and elsewhere that always accompanies the first cyclical downturn in business in the recession. The result was one of the largest inventory liquidations in history.

While all recessions are caused by credit expansion, they do differ. Most analysts fight the last war and are watching inventories carefully. Since inventories did not expand to the same extent as the last cycle, analysts have a sanguine attitude on the next recession despite the huge expansion of credit and the wild activity in most financial markets. Will this one be the same? Though inventory increases did contribute to the last recession, the reader should keep in mind that a recession is more related to overall magnitude of credit expansion. To get a clearer picture of the actual shape of the next recession, one should look to see where the largest distortions occurred.

The Great Consumer Collapse

As a matter of fact, we already have a great deal of evidence about the probable shape of the next recession. Though each credit cycle is roughly similar as far as financial deterioration in each economic sector and the broad economic distortions, there are usually a few extremely distorted areas that give some hint as to the shape and magnitude of the recession. In the last cycle, as described above, it was an inventory problem. Analysts now look back at that recession as the "great inventory liquidation." The 1980–1981 bust will be characterized, in retrospect, as the "great consumer credit collapse."

If business overinventoried in 1973–1974, this time the consumer overinventoried. Because consumers have finally learned that the proper way to cope with inflation is to trade their paper money faster for real goods, they have gone much further into debt than in any other cycle. The growth in mortgage debt was truly extraordinary from the trough in 1975 through 1979, with the annual rate growing from $40 billion to $117 billion in 1979. There was also a big boom in all other kinds of consumer bank debt, as consumers bought ahead on all kinds of consumer durables. We also saw the biggest consumer balance sheet deterioration in history.

As a result, the next bust will see at least a 50 percent decline in consumer credit growth. We will also see record numbers of personal bankruptcies. Because more lenient personal bankruptcy laws were passed in late 1979 (just in time to spell even more trouble for lenders), lenders will have to write off billions of dollars of bad consumer loans. We will also see record numbers of mortgage foreclosures, especially on secondary homes, condominiums, and speculative real estate. Personal bankruptcies were already strongly on the rise in late 1979 before the recession was even upon us.

In addition to normal cyclical consumer credit expansion and balance sheet deterioration, there has been a great deal of new and more disturbing consumer behavior in the past several years. The last cycle has been characterized, for example, by far more speculative real estate activities. There has been a substantial acceleration in second mortgage activity on homes as consumers have traded on the rising equity values of their homes. Down payments have been lower, meaning less starting equity in homes. Some families have purchased far bigger homes than they needed, for speculative purposes. Many others have purchased second homes on speculation. House payments have been structured where they are permanently dependent on a continuing second family income and, in many cases, on "moonlighting" incomes for both husband and wife. The debt service is also higher on homes due to higher property taxes, which have risen with the value of homes, and due to much higher mortgage rates. Consumers have also been engaging in a great deal of "buying ahead" of all kinds of consumer durables such as appliances, automobiles, recreation vehicles, home entertainment equipment, and other luxury items as the inflationary psychology has become embedded in their thinking.

As a result of this, the consumer is seriously overextended. Debt service as a percentage of income was not only at a record high by late 1979, but it was not even fully reflecting the total amount of new obligations taken on. The average maturity of consumer debt has also been substantially extended in recent years, and family income has been increased by additional working members. In spite of this, the percentage of total family income required to service interest and debt repayments is worse than ever. And this record high burden exists before the recession has even gotten underway. When unemployment rises and average earnings decline, the burden will be unbearable for many. Of the roughly 21 percent of disposable income represented by consumer debt, 15 percent is installment debt that will collapse quickly in the credit liquidation that must follow.

In sum, the overextended consumer will be the major factor in the next recession. The distortions to be corrected in this sector are as great or even greater than those existing in inventories in the last recession. Consumer spending, moreover, represents a far larger proportion of the GNP. The time required to cure the consumer problem will also be far greater than that needed to put inventories back into balance. Business can react far quicker to problems of this kind by liquidating inventories, laying off workers, and other cost-cutting. What can the consumer do but pull in his belt a little tighter? In fact, another important factor in the last cycle was the extraordinary rise in the price of necessities such as food, fuel, and shelter for consumers. This, combined with the overextended balance sheets, portends a severe crunch in consumer discretionary spending power which, in turn, spells trouble for many major industries during the next recession.

Major Industry Corrections

Adding substantially to the seriousness of the 1980–1981 recession and its aftermath will be two major industries—automobiles and housing. Both industries have serious problems. Both are heading into a serious cyclical correction at the same time. And the troubles of each are closely related to the consumer credit problem as well as to excessive government intervention.

Looking first at autos, there are a multitude of problems all coming to bear on this industry at once. Tracing through them is a very useful exercise for seeing just how destructive government intervention can be. It can also alert the reader to future problem areas. The auto industry is a kind of microcosm of the broader problem of government intervention.

For years now the government has imposed a multitude of safety and environmental requirements on the auto industry. Often, the industry has been forced to undergo a number of changes in the design of many of the mandated alterations in the auto design to meet vacillating government bureaucratic whims. It has been expensive. Retooling has been extensive and it has added thousands of dollars to the cost and final selling price of most autos. Consumers have been forced to go much deeper in debt to own their automobiles, and the 48-month auto loan has become the standard in just a few short years. Millions of autos have been recalled over the past few years, which has also added greatly to costs.

Next, the years of persistent inflation, also engineered by the government, has built strong inflation expectation psychology into consumer buying habits. The more auto companies had to raise prices to pass on the higher government-imposed costs, the more inclined consumers became to "buy ahead" before prices rose even further. As a result, consumers went on a huge auto buying binge in the last credit cycle, adding to their debt substantially and adding to the volatility of the auto industry.

Then came the energy problem, another government creation. For years, environmental changes reduced auto mileage at the same time that energy problems were intensifying. You guessed it. Next, the auto industry was under orders to reduce the weight of cars and make other changes to increase mileage, adding even further to production costs and uncertainty in the industry. By the spring of 1979, the economics of the auto industry were so thoroughly distorted that economists' predictions on the economy were thrown into disarray by auto inventory problems. Suddenly, auto companies were left with record numbers of large autos they could not sell and a shortage of smaller gas-efficient autos simultaneously with increases in foreign auto sales.

Today we are at the beginning of 1980 and poised for another postwar recession. Even before the recession begins, one of the Big Three (Chrysler) would be out of business without government assistance. A total of 468 Big Three auto dealers went bankrupt in the 1979 model year *before* the recession has begun. The Ford Motor Company has announced that it is losing a billion dollars on North American auto operations for both 1979 and 1980. And General Motors, the paragon of efficiency, has seen its long-standing superior after-tax margins cut in half. Balance sheets in the entire industry have been seriously impaired. Finally, in spite of numerous plant closings throughout the fourth quarter of 1979, the industry enters 1980 with the highest inventories in history.

What lies ahead? A very bad cyclical correction and problems that will last well into the 1980s. First of all, the consumer is facing an extended retrenchment in his spending, and he is already overly burdened with auto debt. His discretionary spending power will continue to be seriously impaired through most of 1980. He is probably well "bought ahead" in autos anyway. With gasoline prices staying high and rationing a real possibility, the miles driven will decline or, at a minimum, will stop growing for some time. This means he will keep his autos longer. The auto companies must reduce their inventories and change over their plants to the production of smaller cars. This will require substantial retooling costs at a time when balance sheets are already strained. Outside financing will be necessary at a time when interest rates are high and the price multiples of their stocks are low. When they finally do change over, there will be much lower profit margins on the smaller cars.

The housing story is much more familiar and requires less detail here. Suffice it to say that the government, through substantial continuing stimulation, has thoroughly distorted the entire industry. Where the industry was once contracyclical and, therefore, helped to balance the downturn in other industries during a recession, the government has turned it into a cyclical industry. It now turns up and down along with other major industries, thereby adding to the volatility of the business cycle. Then, through the creation of substantial inflationary expectations among consumers and the supplying of credit to satisfy them, the government has succeeded in creating, during the last credit cycle, the greatest speculative boom in housing prices in the history of the country.

By the end of 1979, then, consumers had substantially overextended themselves with mortgage payments, housing had at least temporarily been priced beyond the reach of millions of other potential home buyers, mortgage rates were at record high levels, and the economy was poised for a credit crunch and a serious recession.

The cyclical correction in housing, for these reasons, should have a major impact on the entire economy. There will be a 40 percent–50 percent reduction in housing starts as well as a lower turnover of existing homes in 1980. Because both the auto and housing industries generate thousands of jobs, the concurrent weakness in both industries should feed on itself. Lower housing prices, or, at a minimum, a flattening in the rise, should weigh heavily on consumer psychology, since the consumer's perceived wealth will be lower. We must not forget that there are billions of dollars of follow-on expenditures that accompany the purchase of a home—furniture, air conditioners, landscaping, appliances, and many others. All these industries will also be adversely impacted.

Related Industries

The trouble doesn't stop there. Steel is still another major industry in serious trouble. Not only does it have terrible balance sheets, but also there is worldwide overcapacity, with new producers like Brazil and Korea also coming in. Meanwhile, the productive capacity of the U.S. steel industry is woefully uncompetitive, and it is also shielded from excessive foreign competition by the U.S. government through a target pricing scheme that keeps out lower-priced foreign imports. Even so the industry continues to weaken.

Add to this sad state the problems of major customers like construction firms and autos and we begin to appreciate the potential disaster of the next recession. The auto industry, in addition to having less steel demand because of the recession, will continue to use less steel in favor of lighter metals and plastics for fuel conservation purposes. With less demand from the housing industry and from manufacturers of appliances, there promises to be a major correction in the steel industry as well.

Finally, tie into this sad story a major correction in the suppliers to the auto industry who will be severely squeezed by the mainframe auto producers in their drive to restore profit margins. Balance sheets in the rubber industry, for example, are even worse than those in the steel industry. Then mix it all together and you have the great consumer collapse.

The Banking Sector

The correction in the consumer sector is, of course, only one aspect of the corrective portion of the credit cycle. Just as in prior credit cycles, all other economic sectors must also correct the abuses of the prior credit expansion. Banking liquidity, for example, has once again reached new postwar lows. Bankers have continued the extremely aggressive lending and borrowing habits they developed over the past few decades with even greater fervor. Once again they will pay the price in the coming correction. In fact, the correction in the banking industry as well as the entire finance industry promises to be extremely severe and prolonged in the current cycle.

Bank failures will reach new postwar records once again. Savings & Loan associations and other thrift institutions will undergo severe pressures. Problems among smaller banks will be particularly widespread. Their balance sheets have deteriorated in the most recent credit expansion far more than in any prior cycle. In the past, smaller and more conservative country banks were a source of stability relative to the larger money center banks. Though they too have run down their balance sheets over the postwar years, the deterioration has been far slower than in the larger banks. At the peak of each credit cycle, they actually served as a source of funds for the larger banks. Now, their loan ratios and other measures of liquidity are nearly as bad as the larger banks. Much of the problem is related to aggressive consumer credit demand. Consumer loans represent a much more important proportion of the loan portfolios of such banks, and it is difficult for the average small town bank to turn down loans to their customers. The last cycle has seen the greatest rise in farmland prices in the nation's history and in farm credit as well. Here, too, the smaller banks bore the brunt of such demand.

There will, in fact, be such a major shake-up in the entire financial sector that it will extend right through the recession and into the next economic recovery. There are some 14,000 commercial banks, 4500 Savings & Loans, and 500 mutual savings banks. Throughout the early 1980s they will all be engaged in a massive life-and-death struggle that will see the disappearance of thousands of units through failure and mergers. As this is written, the tempo of bank mergers has already accelerated substantially before the recession has even begun. Let's look at some of the reasoning for such a dramatic prediction.

First of all, we are starting with banking balance sheets at all-time record lows in terms of quality. Liquidity indicators are at record lows, of course, and the capital positions of most banks are severely strained. As mentioned, if bank capital were written down to more accurately reflect the questionable nature of many loans and if investment portfolios were not carried at cost, equity capital would be extremely deficient. Since little more earnings growth can be gained by running down the balance sheet, many bankers will feel the time is ripe for selling out.

Competition is also heating up in the entire industry. Money market funds have become powerful competitors for savings funds. In fact, there has almost been a stampede into such funds by investors and savers. There are also many actual and prospective changes in government policies that have been and will be promoting even more competition. Many thrift institutions have been allowed to use NOW accounts or what amounts to interest-paying checking accounts. There are strong moves to permit the use of such accounts on a nationwide basis. Moves to liberalize branch banking laws in various states so as to allow more statewide and nationwide competition have steadily gained support. There is growing support for lifting Regulation Q ceilings on savings accounts that could overnight raise the cost of funds to banks and savings institutions. It would also erase the ¼ point advantage in attracting savings which Savings & Loans have enjoyed. The list of such proposed moves is growing steadily. This is not to say that any of them are bad. The problem is that the government often moves too quickly in such matters and thoroughly disrupts an industry. In this case, the vulnerability of the industry is already quite high and the adjustment process will be painful and perhaps disastrous.

The earnings of both banks and thrift institutions are now very sensitive to changes in interest rates as well as external shocks. Their interest rate spreads (the difference between the cost of money and lending rates) have narrowed drastically in recent years due to competition, and there is little flexibility to meet shocks. Yet, there will be many shocks ahead. There is a proposal, for example, to slash the size of savings certificates from $10,000 to $1000. Imagine an overnight write-up of interest costs from the 5.5 percent on passbook savings funds to market interest rates on savings certificates. In early 1980, the average yield for

Savings & Loans on their mortgage portfolios was only 8.9 percent while the cost of money was obviously much higher.

In sum, we are entering a trying period for the entire financial industry. Part of the problem will be the normal cyclical correction of the credit abuses of the expansion. Each correction has been worse anyway, and this one will be no exception. But the long term is catching up with the industry and there are also some special factors that will be superimposed. As a result, we will see commercial banks, thrift institutions, credit unions, money market funds, mortgage bankers, and commercial loan companies all battling it out for survival. They go into the period in especially precarious financial shape with interest rate swings continuing to be volatile and unpredictable. At such a time when liquidity will be more important than ever, it is very low within the entire industry. While the government should be encouraging a build-up in liquidity, its policies are just the opposite. In late 1979, reserve liquidity requirements for Savings and Loans were reduced to 5.5 percent from 6 percent. Permission was also given for them to borrow outside funds up to 20 percent of assets as compared to less than 10 percent previously. The industry will surely come out the other end of the cycle with far fewer members. In the meantime, the shaking-out process will add considerably to the recession and the ensuing recovery will be adversely affected as well.

The Corporate Sector

The news is not much better in the nonfinancial corporate sector. Corporate liquidity again reached new postwar lows, and the correction will again reach record proportions. We are clearly looking into the face of record postwar bankruptcies and record defaults of business loans at the banks. Marginal borrowers, unable to get the credit they require, will fold. All the unwise and overleveraged investment fostered by the huge credit expansion will be liquidated. And corporate profits will fall substantially.

State and Local Governments

Bad news is in store for state and local governments. In the year 1979, we saw a complete reversal from an aggregate budget surplus for such governments to a sizable aggregate deficit. The problem will worsen in the recession. Debt financing for state and local governments doubled in the four-year period from 1975–1979. Since the growing tax revolt is much more effective on the local level, considerable pressure is being placed on finances and the ability to raise taxes. Pressures on the federal government are also making revenue-sharing sources of funds more unreliable, especially any increase in such funds. Public employee unions are still growing increasingly militant on raises and other benefits. By the end of 1979 we were beginning to see defaults: Cleveland, Wayne County in Michigan (the county in which Detroit is situated), and the Chicago School Board. The New York City problem, of course, has never really disappeared. We have also seen bond rating reductions in Pittsburgh, New York State, and else-where.

Conclusions

Putting all this together, then, we are about to pay the price once again for one more in the long series of increasingly larger credit expansions. Like each one before, the economic distortions of the credit expansion will have to be liquidated by new postwar record bankruptcies and loan losses in every sector of the econ-omy. First, the last remaining available credit in the economy will be rationed out in a final surge of interest rates and credit crunch. Then, we will see the scramble for liquidity and a cyclical decline in business. Commodity prices will decline and, with a lag, consumer prices will even moderate. Consumers will reduce spending sharply and attempt to bring some health back into their finances. Business will slash inventories and other costs while floating large bond issues to fund their short-term debt and restore some semblance of order to their balance sheets. They will all swear that they will never do it again. Bank lending will decline and banking liquidity will improve. The financial press will say that bankers are reforming and we will never again see the same problems. Bank lending will fall, not because bankers have reformed but because there will be little demand. In short, it will look just like the deflationary collapse many have been expecting for many years now.

The Supercrunch?

As this scenario unfolds, the big question in the minds of many people will be: Is this the Big Bust? Will it be the end of inflation and the beginning of deflation? Indeed, the risk is there and it grows greater with each cycle. As we have described, the recent credit expansion was the largest in history, the distortions to be corrected more widespread than ever, and the visible adverse effects far worse. In addition, we have the special problems in the consumer and banking sectors that are potentially more debilitating. The Middle East is a potential powder keg. Given the huge and unmanageable Third World debt levels, the precedent of the Iran default on its debts could be only the tip of the iceberg. How easy it is to say that the new regime is not responsible for the debts of the prior rulers, especially in light of the limited life span of politicians of many developing countries. Each credit cycle builds new and larger distortions to correct and, in addition, the problems of the prior cycles are never completely cured. Many of the bad bank loans of the last cycle are still on the books. We certainly have all the ingredients of the final crunch. But it is important to remember that the risk was also there in 1975. Why didn't it happen then? Or why didn't it happen in 1970? The key question in this govern-ment-dominated economy is: "What is the government going to do about it?" Every inflation creates with it the deflationary seeds of its own destruction in the form of the distortions we have been describing. Will the government policy-makers allow the deflationary pressures to get out of control?

The Bail-Out

The answer to that question in each cycle has been negative. Each time, before the recession and debt liquidation have gotten out of control, the government has stepped in with another credit fix. Because all the distortions are not really corrected, each fix is a little larger, and this sets the stage for an even bigger credit boom/bust to follow. All one has to do is watch the political news in the papers to know ahead of time whether the bail-out will occur again.

In late 1979, before a serious recession had taken hold, plans were being made for the bail-out. This was going on even while every politician was still calling inflation "Public Enemy No.1" and while the U.S. government was announcing a bold new plan to end inflation and save the dollar. Only weeks after Fed chief Volcker announced bold new Federal Reserve policy-making changes to end inflation forever, he was quoted as saying: "Higher inflation means the Fed must supply more money to sustain economic activity." This is exactly the kind of theory that led to hyper-inflation in many countries. As soon as the monetary authorities try to increase growth of money to the level of the rate of inflation, a complete loss of control cannot be far behind.

What other kinds of news announcements signal the intentions of the government to institute a bail-out? In late 1979 there were many. Stand-by programs for local public works were announced that would be triggered by set unemployment levels. A bail-out plan for housing starts, replete with interest rate subsidies, government purchases of mortgages, and other measures calculated to restore as many as 400,000 housing starts, was announced. The Chrysler bail-out plans also do not signal a hands-off government plan. At the same time, spending increases in many areas were announced and talk of tax cuts was frequent. We could go on, but every cycle has been the same. There is no evidence that the most recent cycle will be any different.

The next important question, then, is whether the government still has the power and the tools to accomplish the task of restimulating the economy once the bust begins. Many people believe that it does not have the power to do it again. They concede that the government will not change its spots in spite of all the pressure of tax revolts and weakening acceptance of Keynesian economic theories. They agree that the government will plunge ahead anyway. It still has the will, they say, but it no longer has the means. Are they right? Let's examine their reasoning briefly.

The Imminent Deflation Case

Most "deflation now" arguments revolve around the notion that the government can no longer "push on a string," that it has lost the power to stimulate the economy by inflating. Since the government inflates primarily through the banking system, the deflation argument presumes that there are no longer sufficient numbers of credit-worthy borrowers to allow this to continue. Though the Fed will try to expand reserves, banks will refuse to lend, many businessmen and individuals will refuse to borrow, and the mountain of accumulated debt will begin to collapse. With the debt liquidation feeding upon itself, an uncontrollable deflationary collapse will ensue. Indeed, as the title of this book implies, the risk of such a reversal of the long-term trends is always present. But it does not have to happen exactly this way, and certainly not necessarily in the immediate future.

There are a number of holes in the deflation argument. First, though balance sheets are deteriorating, it is difficult to say just where the limit is. Bankers, individuals, and businessmen have all been ingenious in keeping their balance sheets afloat. Bankers have found new ways to raise funds to lend when needed, including foreign sources. Families now have more working members than just five years ago. Though many marginal businesses are liquidated during each recession, new businesses are created with new government infusions of credit.

Second, businessmen will nearly always borrow if the price is right. Supply and demand for loanable funds will be balanced at some interest rate just as for any commodity. And the government still has the power to temporarily reduce the real rate of interest until the price seems right.

Third, bankers detest idle money and will always lend when the spread between the cost of money and the interest they can charge is attractive. As long as they are allowed to raise the interest rates to the marginal borrower to reflect his higher credit risk, and can borrow the funds at a lower rate, the bankers will make the loans.

Fourth, bankers can help the government inflate the economy without even lending to private borrowers at all. They can buy government securities (lend to the government). Together, banks, the Federal Reserve, and the Treasury can flood the market with government securities and have the same inflationary effect as expanding money and credit by lending to private borrowers. They did this in the 1974–1975 collapse when deflation threatened. They reliquefied the banking system with government securities to replace the private loans that were liquidated, waited until business and individuals cleaned up their balance sheets and developed the courage to borrow again, and then liquidated the government securities to put out private sector loans once again. Though private debt was liquidated during the recession in great amounts, *total* credit continued to rise at a fairly high rate all through the recession.

Finally, even if the credit inflation techniques of today should fail, the government still has many other inflation techniques. It could, for example, go back to currency inflation, printing money directly. It could sell off its gold (as it is now doing), loan directly to troubled corporations or guarantee their loans (Chrysler, Lockheed) turning marginal borrowers back into credit-worthy borrowers, print new forms of money like food stamps or even ration coupons, or any combination of all the above techniques. It might again submerge price inflation with price controls. In short, desperate politicians can be as ingenious at baffling and dumbfounding the public with new inflation techniques as the free market can be in getting around government controls. Though the public is rapidly learning what inflation is all about, it has much to learn, and illusions about money are still high.

A variation of the deflation argument is often used in the international area. When confronted with some of the arguments given above, they claim that the U.S. government may be able to pull it off longer domestically, but the Eurodollar market is beyond its control—and the Eurodollar market is about to collapse. But the answer here is roughly the same. International bankers and foreign central banks are no more willing to blow the whistle on the game than are our domestic bankers. They too have many tricks up their sleeves if collapse threatens. The Eurodollar market is a useful institution or it would not have developed. One must also remember that the same philosophies and defunct economic theories that support continuing government intervention and inflation techniques in America are accepted in other major countries. In the final analysis, politicians of the world will cooperate when the pressures become too great. We also have international agencies like the International Monetary Fund to bail us out on an international scale with such things as direct loans to Third World countries and Special Drawing Rights.

In summary, there are many convincing arguments against an immediate deflationary collapse just as there were when we wrote our first edition. Nevertheless, the risk of such a collapse is high and one should take steps to protect oneself from such an event. It's just that it is too difficult to time when the deflationary collapse will occur. Besides, there are even more painful alternative conclusions to our long economic deterioration. One such possibility is runaway inflation.

The Runaway Inflation Case

One thing to keep strongly in mind is that the credit collapse, the massive liquidation of our accumulated debt, can also occur through hyper-inflation. High rates of inflation wipe out the real value of debt just as surely as forced deflationary-type liquidation. Lenders have already painfully learned that making long-term loans at fixed rates during high rates of inflation can be disastrous. Long-term bonds are among the worst investments in inflationary periods.

Just as there is a risk that the government could somehow lose control on the deflationary side, I find that there is an even greater risk that control could be lost on the inflation side. There are literally no strong organized groups that support ending inflation at any cost. On the other hand, we have strong labor unions who will strongly resist rising unemployment, holding down wage increases, or scrapping the minimum wage. Then we have every major pressure group that benefits from government benefits against reduced spending, including the government itself. As a nation, we also believe that the depression cure is worse than inflation. We are always looking back over our shoulders with a morbid fear that another Great Depression will occur. Finally, there is still a fairly widespread inability by many to distinguish between real increases in wealth and the illusory gains of inflated dollars. Even sophisticated analysts are debating about the real cause of inflation. Consequently, the government can continue to offer false cures and scapegoats to take the heat off. As long as the government is willing and able to treat economic problems by throwing money at them-and get away with it, every deflationary argument can be turned into an inflationary argument.

The Progressive Nature of Inflation

Another important point to remember is that inflation, once it is well under way, is progressive in nature and naturally feeds upon itself. The growth of government

212

itself, the starting point of the process, is progressive. It is the nature of politicians to demonstrate their worth by proposing new programs. So every new administration and Congress showers us with new programs while the old programs continue even if their original purpose has disappeared. This is true because it is the nature of the government bureaucrat to hold on to his job and to demonstrate his value by expanding the size and scope of his department through requesting more personnel, more responsibility, and more appropriations. So nearly all of the old programs continue to grow in size. Most programs also develop a fiscal constituency that demands higher benefits that no ambitious politician can resist. Each government intervention also creates distortions that require further government intervention to cure. It is a strong self-sustaining process that grows in a progressive manner. Our assumption is that this process cannot be stopped spontaneously inside government circles. Only the groundswell of resistance that is beginning at the taxpayer and voter level will accomplish it.

The inflation process creates potentially deflationary economic distortions by rearranging economic resources in ways that the free market may not necessarily have used. Since the government intervenes before each recession corrects all distortions, it requires a greater creation of credit each time to keep the recession under control and to expand the economy afterward.

The growing accumulated debt burden requires an increasingly larger credit infusion to keep it from collapsing. There is an independent self-enforcing process here within the larger one. Increases in money and credit result in higher prices, and the higher prices stimulate the demand for more money and credit. Higher prices mean a higher nominal value of inventories to be financed. Price inflation stimulates speculation, much of which is financed by credit. Everyone gradually learns, as inflation persists, that borrowing money and repaying in cheaper dollars is a good way to hedge against inflation.

That brings us to the next important source of the progressive nature of inflation. People do *learn and adjust to* their environment. An individual's currency cannot be depreciated continuously at high rates without his eventually learning what to do. He eventually learns that many of the gains he thought he was making, like higher wages or profits, were not *real* gains at all but simply price gains. His money illusion eventually disappears. He then begins to retreat from the currency. It begins with a trickle, but gradually gains momentum. He spends his money just a little faster and he learns to save less of his income. He begins to borrow more and gets used to carrying an ever larger debt burden. In the meantime, he puts more money in real assets like his home, auto, gold, silver, and so on. He gradually learns that it is better to buy now rather than later when prices are higher. If he doesn't have the money, he borrows it. The process continues to accelerate because it is a one-way street. Once someone learns the secret of defending against inflation, he continues to practice what he has learned. And each year, more people learn the secret. We also get such things as cost-of-living clauses in wage contracts and cost-escalation clauses in contracts of all kinds that make further price and wage increases become automatic. All this means that the government is required to use increasingly larger amounts of new money and credit to get the same temporary gains in the economy. This, of course, accelerates the retreat from currency and requires even more inflation stimulus in the next cycle.

Because of all the progressive factors described above, the lag time between the increase in money and the resulting increase in prices also steadily shortens. Businessmen learn to raise prices faster than their costs rise in order to maintain profits. Businessmen and individuals learn to economize on cash balances, keeping less in actual cash and more in real assets. That's why in Chile, Argentina, Brazil, and other countries suffering from high continual rates of inflation, the lag time between an increase in money supply and prices is a matter of weeks. In the United States, it used to be as long as two years. In economic terms, the *velocity* of money is increasing as it always does in any inflationary environment.

The international sector is also a source of progressive inflation and promises to be even more so in the future. For years, the United States has been exporting at least part of its inflation by sending our excess dollars overseas. Through "cooperation" and gentle arm-twisting, other industrialized countries have been persuaded to absorb a large portion of our dollar creation. This could only be done at the expense of expanding their own money supply, which in turn forced them to absorb the price effects of our dollar creation. As a result, we feed worldwide inflation. This feeding has its limits too. With the continued weakness of the dollar and the falling prestige of the U.S. throughout the world, our trading partners are increasingly rebelling against the accumulation of dollars. They are inclined more toward the European Monetary Union, gold, and alternative strong currencies like the Deutschmark. They will also be trading more of their excess dollars for real assets in the United States, including buying into our companies. This means that there will be more immediate price inflation in the U.S. with each increase in money because we will not be able to export our inflation as readily as in the past.

The Stages of Inflation

In order to put all the factors in the inflation process described above into perspective, it is useful to discuss the three stages in any inflation process. They can be observed during any short cycle of inflation or during a long-term inflation spanning many cycles.

The *first stage* may be called the stage of ebullience or innocence. It is a pleasant stage in which money rises faster than prices as consumers hold on to the larger cash balance created by government monetary policy in the hope that prices will eventually recede. During this period, many businesses may prosper simply because of easy money policies. Businessmen react to what they believe to be permanent increases in real demand for their products. Their suppliers at the same time are selling their services too cheaply, not realizing the future implications of the rise in the money supply. Costs, consequently, do not rise as fast as final consumer prices and profits grow for many businesses. Economists approvingly nod, saying that "a little inflation is a good thing." Beneath the surface, however, inflation is causing distortions in relative prices and wages throughout the economy and future problems are already being formed. If the inflation process ended there with short-term inflation, there would be a mild recession that would correct the distortions and the country could return to normal stable

214

growth. But, as we know, the government did not allow the recessions to cure all the distortions and the inflation was not a "one-shot affair." The inflationary policies of the government have endured for over forty years. On a secular basis, we are quite obviously well past the first stage of inflation.

The *second stage* is less pleasant and may be called the stage of enlightenment. Government continues to print money at high and accelerating rates and the people slowly begin to learn about the implications. Workers begin to demand higher wages to offset the past recession. Lenders want to add an inflation premium to the interest rates they charge to adjust for future depreciation of the dollar and their loaned capital. Consumers not only begin to learn to spend their money faster and save less, but they also learn it is better to borrow and spend now and deplete their cash balances. Demand for credit rises. Prices are now rising almost as fast as the growth in the money supply, though the lag effect between the two is still fairly long. In spite of this, the government must continue to accelerate growth in money from cycle to cycle to offset the adverse effects from the prior economic distortions resulting from credit expansion in the past. At the same time that private credit demands are rising, therefore, the government is also competing more aggressively for the same savings to support its own borrowing needs. Near the end of this stage, all the ill effects of inflation appear, though many are still not obvious to the majority of the population. The debt service of all the prior excessive credit becomes a burden and all the symptoms of recession are manifest. Now, it becomes just the opposite of the first stage. Inflation steadily loses its temporary stimulative properties and production becomes disorganized. Many illusions begin to disappear. Businessmen learn that their burgeoning profits are at least partially illusory. Capital assets are underdepreciated and taxed away by the government. The capital base of the nation is steadily eroded.

The *third runaway stage* of inflation is characterized by a growing loss of control. People in large numbers are now learning how to protect themselves. They learn slowly that while the prices of their homes, gold, silver, antiques, and other assets are rising, the value of the currency is becoming worthless. This is a subtle but important difference. Once learned, money illusion is gone completely and the results can be devastating. Selective real asset investing is replaced by a full retreat from the currency. People are now not simply buying assets any longer but *selling* the currency for whatever they can get before it goes even lower. Inflation expectation becomes rampant as all hope is given up that inflation will subside.

This final stage of inflation puts the final touches to the destruction of the value of savings, destroys the value of all fixed-income assets, leads to widespread poverty, destroys the middle class, and widens the gap between the rich and the poor. This condition then exacerbates class tensions and calls for radical change in the political structure of the country. As is so often the case, government intervention, no matter how well-intentioned, turns out to be perverse. It begins by trying to create equality, but actually increases inequality.

In this final stage people and politicians finally learn that uncontrolled inflation is far worse and more destructive than the recession cure that they so carefully avoided throughout the process. The final stage of inflation doesn't necessarily have to end in the wild hyper-inflation such as in post–World War I Germany or other famous inflations of the past. But it is here where the risk is the greatest. At this stage, prices are rising much faster than the money growth, high as that is. This is true because, unlike the second stage where people were merely trying to offset past inflationary losses, they are now anticipating future inflation and taking steps to protect themselves from what they *expect* will happen. When this becomes widespread, of course, the expectation is self-fulfilling. Business in this last stage becomes disoriented and far fewer goods are produced on which to spend the increased money supply. The lag between money and rising prices now becomes extremely short, leading, in extreme cases, to workers being paid daily or even hourly so they can get rid of the money faster.

The seemingly odd result of all this is a common complaint that enough money is not being printed. In spite of busy printing presses, there really is a *shortage* of money because its value is falling faster than money can be printed to replace it. As economists say today, the *real* money supply is falling though the *nominal* supply is rising. The temptation of the government is to bow to political pressure by trying to catch up with prices. This is the fatal policy error that can throw the nation into hyper-inflation. The more the government increases the money supply, the faster prices will rise. The process can only end in complete destruction of the currency.

What are the chances of the U.S. making the same error? Most economists will say it is impossible. Of course, they are the same ones who stubbornly insist that gold is only a "barbarous relic" of the past and not real money. Walter Heller, economic advisor to Kennedy and Johnson, for example, proposed a solution to the inflationary bulge in 1974 that was very similar to comments made by officials in the Weimar Republic. The problem, he said, was that *real* money supply was not rising fast enough and it should be raised. Fortunately, he was not advising the administration at the time. The comment in late 1979 by Federal Reserve chief Volcker is equally frightening: ". . . higher inflation means the Fed must supply more money to sustain economic activity."

Are we about to lose control and go into hyper-inflation as many fear? At this stage of the long adverse trends, we never know for sure. Like the deflation case, all of the necessary ingredients are there and the risk is high. The government is the big factor here too, and a serious judgment error can tip the scale. There are also fewer safeguards against runaway inflation than there are against a deflation. In spite of all this, however, I don't think the nation is on the brink of runaway inflation either.

Balancing the Extreme Views

This is, of course, what makes long-term investment and personal financial planning so difficult in the current economic environment. There are two extreme alternative conclusions to our long-term economic problems. Either is possible and either could happen at any time. Even if one is perfectly confident as to which conclusion will occur, the timing is difficult. Many analysts have been predicting an *imminent* hyper-inflation or deflation for over ten years. The government, however, has been ingenious in finding new ways to inflate and hide the results or in successfully casting much of the blame elsewhere. In so doing, it has been able to avoid a deflation. On the other hand, the free market has been successful in at least partially adjusting to the inflation.

There is obvious danger in committing oneself completely to one extreme or the other. Even if one is right in his choice, he could be wiped out while waiting if his timing is wrong. A deflation, for example, could be preceded by an inflationary blow-off that could wipe away most of the assets of the investor who correctly prepared completely for the deflation. Given the high volatility characteristics of the last stages of inflation, sharp cyclical disinflation could wipe out the heavily leveraged investor counting on hyper-inflation to bail him out. How does one balance the risk? We will answer that question in the next chapter.

Light at the End of the Tunnel?

But what of the other equally extreme view that we will work ourselves out of the mess while avoiding either extreme? There are many who say that the events of the past years have already set in motion movements that will force the government to stop what it has been doing. Through a long and controlled deceleration of the money supply and the growth of government, we will enjoy a soft landing.

This is an extreme view because no other such persistent inflation as we have suffered in the past several decades has ever ended that way. Moreover, there is little concrete evidence to say that things are any different today. Many point to the growing tax revolt highlighted by Proposition 13 in California. There is little doubt that this is encouraging. Local governments have been put on notice to hold back unnecessary spending. It is also easy to say you are against big government and against government spending in the aggregate. Yet, we still see more activity than ever by special interest groups to maintain and increase their *individual* government spending programs. In this context, Proposition 13 was just another exercise in interest group warfare. Property owners sought tax relief against the rest of the state and succeeded in reducing their tax burden. But other taxes went up and the tax burden was simply spread over a bigger group. In fact, the overall tax burden was higher two years later. Teacher salaries, public employee salaries, and other spending was higher. As a result, other less politically strong groups were burdened by shifting the tax burden. Landlords were pressured to pass along the tax cut and in Los Angeles they were subjected to rent controls. Business interests were pressured to forego any benefit from the property tax reduction. Like almost all tax reforms we have seen, the political realities end up penalizing business and ultimately investment and growth. Proposition 13, as a kind of microcosm of tax reform, was no exception.

Any supposedly conservative movement must wait for documentation by the eventual recession test. It is easy to be against taxes but quite different to reject government help when it is really needed. Most of the politicians who have taken on a new conservative image also admit that they will stimulate again rather than face higher unemployment. Even in the absence of the recession test, successful tax revolts have not been followed by equally enthusiastic support of the spending cuts necessary to balance the budget. This was true in California following Proposition 13, which was passed in the light of a huge surplus on the state level, a surplus that is now disappearing. The real test is still ahead. On the national level, every recession test has quickly flunked. No sooner does unemployment begin to rise than government stimulation increases.

We remind the reader again that the attitudinal roots of our economic problems run very deep and the institutions these attitudes create are firmly established. Isn't the government still viewed as the ultimate problem-solver instead of leaving it up to individual initiative and the free market? One need only review the energy crisis and the way that is being handled to know the answer. This crisis has given us several new giant government agencies and has set new precedents for continued intervention of government in the private sector. Is the government still held to be responsible for the welfare of the individuals in the nation, for maintaining economic growth, for ending recessions, for attacking inflation? The answer is obvious. If we were truly far enough along in changing the underlying problems, we would see much more support and even organized movements to reduce the presence of government in the private sector. Instead, we see the opposite. The Commodity Futures Trading Corporation, for example, has sprung up in recent years to spread a new regulatory blanket over previously unregulated commodity markets, markets that have contributed immeasurable increases to our standard of living. The new agency's beginning staff was larger than the combined staff of all the commodity exchanges in the country. Like all good socialist countries, we now have a new Education Department that will be followed by much greater federal control over education. Since our last edition, OSHA, EPA, the FTC, and other alphabet agencies have accelerated direct government regulations dramatically. Rent controls continue to spread across the country. Debate on a national health plan is centered on its form and beginning cost only, not on the idea of having one. No politician has dared to attack the existence of the totally unworkable Social Security system. In fact, benefits have been steadily raised, especially in election years, until the Social Security recipients are one of the few groups who have stayed ahead of inflation. Whenever voters are polled on whether they would prefer recession or wage and price controls, the majority invariably goes for controls.

If there is one ray of hope, I would say that we have passed some kind of watershed in economic theory. Keynesian economic theory and the policies it evokes have been called into question by the academic community. There are still plenty of Keynesians at the colleges, however, and even more in the government. It will be difficult and take time for them to change, if they ever can throw away what they have taught and practiced for decades. It may remain for the younger academics to finally change things, and, again, that will take time. For one thing, even the most enthusiastic rebels against Keynesians are still not quite sure what to replace it with. It is encouraging that Austrian free market economics, which was around long before Keynes, is slowly and steadily gaining public support.

Specifically, there is much more attention given to the *supply* side of the supply/demand equation. Keynesians completely ignored that side in favor of concentration on demand and demand management. As a result, they have nearly succeeded in destroying the ability of the country to supply goods and services. On a negative note, even if the supply enthusiasts gain the upper hand, there is still the risk that policy-makers will simply turn to supply management instead of demand management and foul things up even more. Certainly government management of the energy industry is an exercise in supply management. As the government creates more and more shortages with its policies, what is to stop them from attempting the same thing with the steel, aluminum, or forest products industries?

No, we concluded six years ago that we had not begun to attack the basic problem seriously, and we must conclude the same today. We are now as far from turning the basic underlying problem around as we were then. Moreover, the economy is much weaker now and much more vulnerable to government mismanagement.

Continuing Stagflation

We find ourselves in a situation where the many years of government abuse could take us at any time into a hyper-inflation or a deflationary collapse. Which would occur first is extremely difficult to foretell and, even if one could pick the alternative with certainty, the timing is difficult. It also appears to be unlikely that we will see a soft landing or easy way out no matter how much enlightenment there seems to be about the problems. Where does that leave us? Unfortunately, these are the same choices I outlined in the original work, and my conclusion must still be the same as it was then. We will continue to muddle along making the same mistakes but paying increasingly higher penalties. Government will not attack the basic underlying problem, which is itself, but will simply treat the symptoms when they become adverse.

Though we do not have any better idea as to timing than six years ago, we do have a much better idea of the shape that adverse credit trends and continued government intervention take. We have the experience of two additional credit cycles that have given us useful insights. We have grown to appreciate the ingenuity and resourcefulness of desperate politicians in creating patchwork solutions to hold the economy together while simultaneously casting the blame elsewhere. We have also developed an even greater admiration for the ability of free markets and individuals to foil the government and adjust to its policies and their adverse effects. The immediate future will bring a long stalemate between the government and the free market that is commonly called stagflation.

This term was originally coined to describe a recession in which inflation fails to disappear as it was supposed to in Keynesian economic theory. Stagflation is a combination of inflation and stagnation. It is much more descriptive of the long-term inflationary problem brought about by excessive govern-

219

ment intervention and credit abuse. Such an environment gradually erodes the capital base of a country and leads to long-term economic stagnation. The Keynesians, in coining that term, did not know how prophetic they were, for that is exactly the condition they have wrought. Stagflation also perfectly describes the pitched battle between the government and free markets. With its interventions, the government creates the many economic distortions we have described. The government creates inflation, and the free markets provide or create inflation hedge vehicles for investors to protect themselves. Government policies cause rising volatility in financial markets and the free market creates such things as financial futures, currency futures, and other protective tools. Most importantly, government policies raise investment risk, penalize savings, create uncertainty, and generally reduce incentives for long-term investment. The free market correctly responds by saving less, investing less, spending more, and speculating. The long-term effect is inadequate capital formation, declining productivity, and stagnating economic growth.

Why Inflation Breeds Stagnation

If we assume continuing stagflation for our future investment planning, we should take a few minutes to explain stagnation. One has to begin his understanding of stagflation by rejecting the very basic economic principle that has dominated postwar government policies—namely that inflation can be used to offset unemployment. We touched upon this in our discussion of the Phillips Curve. Inflation is a basic cause of both unemployment and the slowing of real economic growth over the long term.

The first reason for this, and the most important one, is that most economic growth must come from savings and investment. A growing nation must offer an economic climate that makes people confident enough in the future to refrain from consuming in the present (saving) in order to consume hopefully more in the future. The resources this releases can then be used to build new plant and equipment (investment). Through direct regulation, high taxes, inflation, and the creation of an uncertain environment, however, the government has created the opposite environment.

The second reason is that government-created money and credit enters the economy in a very uneven and arbitrary fashion. In so doing it misdirects resources away from where they may have flowed freely. Since free market forces are constantly trying to put resources back where they belong, there is a substantial deflationary drag on the economy. Some pressure is relieved by periodic recessions where some of the distortions are corrected, but the government never allows the correction to run its course. Consequently, the deflationary drag continues to mount.

The huge overhanging debt we have described also constitutes a continuing deflationary threat to the economy. Since the debt has progressed to such a mature stage of financial deterioration, it is having deleterious effects on present and potential economic growth. Many consumers, for example, have bought a higher standard of living and have mortgaged the future to pay for it.

In the international area there are other depressants to future growth. In the past, much of the improvement in the standard of living of Americans has been bought by shipping our inflation overseas. To the extent that our trading partners have accumulated billions of dollars, the United States has taken real goods in exchange. It is already clear that our partners are no longer willing to trade real goods for devalued dollars. This international volatility and uncertainty, brought about in large part by United States economic policies, may also mean lower growth in international trade.

Finally, the real impact of the rise in oil prices has yet to be felt by Americans in terms of economic growth and real standard of living. Up to now, higher oil bills have been offset by higher creations of money, allowing Americans both to pay the higher price for oil and to continue consuming other goods at the same levels. This cannot continue much longer. All the dollars collected by OPEC members will eventually be turned in for real goods in this country, which will mean less for Americans to consume and hence a decline in the real standard of living.

For these and many other reasons, when one makes an assumption of continued high inflation rates, as many experts have, an assumption of continued stagnation must also be made.

Growing Instability

Though we assume that the economy can be controlled for the foreseeable future in a stagflation environment, this does not imply a stable situation. In fact, the progressive nature of the problem still exists. The added assumption of stagnating economic growth simply adds to the problem. With restricted increases in the supply of goods and services, every dollar created becomes all the more inflationary since there is less to spend it on.

Throughout the 1980s, real GNP can grow on average not much more than 3 percent, and this prediction is based on optimistic assumptions. We optimistically assume that investment will get a bigger share of the pie than in the 1970s and that productivity will increase faster. With the labor force growing at a slower rate in the 1980s, we must substantially increase productivity by 2 percent per year. In contrast, productivity grew at 0.6 percent in the 1970s.

The defense share of the GNP also shrank during the 1970s from 7.5 percent to 4.5 percent at the end of the decade. It is already obvious from the world situation and comments from Washington that the share for defense will be growing in the 1980s. Putting this all together, if investment and defense have to get a bigger share of the GNP it means there will have to be less consumption. Adding to the growing financial instability, then, will probably be a great deal of turmoil as every pressure group battles to maintain its share. The pressure on the government to continue inflating will be very high.

The Stagflation Assumption

So, we find ourselves with continuing stagflation within which to make our financial plans and investments. Though we presume that the economy will not quite get out of control, the situation is precarious enough that one cannot completely rule out one of the extreme cases. One must also take this into consideration in one's planning. I conclude that we will see a fairly long period of more of the same: high inflation, sluggish economic growth, and plenty of confusion. It will end with something resembling runaway inflation, an inflation blow-off. Following that, we can expect a deflationary environment. How does one survive such a climate? We will try to give a few helpful suggestions in Chapter 14.

Chapter 14

Surviving Stagflation

Just how does one survive stagflation? The first step is to fully understand the deep-rooted causes and dynamics of our economic problems. Then you can settle down to objectively monitor the economic developments as they occur. You can stop looking around every corner for a sudden cure. The problems aren't going to disappear quickly and they will most probably get worse. With this understanding of the big picture, you should be able to calmly structure an investment plan to survive and even prosper in the period ahead. It will be a period when calm reasoning must prevail over emotions.

In this chapter we won't try to list all the specific investments that should be used, or the mechanics of investing in each. That isn't the purpose of this book. There are plenty of good books and market letters to do that. The most attractive investment vehicles, moreover, will be shifting constantly in relative attractiveness in the volatile period ahead. We will discuss some vehicles broadly, particularly as they relate to the economic conditions we are expecting, and try to give the reader an investment framework within which to work.

Making the Stagflation Assumption

The most important starting point is to take a reasoned stand on the most probable course of the economy. That assumption should be, as we discussed, a continuation of stagflation, a continuing stalemate between government intervention and free market forces. Government will continue to intervene in the private sector, causing all kinds of new distortions while the old ones get progressively worse. Inflation will continue to be a problem, but there will be periodic disinflationary downdrafts where it will appear that inflation has been licked. The price effect of inflation may be submerged by controls for periods of time, but it will always be there. There will be economic recoveries, though weak ones, and there

223

will be increasingly troublesome recessions. Through it all, long-term economic growth will stagnate. There will be bull and bear markets in both bonds and stocks, but the economy will not be healthy.

Once you make the assumption of continuing stagflation, you can then stop running scared from alternating fears of hyper-inflation and deflationary depression. This will be extremely important at major cyclical turning points. Under our assumption, there will be lots of volatility and many highly emotional peak and trough turning points in the economy and the markets. It is at such points that extremists generally make costly mistakes. When cyclical inflation peaks and investors should be lightening up on inflation hedge trading and investment positions, those who fear hyper-inflation load up their positions even more heavily. The sharp price gains always present at the peaks seem to be confirming their worst fears. They passed up the opportunity to take good profits and to switch into other investment vehicles that would add further to their profits on the downside of the inflation cycle. They may even have sizable paper losses on inflation hedge positions taken late in the cycle. Worse yet, they may sell out in disappointment at the bottom just when it is time to think about adding to inflation hedge positions for the next cyclical upsurge.

At the other extreme, as the economy reaches the depths of the correction of the previous credit expansion, amid bank failures, bankruptcies of nonfinancial corporations, huge loan losses, and heightened fears of the big bust, the deflation extremist is making the same mistakes. When he should be looking for under-valued stocks and perhaps laying plans to rebuild inflation hedge investment positions for the next surge in price inflation, he looks upon the climate as confirmation of his fears that the big bust has arrived, and raises more cash.

The stagflation assumption gives you a continuing framework against which all these highly emotional developments can be calmly assessed. As mentioned earlier, committing oneself fully to the wrong extreme can be financially fatal. Picking the right extreme at the wrong time can be just as bad.

Playing the Stagflation Game

Once you've settled into the stagflation assumption, you can also begin to objectively analyze government policy moves to your advantage. Using good free market economic analysis, one can turn government failures into investment windfalls. Though the government is an important key to economic and financial trends, you don't really have to play the Washington game by trying to anticipate new government policies. Let the government announce its new interventions. Then begin to analyze what the free market response will be. All you really have to know about economics is the law of supply and demand and that the free markets will win out in the end. Whenever the government interferes with free markets, it sets into motion forces that will eventually reverse the result the government intended. In so doing, an attractive investment vehicle will usually be created that the alert investor or businessman can turn to his advantage. Importantly, there is a long lag between government intervention and the eventual free market response. This gives you plenty of time to act. Some opportunities may be excellent investments while others may simply be good business opportunities for the entrepreneur. For example, the growing volatility in financial markets caused by persistent government inflation policies is in the process of creating a very viable financial futures market where bond owners will be able to hedge their bond portfolios, where speculators can play the interest rate swings and entrepreneurs can start a new business or service. Institution of rent controls may stimulate condominium sales or serve as a warning to liquidate your investments in rental properties in the area. Price ceilings will create shortages that may open up an investment or business opportunity. Government intervention in housing markets tending to push up prices of individual homes creates investment opportunities in mobile homes and manufactured housing. The list is endless. For every government action there will be a free market reaction either to ease the burden of the adverse effects of the government policy or to find a way around the government intervention with private decision-making. In either case, there will probably be a way to profit from it.

Stagflation Projections

There is another important way to profit from the stagflation assumption that is similar to the previous exercise. Once you decide that the government will continue to intervene and that it will be business as usual for some time, you can begin to build a whole set of projections from the original assumption. Once you can build a whole set of assumptions into an overview, it is not difficult to structure an entire investment portfolio of various vehicles to protect yourself against the adverse conditions you project and to profit from others.

To illustrate what we mean, let's simply compile a list of projected conditions that must naturally follow from the assumption of continuing stagflation. As we go through this exercise, you will see that one projection will naturally lead to another logical projection. Keep it up individually or in a brainstorming group and you will shortly have an accurate description of the future climate. You will also get a lot of interesting investment ideas. If you do the exercise consistently from now on, the list will grow. There will also be different ones to go along with new government policies, so it will be a continuing process that will supply you with a growing list of investment insights.

Let's begin our list of projections by first repeating some of the obvious basic conditions that will accompany stagflation and then proceed from there simply by letting our mind move from one basic projection or premise to the next. Once again, we are not predicting but only *projecting* what must logically follow from each assumption.

1. The government will not attack the basic problem, which is growth of government itself, but it will actively intervene to treat and attempt to suppress the ill effects of its policies.

2. The tax burden, therefore, despite the tax revolt and all kinds of tax "reform," will continue to rise or most certainly will not fall. So an important part

of any investment portfolio should be tax shelter investments to offset this important adverse condition. Rest assured that the free market will continue to manufacture all kinds of new tax shelter investment vehicles. You should, therefore, be on the alert for new ones as the government will also continue to work toward closing down old tax shelters.

3. The growth of the money supply will remain at high levels. Since tax burdens are already painful and taxpayers are revolting, even more pressure than previously will be placed on the Federal Reserve to finance the government with more money. Since supply of goods will also be constrained, each new dollar will lead all the more to price inflation. Each new dollar will also cause more deflationary distortions that will require all the more money creation to offset.

4. A high and steadily rising trend rate of price inflation is the obvious next projection. A healthy proportion of every portfolio must, therefore, consist of meaningful inflation hedges. Because the climate will also be one of high volatility and changing relative attractiveness of inflation hedge investments, you should be well diversified and constantly on the look-out for new forms of inflation hedges that, again, the free market will be providing.

5. Government controls of all kinds will steadily proliferate as Washington will attempt to suppress the effects of inflation and its intervention generally. There will be strengthening of the old forms of control, but also many new innovations that you must look out for and try to anticipate.

6. The growing and continuing threat of controls must be one of the considerations you allow for in every investment commitment. Try to stay in areas where it would be most difficult for the government to control. With common stocks, for example, it is more difficult for the government to control a highly fragmented industry than one that is already concentrated. An industry that is already partially controlled is an obvious risk. Industries with rapid new product development are almost impossible for government price regulators to control. Industries dealing in consumer necessities, where political pressures can be high, are especially vulnerable. Industries doing large amounts of government contract business are other obvious problem areas. This also means you must be well diversified at all times. With the possibility of sudden and arbitrary government actions, what might have been an excellent inflation or deflation hedge may be turned overnight into a losing proposition.

7. On a more positive note, remember that every new government control will run into the free market process. The controls will be circumvented eventually by the indomitable human spirit. In the process, there will be new investment vehicles. Though it is obviously bad for the country, as an investor you should look upon each new control as an investment opportunity.

8. All this naturally implies very volatile and choppy business cycles and shifts in economic trends. Weak expansions and violent contractions on a regular basis will be the rule. As an investor, therefore, you must be ready to make frequent shifts in your own portfolio and changes in the weightings of your holdings.

9. Economic growth on a longer-term basis will be sluggish or stagnant. There are many investment implications inherent in this projection. The technology industry, for example, will remain a relatively attractive area for many reasons.

With incentives for costly major brick and mortar investments lacking and profits squeezed, business will be looking for quick and cheaper ways to increase efficiency and profits. Technology is an obvious answer. It is also one area where costs are falling.

10. We will continue to see high volatility in all financial markets and investment risk will remain high.

11. High levels of business risk necessarily mean that investment horizons will remain short. When uncertainty about the future is great, a dollar today is simply worth much more than a dollar tomorrow, more so than usual. The longer the investment horizon, the more uncertainty and the greater the risk premium that must be charged. For example, a businessman putting up a new plant in Iran or Botswana may insist upon a rate of return high enough to return his investment in, say, two years. On the other hand, with the same investment in Belgium or France, he may be willing to write off his cost over ten or twenty years. It is simply a matter of the certainty of return.

12. Looking at common stocks, for example, this also means that there would be a greater emphasis placed upon current dividend return than in more certain times. Perhaps you've already noticed that current yields on stocks have been rising for the past several years. On the other hand, in the 1960s, when the New Economists had convinced the nation that the business cycle was dead and the government could keep the economy going for years through "fine-tuning," yields were at an all-time low and the entire orientation in investing was the growth rate in earnings and the income statement.

13. The combination of high risk and slower growth means that investors will be less willing to pay for future growth. As a result, low price-earnings multiples on common stocks will remain. The multiple is simply the discount factor by which future income streams are given a present value. The higher the percentage return an investor requires to reward him for risk, the lower the price-earnings multiples. When selecting stocks, therefore, no matter how good the future prospects look, remember that investors will discount that growth heavily and there is a limit to what current price that future can command.

14. For all the above reasons, investors will continue the trend that has already been in place for several years. They will pay increasing attention to balance sheets and balance sheet ratios and less to earnings per share growth than in the past. Price-to-book value will be more important than the price-earnings ratio. This tells you something about what kinds of stocks to own.

15. Disincentives to save and invest will continue. Capital formation, or the building of plants, equipment, and all the projects aimed at producing more goods and services, will remain deficient. Aside from the perverse effects on inflation and the general growth in the standard of living, there are also many specific investment implications in this projection. Some of them follow.

16. Capital in place, the existing plant and equipment, will take on increasing value. Even capital that may not have an attractive rate of return now will be showing better returns in the future because it will have less competition.

17. Companies that already control large amounts of physical capital will become more valuable in the eyes of investors. Their price-earnings multiples

227

relative to companies without the same assets will rise. This is one of the reasons why multiples of the "nifty fifty" companies of a few years ago, most of which were more noted for steady and reliable growth than asset control, have been falling relative to the rest of the market.

18. We will continue to have a growing asset orientation among investors. This has already been going on for several years.

19. Buyouts and mergers will continue at high rates in this anticipated environment. This, of course, has already been going on for some time. Many analysts have looked upon it as a phase, but you can see from what was discussed above that this represents a natural extension of all economic forces presently operating. In fact, given the risks of investing in new plants—high interest costs, delays in construction due to government regulators and labor strife, uncertain markets and supplies, and all the other disincentives mentioned—I would consider it irresponsible management to build a new plant when it may be bought, especially below book or replacement value. If you watch merger trends, you will even see a growing number of new kinds of mergers. Many corporations are simply buying out the assets themselves and leaving the corporate shell to the stockholders. Many groups of officers are buying out their companies or their company assets. Then there is another reason for mergers. Companies simply do not have the desire to invest in expansion of their basic business and are, instead, using their excess cash to buy out other companies.

20. The years ahead will see many problems with shortages. We will see spot shortages in many materials due to bottlenecks, and some prolonged shortages in others due to periodic malinvestment as well as deficient overall capital formation. This will lead to many good investment ideas for the alert investor.

21. Raw material and natural resource investment, for these reasons, will continue to be good inflation hedge vehicles when carefully selected with caution because of the cyclicality of such investments. This is one more reason behind the overall asset orientation in common stock investing ahead.

22. For the reasons above plus the great interest in speculation which always accompanies inflation, commodity markets will continue to be popular trading mediums. We'll see new futures markets invented to hedge against new risks.

23. Gold and other precious metals will continue to be good insurance positions as well as good trading vehicles. They will not be the same one-way streets they have been for the past few years, especially relative to other investments. Price moves will be volatile.

24. Interest rates will remain high and volatile. The secular trend will also tend to be rising. This will continue to have broad investment implications for many investments and industries. We've already described the broad structural changes that are likely in the financial industry.

25. Fixed rate mortgages will disappear from the scene almost completely in the very near future. They will be replaced by variable rate mortgages where rates are tied into some interest rate or by loans that are renegotiated periodically or some variations of the two. Long-term lenders will no longer be willing to put out long fixed-rate loans. Lock in all the long-term mortgages you can in the near future, particularly at the next cyclical bottom in rates. It will be the last chance.

228

They are assets in an environment of continued high inflation rates.

26. Long-term capital markets will gradually disappear if this environment continues and worsens. It's already happening slowly but steadily. Institutional bond portfolios, for example, are carrying steadily rising proportions of shorter-term securities. The demand for short-term securities is also growing rapidly relative to bonds. The skyrocketing money market funds are one indication of this force. Lenders, in this case, primarily ex-depositors at banks, prefer to hold their funds in high-yielding and liquid securities.

27. Interest rate futures will accelerate in use strongly and grow to be the largest of all futures markets. Perhaps this is one hope for the capital markets. If U.S. investors and lenders are innovative enough to develop the vehicles and markets to hedge their fixed-income investments, the markets may be able to survive for a long time. Such protection may also take the form of various kinds of protective clauses written into the bond indentures, such as a gold hedge clause where interest and principle will be guaranteed to be paid in dollars or gold depending upon the desire of the lender. Other hard assets may also be used. Eventually, even this will fail if inflation is not brought under control.

28. With continued high interest rates and volatile currency flows around the world, currency disruptions will continue and currency futures will continue to grow in usage. We will see new kinds of hedging techniques in import/export trades. International trade will suffer anyway as nationalistic feelings grow along with protective barriers to trade and currency flows. A positive possibility may be a new international monetary system with gold again playing a key role. This will not necessarily solve the domestic inflation problems but it will bring a period of respite to the international arena.

These are only a small sampling of the projections that logically follow from the key assumption of continued stagflation. Each one, with a little thought, can stimulate dozens of others. With continued analysis, the list should be growing and it should be changing over time as new government policies create new reactions. But don't be quick to dismiss any of them. They will take time to develop and will remain far longer than you think. Write them down. Review them constantly and test them against current events. Build an entire scenario and a full set of conditions. Then structure your investment portfolio to protect yourself from the adverse conditions and to profit from others.

The important thing about the conditions I've outlined above is that they are not predictions or guesses or hypotheses. They are *projections.* They *will* happen for the most part as long as the basic causes and underlying trends are not reversed.

Putting it All Together

So far, you have the first basic ingredient to surviving the climate ahead. You understand the true roots of the problem and the entire process underlying nearly all of the economic problems of the past decade. From the basic assumption that the next decade will more than likely be the same, you can logically structure a fairly accurate framework of most likely conditions for investment as well as one to analyze most of the future changes of government policy. Now, just put it all together into a continuing portfolio of investments that will take advantage of the environment. I must offer, however, three more general rules to fit it all together.

I. Time Horizons

The first rule is to keep reminding yourself to step back and see the big picture while taking a longer-term time horizon when viewing both the economy and your investment portfolio. It's far too easy to get caught up in the emotions of the moment and the day-to-day news announcements. If you do that in today's environment and the most likely one ahead, you will almost become a manic depressive, unable to fit events into a proper perspective and usually zigging when you should be zagging. Listening to Wall Street experts is even worse, for their time horizon is invariably extremely short. At every cyclical peak there will be talk of immediate hyper-inflation, and at every trough the 1930s revisited will be the cocktail party conversation. In the aftermath of every credit crunch, you will also hear promises that business, bankers, and individuals have all learned their lessons. And you will hear the perpetual Washington rhetoric that there is a new plan.

Just step back, look at the basic problems we have talked about, and ask yourself: What has really changed? Look at the list of probable projections we've given, together with those you've added, to remind yourself of the magnitude of the problems and the time required to reverse them. I keep a "business as usual" clipping file. Every time I see an article or announcement on a new government program, new regulations, new bail-outs, or new record levels of debt, I put it in the file. I also keep a "light at the end of the tunnel" file. When the latter gets fatter than the former, perhaps it's time to reassess.

II. Playing the Credit Cycle

Then there is also the opposite time horizon problem. Once you become painfully aware of the serious and deep-rooted nature of our economic malaise, there is a tendency to justifiably become so pessimistic that you become totally committed to one of the extreme views of hyper-inflation or deflation and prepare accordingly, or to get frozen into inaction, especially at major cyclical turning points. You may load up on a five-year supply of Spam, tuna, or freeze-dried food, stash currency in a safe deposit box and other drastic preparations depending upon the extreme you choose. As mentioned earlier, this runs the risk of being wiped out completely if you guess wrong or if your timing is off. If you had prepared for deflation, it would have been disastrous already and it will get worse. If you prepared for hyper-inflation, you've probably done very well so far but you did run a risk. With the highly volatile environment ahead, the risk is still very high. If your leverage is too high, for example, a serious recession could be enough to cause considerable financial pain. Most importantly, you miss many important investment opportunities in the meantime.

Our stagflation assumption presumes high volatility and sharp cyclical swings. Keep the long-term picture in mind but don't forget that there will still be cycles as well as cyclical opportunities and risks. Make sure to distinguish between cyclical changes and the long-term trends. Some investments are extremely attractive for the long pull under our scenario, but they can be horribly bad investments for a year or two during the cyclical counter-swings. Holding right through the cycle will lose a lot of your accumulated profits. There is also the risk of being frightened out at the wrong time. On the other hand, investments like long-term bonds are bad investments over the long pull but can be very profitable low-risk investments for a good part of each cycle. You should be ready to switch investment vehicles or their weighting in your portfolio at the right phase of each cycle. It is very important not to get locked into an inflexible position, especially one that is not diversified. Economic conditions are bad and will remain so for a long time. But the problems come in waves.

Fortunately, the government has provided us with a highly developed framework for timing all our portfolio adjustments. In financing government spending with credit, the government has created the now highly predictable credit cycle. In *Free Market Perspectives,* * my monthly investment letter, I have monitored this credit cycle continuously for a number of years and have found it to be extremely helpful in timing moves into and out of major investment vehicles at all important cyclical turning points. With a good dose of continuing free market economic analysis added to my credit analysis, I've had a good head start on spotting new investment vehicles as they have evolved.

Credit is not only the proximate cause of our problems but also the grease of our economic machinery. The relationship between money and credit flows and our financial markets is very direct. It is for this reason that a credit-based analysis of economic trends is the most useful approach for investments and personal financial planning.

The credit cycle also unfolds in a very predictable manner of cause and effect. At one phase, public debt is rising faster than private as the government is pumping new credit to offset private debt liquidation. Aggregate balance sheets are improving during one phase of the cycle while deteriorating during another. The turning points are extremely significant for investment timing. The cycle tells you when banks will be accumulating or liquidating government securities. It obviously gives you exciting insights into interest rate trends and spread relationships between different maturities of issues and between different quality issues. It also tells you when they should be widening or narrowing, which will be helpful when trading financial futures or bonds outright. You can tell when high quality bonds are attractive and when it is safe to buy lower quality bonds. Most impor-

Free Market Perspectives. Published by HMR Publishing Co., P.O. Box 471, Barrington Hills, Illinois 60010.

tantly, it gives you valuable insights in predicting cyclical turning points in interest rates, stocks, commodities, and other assets. Finally, a close study of credit trends constantly reminds you that there is a cycle.

III. Diversification

The third important rule is to *diversify*. Regardless of the economic, political, or financial environment, this should always be one of your first personal investment rules. Continuing stagflation means strong and violent cross-currents, abrupt and arbitrary government intervention that can derail even the best of investments overnight, and lots of new investment opportunities. Diversification, therefore, is more important than ever. Finally, we presume stagflation as the most *probable* condition over the foreseeable future. But we do not deny the *possibility* that runaway inflation or a deflationary bust may occur sooner than expected. Certainly the ingredients are there for either, and government miscalculations could trigger it. In fact, one or both of the extreme conditions will eventually occur, since stagflation is not a stable economic situation. Only with proper diversification can you effectively hedge your investments against both extremes as well as continuing stagflation.

Now you have what I believe is a complete intellectual framework to survive the continuing conditions that are most probable for the 1980s. You understand what stagflation is all about. From that basis you have a fairly detailed description of the most likely set of conditions that will prevail over the near future. You also have the tools to add to the list of expected investment conditions as the government finds new ways to intervene and the free market develops new responses. And finally you have the three most important rules to bring it all together into an effective financial plan for the 1980s.

You are also prepared for any surprises. By always looking at the big picture and using a longer time horizon, you shouldn't be fooled by false and temporary palliatives into abandoning your plan. By playing the credit cycle properly you are at the least properly prepared for one of the extremes. And with proper diversification, even if your timing and economic analysis is terrible, you never leave yourself open to debilitating overall losses in your portfolio.

Investment Vehicles

What are the individual investment vehicles to be selected and their proper portfolio mix? Both the mix and the individual vehicles selected will, of course, depend upon your individual financial situation. Both the mix and the vehicles should also be changed over time and in relation to the phase of the credit cycle. There are plenty of good books by experts in every investment field as well as market letters and advisors, but we will comment briefly here on some of the major vehicles.

Real Assets

With a continually falling currency value, both in the U.S. and in other countries, you must always keep the value of "real assets" firmly in mind. This includes gold, silver, other precious metals, land, buildings, machinery, collectibles, and natural resources. Their continued rise in value is axiomatic under our assumptions simply because they are only reflecting the depreciation of the currency. No matter what investments you select or the mix of them in your portfolio you should always have a substantial holding of real assets. Some make more sense than others and their relative values will shift. Some will get overplayed for a while and should be de-emphasized, while others may just be coming into favor again. One key is to avoid becoming emotionally attached to any one of them, especially gold or silver at recent high prices. The other key to remember is that the value of our currency is falling and that not any one physical asset type is an extremely good investment. That is, people are simply retreating from falling currency, whether they think of it in those terms or not. For these purposes there are many different real assets that will fill the bill. Some are more convenient than others to hold. Some are more fungible or tradeable than others. Some are more historically recognized as investment vehicles than others. But they are all real assets that in the long run will be better than paper currency. Consequently, no matter how bad or how good an asset may look, there is a price for everything and, over time, assets will sell in some relationship to each other. As some get out of line they may be good sales or purchases.

My view of gold is simple. It is real money—the only real money over time—and therefore it should be the ultimate liquidity position. It is prudent to keep a portion of funds, whether you are a bank, business, or individual, in liquid assets in case of unforeseen difficulties. That is the primary use of gold, especially in uncertain times. Doubters claim that it is barren and does not pay a current return. But that is not the role of the liquidity buffer in one's financial plan. Beyond that liquidity buffer, gold must compete against other alternative investments for inclusion in your overall investment portfolio. For a long time, the price of gold was artificially held down by governments of the world. For some years now it has been allowed to seek its own level. At any given time from this point forward it may or may not be fairly valued relative to other assets. I suspect that from present levels ($680 per ounce) there will be many other real assets that may be better investments in the 1980s. But the gold liquidity buffer position must always remain a part of the financial plan.

Silver, in my view, is somewhat similar. It is somewhat less attractive than gold as an ultimate liquidity repository although there has always been some historical relationship between the two. But as a commodity, based upon its own supply and demand fundamentals, it is more attractive than gold.

All other real assets must be analyzed on their own supply/demand fundamentals and on the basis of their price movements relative to each other. Each may also have its own cyclical characteristics which must be taken into consideration.

Looking into the 1980s, I see continued high interest in almost all the real

233

assets. Many individuals have yet to consciously increase their holdings of real assets. Institutional investors, who control billions of dollars, have been left at the starting gate. But if our scenario continues to unfold as expected, institutions will become a much bigger force in the purchase of real assets either directly or indirectly. There is already substantial planning and discussion among institutions on this subject. Several banks have started funds to purchase equity real estate positions and art for personal trust clients. Many have been buying gold. We will probably see bond indentures that have a clause indexing payment and principal to some real assets. Whichever way it develops, there will be at least one more extended rise in real assets of all kinds as institutional money managers take their positions.

Common Stocks

Over ten years ago, common stocks were sold to the public as the ultimate inflation hedges and they were priced accordingly. Investors found out differently. In dollar terms stocks are still lower today than they were in 1966. In real terms, they have lost half of their value since then. There are at least two important primary reasons for this action. First, stocks were simply priced too high relative to other assets. They reflected the long postwar boom as excessive liquidity was run down and peacetime production caught up with the shortages of the war. The rhetoric of the New Economists also convinced investors in the 1960s that growth could continue unabated with the help of the government. Second, the inflation rates that followed were *unanticipated.* If you look back in time at the behavior of stocks during other inflationary periods in this country and others, you will find that stocks generally do poorly when inflation rates are not anticipated, but then improve substantially when high rates are anticipated.

For the 1980s, stocks will be much better investments than in the 1970s. They are now much more realistically priced in relationship to the economic environment. More importantly, they have lost considerable ground on most other investments except for bonds. As mentioned, all assets must sell in some relationship to each other and stocks have clearly lost ground. This is not to say that the climate will be conducive to profits or overall corporate health. It will continue to be a difficult environment for most companies. But much of the "water" is out of the prices, and both corporations and individual investors have a much more enlightened view of the ravages of inflation.

It is often overlooked that common stocks represent an equity position in real assets. If it will make continuing sense to own a variety of real assets in the expected economic environment, then it makes even more sense to buy real assets at a discount from their stated and especially their replacement value. This is exactly the case with many common stocks. It is even more true at bear market bottoms. But, as we mentioned earlier, there is already a strong and growing asset orientation to common stock investing as investors are gradually awakening to these opportunities. The merger and acquisition activity of recent years is another indication of the growing awareness.

Stocks from this point forward may even represent a multifaceted hedge against the economic environment. If, as we expect, inflation continues to worsen with each wave, stocks eventually will have to move up significantly. It is interesting to note that in the disastrous Weimar inflation most of the damage to stocks occurred earlier in the inflation. In the last violent inflation stage, they moved higher dramatically. Throughout the entire period those stocks that controlled considerable assets did much better than the average, and investors holding them during the entire period did not do too badly. If, on the other hand, our assessment of future economic trends is wrong, and things turn out much more positively than expected, stocks will move up strongly. In fact, for that to happen in my opinion, substantial investment incentives would have to be offered by the government to get more capital formation and productivity, which is already being discussed. This would particularly benefit companies with strong asset positions and basic industries. In the event of a sudden deflationary collapse, there would still be risk in stocks, and that is one reason why you must be diversified. But many real assets would be much more vulnerable. All things considered, we must conclude that stocks must be a significant portion of every investment plan for the 1980s.

Selection

Having said all this, we must still caution that the overall economic environment will not be a pleasant one for corporate managers. With inflation, volatility, arbitrary government intervention, and sluggish growth, business planning and economic calculation will still be difficult. But managers just finished a decade with a similar climate and are a little better equipped to adjust to it. And the risk is reduced by the more realistic pricing of shares.

The trick will be to concentrate among the right sectors and industries as well as individual stocks. As we have said, concentrate on the quantity and quality of the assets the company controls and the supply/demand characteristics of the assets. Then, make sure you are not overpaying for the assets. Many of the asset-rich industries are also very cyclical in nature and you should be prepared to adjust your holdings to the credit and business cycle. Since we presume very volatile business conditions anyway, you should be ready to change mix on all your asset holdings as mentioned.

If you watch carefully, government policies will be creating investment opportunities in various industries, and you should move into these areas with your investments whether with real assets or common stocks. Let me give a few current examples.

Defense Stocks

After many years of high inflation and other government abuses, the dollar has fallen from its former stature. As a result, the United States has lost substantial stature in the world community. With the dollar losing its former role as a weapon, we will be forced to find other more direct weapons. The situation in Iran is only one example of what will probably be many in the future. As a result, defense spending will be increasing throughout the 1980s and the companies in this industry will be attractive. Higher defense spending plans have already been unfolded in Washington, and it will be a political issue in the 1980 elections.

Technology Stocks

High technology companies will also be attractive for two reasons. First, they are often the same companies who will be doing much of the higher defense business. Second, they will be the beneficiaries of government attempts to restimulate investment as well as benefiting from business attempts to offset the stagnant growth anticipated. Business incentives will probably still not be strong enough to create the huge increases needed in expensive brick and mortar investment. But business will be looking for cheap ways to increase profits. In this respect, high technology fits the bill nicely. With computers, especially microprocessors, there are many cost-cutting possibilities.

Natural Resource Stocks

This will continue to be a very attractive investment area via common stocks just as it is with real asset positions directly. In the future there will be increasing experiences with spot shortages, and some of these industries may be much more attractive than others for a time. Watch industry supply/demand trends on a worldwide basis for various natural resources. Watch also capital spending plans for each and capacity utilization readings. A diversified portfolio of natural resources would be a very desirable long-term inflation hedge position in your overall financial plan. Again, this industry is also very cyclical and there are better times than others for taking positions. There are also points in the cycle when they should be sold or reduced.

Housing

There is no better example of just how badly an industry can be distorted with government intervention than housing. As a result of many different government policies, housing has already been priced way beyond the financial means of a large proportion of the population. First home buyers will continue to be hard-pressed. But if you look hard enough, you can find an investment opportunity. In this case, manufactured home building will be coming into its own in the 1980s. Mobile homes as well as all the other means of pre-fabricating, in whole or in part, will be affected by financing arrangements that are being changed to allow more flexibility in the financing of such homes.

Stock Characteristics

In addition to looking for attractive industries or sectors based upon government policy directions and the economic conditions projected from the stagflation assumption, there are important characteristics that you should look for in individual companies. In our first edition, we published an extensive safety checklist of such characteristics, most of which are still valid today. Here are a few of the more important ones:

1. Avoid a heavy representation in financially oriented stocks generally. Rapidly changing interest rate spreads and high volatility make their business increasingly difficult. There is also very little real asset value behind them. Those with low *returns on equity* (less than 10 percent) are particularly vulnerable since there is little margin for error. Marginal companies in this area can go out of business over a weekend with little warning.

2. Avoid slow-growing consumer companies no matter whether they happen to be a household word or not. They are not growing fast enough to offset inflation and they have seldom become sufficiently undervalued because of their more stable earnings.

3. Be especially careful of companies with heavy foreign exposure because of growing international instability.

4. Insist on excellent balance sheets and standard financial ratios.

5. Avoid industries or companies being supported by the government. Current examples are the steel industry, with "target pricing" protecting them from foreign competition, and Chrysler.

6. Growth is still a very desirable characteristic for any company regardless of industry, but insist upon projected growth rates much higher than the expected inflation rate and don't overpay for the future.

7. Strong product positions will be important in what will be an increasingly competitive business environment to gain a share of shrinking economic growth.

8. A low political profile is a desirable characteristic in an era of growing government controls and consumerism.

9. Be careful of companies that merely process and sell raw materials but do not have control over their source of raw materials. They will be squeezed in an environment characterized by growing shortages of all kinds.

10. Avoid companies with a high labor content in their product, especially if the workers are organized or are likely to be organized in the future. Labor understandably will become increasingly militant.

Fixed Income Investments

Here is an example of why you have to be able to separate the cycle from the longer-term trend. Because of their very nature, bonds have been in a bear market for several decades that will continue as long as the long-term trend rate of price inflation is up. There is no permanent place for bonds in an investment portfolio in the environment we expect ahead. Yet, periodically, over the past decade or so, one well-known analyst or economist has announced that the secular bear market in bonds has ended, only to regret it later. Usually, the error arose because he didn't fully appreciate the embedded nature of our problems as discussed here or he mistook a cyclical peak for the end of the long-term trend.

The cyclical aspect of bonds is quite another story. With the violent interest rate swings that have come to characterize the credit cycle, there are sensational trading opportunities with bonds. A *one-year remission* in the inflation rate will lead to a very profitable *cyclical* bull market in bonds, especially if you use a little leverage. With financial futures now available, there is also another leveraged play. The kind of credit analysis we have been recommending here is particularly helpful in calling the cyclical turning point in interest rates and is one of the key objectives in our market letter. Usually, when the recession is over, and about halfway through the ensuing economic recovery, balance sheets start to decline again, and this marks the point at which interest rates turn up for the cycle.

Fixed income vehicles with short maturities (under a year), on the other hand, are valuable investment vehicles even in the stagflation environment. The objective of any financial plan in this environment is to beat inflation. Your money must be kept working as hard as possible at all times. Since you should also be shifting your asset mix to suit the current climate, there are many times when you will be "between" positions. That is the time for using short-term money market instruments. With a good understanding of this area, you will have a better chance of finding the vehicles with the best current yields balanced with safety and protection against inflation risk. This is an area where the free market has been particularly innovative, and there are new vehicles being developed constantly.

Fighting Fire with Fire

Though it may seem blasphemous in the light of all the preceding chapters, an important part of your financial plan should be a judicious use of debt. It is certainly true that debt will be paid off with cheaper dollars in an inflationary period. Lock in some long-term debt whenever it is possible, particularly at cyclical interest rate troughs, and employ it in other assets. Just make sure that your rate of return on the borrowed funds equals or exceeds the cost of the money. Real estate is an obvious way to use debt in this manner. Also use debt on a cyclical basis to get more leverage on your cyclical investment plays such as playing the bond cycle or your margin account with stocks. Reduce your cyclical debt positions whenever you see or approach new record highs in interest rates and you are probably timing the reduction in your cyclical investment plays at about the right time as well.

One note of caution. Our assumption of stagflation implies that it will not all be a one-way street. There will be sharp cycles and, if your timing is off, you could be hurt. Make sure that you can service all your debt, if you have to, for at least two years. Otherwise you probably have too much debt. Remember, a balanced approach at all times is the way to survive stagflation.

APPENDIX

Economic and Investment Newsletters

Listed below is a sampling of regular newsletters for the reader interested in pursuing the economic ideas presented in this book and their investment implications. Together, they cover the whole range of investments and financial markets necessary to build a comprehensive balanced investment portfolio for surviving stagflation.

Free Market Perspectives
This newsletter, edited by Alexander P. Paris, attempts to apply the principles discussed in *The Coming Credit Collapse* to current investment conditions. All the important credit and financial indicators described in this book are monitored regularly. Continuing credit analysis is used to time cyclical movements in all major investment markets and to view all investment vehicles within a proper long-term and cyclical perspective. All government activities are analyzed from a free market economic perspective for their impact on the economy and investments.

Published by HMR Publishing Co., P.O. Box 471, Barrington Hills, IL 60010. Annual subscription $50 for 12 issues ($58 for foreign airmail delivery).

Gold Newsletter
Edited by James U. Blanchard, one of the major figures in the legalization and revival of gold investment in the U.S. Blanchard's monthly market letter is one of the best ways to keep fully informed on all the latest developments in gold investment. Issues include guest articles by experts in the field.

Published by National Committee for Monetary Reform, 8422 Oak Street, New
    Orleans, LA 70118.
Annual subscription $25 for 12 issues.

Harry Browne's Special Reports
Editor Harry Browne is one of the best-known economic and financial writers. His newsletter contains reports covering a wide range of investment topics including the stock market, real estate, gold, silver, currencies, fixed income investments, commodities, options, warrants, and collectibles.

Published by Harry Browne Special Reports, Inc., P.O. Box 5586, Austin, Texas 78763.
Annual subscription $195 for 10 issues.

Market Report
Edited by Peter Cavelti, senior vice-president of Guardian Trust Company in Toronto, *Market Report* is useful for precious metal and currency traders. This especially wide-ranging international newsletter contains an abundance of international financial and economic statistics complete with charts and capsule news items from around the world.

Published by Market Report, 87 Yonge Street, Toronto, M5C 1S8, Canada.
Annual subscription $45 for 24 issues.

North American Client Advisory
North American Coin & Currency Ltd. is one of the largest U.S. dealers in gold and silver bullion coins. North American Diamond is a dealer in certified diamonds and other investment gemstones. Their *Client Advisory* letters cover a wide range of topics relating to gold, silver, and gemstone investment complete with price information and charts. Letters are distributed free to clients.

Published by North American Coin & Currency Ltd., Suite G-2, First National Bank Plaza, 100 W. Washington St., Phoenix, Arizona 85003.

Personal Finance
This letter is a very broadly based investment publication covering all aspects of investment and personal financial planning. It features articles by experts in each field with a wide diversity of opinion and offers a "Capsule Advisory" section in each issue. Another letter, *Tax Angles,* is also available.

Published by Kephart Communications, Inc., 901 Washington St., Alexandria, VA 22314.
Annual subscription $65 for 24 issues.

The Donald J. Hoppe Analysis
Edited by Donald J. Hoppe, this wide-ranging and thoughtful analysis covers international finance, precious metals, stock markets, socio-economics, cycle research, and trading strategies for many markets. Detailed trading suggestions for stocks, bonds, and most futures markets are regular features.

Published by Investment Services, Inc., Box 513, Crystal Lake, IL 60014.
Annual subscription $140 for minimum of 22 issues.

The Numisco Letter
Edited by Walter Perschke, one of the nation's leading authorities on numismatic coins, this monthly newsletter covers all aspects of coin investment. It combines comprehensive "how-to-do-it" advice with specific buy and sell recommenda-

tions. Also published is *The Independent Speculator,* which has buy, sell, and stop loss recommendations on precious metals, currencies, and interest rate futures.

Published by International Financial Publishers, 175 W. Jackson Blvd., Suite A-640, Chicago, IL 60604.
Annual subscription $97 for 12 issues.

World Market Perspective
Edited by Jerome Smith, one of the very early advisors to recommend silver, gold, and Swiss francs. Investment guidance primarily for the investor in precious metals. It is an excellent letter strongly steeped in Austrian economic analysis with in-depth long-term research on its investment suggestions.

Published by ERC Publishing Company, P.O. Box 91491, West Vancouver, B.C., V7V 3P2, Canada.
Sample current issue and subscription information free on request.

World Money Analyst
Edited by Mark Tier. An extremely comprehensive international coverage of most financial markets and investments. A considerable amount of statistics and charts, as well as reasoned opinions, on markets, investments, and commodities around the world are provided as well as recommendations on the probable trend directions in all markets.

Published by World Money Analyst, 1914 Asian House, One Hennessy Road, Hong Kong.
Annual subscription $95 U.S. for 12 issues.

INDEX

Deposit turnover, 44–47, 55
Discount window, 116–17, 118, 132
Disposable personal income, 112
Dollar, devaluation of, x, 9, 13, 52, 147, 154, 161, 168, 180, 191, 214
Donald J. Hoppe Analysis, The, 240

"Efficacy" requirements, 60
Employment Act of 1946, 11, 63, 94, 105, 176
Energy crisis, 148, 172
Equities, 87
Eurodollars, x, 9, 31, 36–37, 124, 131, 182, 196, 211–12
European Monetary Union, 214

Farm products, 172
Federal debt, 12, 100, 101, 104–106, 109–111, 115–121, 128, 133, 148, 154, 176–77, 178, 180, 191
Federal Deposit Insurance Corporation (FDIC), 30, 37
Federal Funds, 30, 35, 38, 52, 118, 132
Federal Open Market Committee (FOMC), 111
Federal Reserve, ix, x, 10, 11, 12, 14, 15, 28, 34, 37, 38, 44, 47, 49, 54, 57, 58, 62–63, 76, 81, 85, 93, 94, 109, 110, 112, 115–121, 123, 124, 125, 126, 127–28, 130, 131, 133, 134, 135, 137, 139, 140, 141, 143, 144, 147, 148, 153–54, 155, 160, 163–64, 179, 180–81, 183, 196, 201, 210, 211, 226; Federal Reserve Act, 116, 153–54
Federal Trade Commission, 78, 79, 218
Fiat currency, 154
Financial panics, 145–46
Financial ratings, 13, 156
Fiscal drag, 129
Fiscal policy, 55, 94, 142
Fixed costs, 150
Fixed incomes, 153
Fixed-income securities, 62, 164, 237
Food shortage, worldwide, 148
Food-stamp program, 103, 149, 153
Ford Motor Company, 205
Full employment, 11, 94, 106–107, 108, 115, 117, 120, 126, 133, 142, 146, 150, 152, 154, 159; full-employment budget, 106–107, 129

General Motors, 205
Gold, ix, 9, 112, 115, 148, 154, 194, 211, 216, 228, 229, 233, 239; gold-standard system, 115; gold stocks, 154

Government employees, 105, 126
Great Society, The, 11, 94, 100, 105, 131, 140, 176
Gresham's Law, 115, 154
Gross National Product (GNP), 14, 75, 81, 92, 95, 97–98, 102, 107, 111, 127, 148, 153, 169, 177, 188, 203, 221; real GNP, 85, 111, 112, 130, 138, 139, 141

Harry Browne's Special Reports, 239–40
Hayek, F.A., x
Heller, Walter, 127
High-powered money, 110, 119, 120, 140

Income effect, 159
Independent Speculator, The, 241
Inflation, x, 148–60, 175, 176, 191, 192, 194, 195, 196, 198, 199, 211, 212–214, 217, 220, 222, 223, 224, 226, 229, 230, 232, 234, 235, 237; in post-World War I Germany, 216, 235; stages of, 214–216; and the stock market, 234; War on, 179
Interest costs, ix, x, 79–80, 81, 175, 178, 179, 191, 193, 199, 228, 229, 231
Interest coverage ratios, 133, 136, 156
Interest-rate ceilings, 37, 38, 186. *See also* Regulation Q
International Monetary Fund, 212
Investment strategy, 192, 223, 225, 226; balance sheet ratios, 227; commodity markets, 228; diversification, 232; dividend return, 227; inflation hedges, 226, 228; judicious use of debt, 238; predicting trends, 231–32; "real assets," 233–34, 235, 238; stock selection, 226, 234–37; tax shelters, 226

Johnson, President Lyndon B., 100, 102

Kennedy, President John F., 100, 102, 127
Keynesian economics, 11, 94, 117, 123, 126, 176, 218–219, 220; Keynesian theory, x, 93, 94, 100, 107, 210
Korean War, 102

Labor militancy, 13, 59, 60, 105, 147, 148, 149, 150, 152, 153, 166, 167, 192, 237
Labor productivity, x, 170–72, 175, 188, 192
Legislative Reorganization Act of 1970, 108
Liabilities management, 13, 27, 29–30, 38, 44, 45, 47, 131, 140
Liquidity effect, 159

Loan-deposit ratios, 25, 27–28, 30, 38, 44, 45, 47, 131, 140
Lockheed, 211

McGraw-Hill, Inc., 168
Medicare, 103
Minimum wage, 149, 152, 171, 172
Minirecession of 1966, 20, 141
Mississippi Bubble, 145
Monetarist theory, 44, 111
Monetary policy, 50, 55, 57, 94, 118, 155
Money market funds, 182, 195, 207, 229, 238
Moody's average interest rate, 81

National Accounts, 100
National debt. *See* federal debt
National-income accounting, 107
"New" bankers, 29
New Deal, The, 11, 175
"New" economists, 10, 11, 94–95, 127, 128, 134
New Frontier, The, 11, 100, 105, 127, 131, 140
New York, Federal Reserve Bank of, 44, 49, 111, 161
Nixon, President Richard M., 95, 103, 106, 155
North American Client Advisory, 240

Occupational Safety and Health Agency (OSHA), 191–92, 218
"Orderly" markets, 118
Organization of Petroleum Exporting Countries (OPEC), 194, 202, 221; Middle East, 209

Paris, Alexander P. *(Free Market Perspectives),* 231, 239
Penn Central, 12, 57, 58, 60, 125, 127, 143, 161, 181
Perschke, Walter *(The Numisco Letter),* 240
Personal Finance, 240
Phillips, A.W., 150; Phillips curve, 150–53, 220
Price and wage controls, 10, 14, 112, 150, 155, 168, 202, 211
Price-earnings multiples, 10, 134
Price stabilization, 117
Profit margins, 35, 85, 150, 167, 171
Profit maximization, 13, 30, 31, 35, 124, 131, 132, 156
Proposition 13, 217–218
Protectionism, 9

Public versus private spending, 98–100, 145; *See also* United States government spending; state and local spending

Quick ratio, 71–73, 75, 91

Real wage, 149, 152, 160
Recession of 1937–1938, 47
Recession of 1969–1970, 22, 60, 61, 66
Recession of 1974–1975, 193, 202, 211
Recession of 1979–1981, 194, 199, 201, 202, 203, 204, 209; and the auto industry, 204–205, 206; and housing and related industries, 205–206; and steel, 206
Regulation D, 38
Regulation Q, 31, 34, 38, 141, 143, 207
REITs, 184
Research-and-development spending, 59, 89, 171–72

Sales growth, 68, 89–90
Savings and loan institutions, 120, 164, 206–207, 208, 211
Savings rate, 61
Service economy, 150, 172
Silver, 115, 233; silver coins, 154
Smith, Adam, 126
Smith, Jerome *(World Market Perspective),* 241
SMSAs, 44
Social Security, 97, 98, 100, 103, 178, 198, 200, 218
South Sea Bubble, 145
"Stagflation," 10, 95, 219–22, 223–25, 229, 231, 232, 236, 237
Standard & Poors, 79
State and local spending, 95–96, 97, 98, 208–209
Stock Market, 58, 137, 164, 224; bear market, ix, 119, 160, 164, 237; bull market, 238; common stocks, 58, 77, 164, 234–37; growth stocks, 12, 75, 129, 133; interest-sensitive stocks, ix, 228; preferred stocks, 30, 58, 77, 135; technology stocks, 236
Stock Market Crash of 1929, 93; The Great Depression, 212
Subsidy programs, 98, 103
Synergism, 134

Tax Angles, 240
Taxes, 13, 100, 105–106, 108–110, 153, 167, 191; excess-profits tax, 140; surcharge of 1968, 142